p.138 depth: present and past
living and fossilized

p.239 ref.

# The Philosophical Naturalists

The early nineteenth century witnessed a period of unprecedented ferment in the life sciences. No longer satisfied with the practice of identifying, describing, and classifying species, European naturalists began to insist on a unifying body of theory, and in some cases a transcendental approach, in their search for "the laws of life itself." In this study, Philip Rehbock examines an important dimension of this crucial scientific movement. Tracing the roots, ascendance, and central figures of philosophical natural history in Britain from 1800 to 1860, he accomplishes the first substantial study of metaphysical influences on pre-Darwinian British biology and documents the sizable conversion of British scientists to the idealist approach. The result is a vital reassessment of nineteenth-century British biological thought that will prove important for all students and scholars of the life sciences, nineteenth-century philosophy, and the history of science.

# WISCONSIN PUBLICATIONS IN THE
# HISTORY
# OF SCIENCE AND MEDICINE
Number 3

*General Editors*

WILLIAM COLEMAN

DAVID C. LINDBERG

RONALD L. NUMBERS

**1**
Death is a Social Disease
Public Health & Political Economy in Early Industrial France
*William Coleman*

**2**
Ignaz Semmelweis
The Etiology, Concept, & Prophylaxis of Childbed Fever
Translated and Edited, with an Introduction, by
*K. Codell Carter*

# The Philosophical Naturalists

## Themes in Early Nineteenth-Century British Biology

PHILIP F. REHBOCK

THE UNIVERSITY OF WISCONSIN PRESS

Published 1983

The University of Wisconsin Press
114 North Murray Street
Madison, Wisconsin 53715

The University of Wisconsin Press, Ltd.
1 Gower Street
London WC1E 6HA, England

First printing

Printed in the United States of America

For LC CIP information see the colophon

ISBN 0-299-09430-8

*To*
*Ralph and Lillian Rehbock*
*the best of educators*

# Contents

## Part II. Organisms in Space and Time

# *Figures*

# *Tables*

# Acknowledgments

Portions of this work, especially those relating to Edward Forbes, first appeared in my unpublished doctoral thesis (The Johns Hopkins University, 1975). That exercise convinced me that, while Forbes might well have been the central figure in the development of what was then called "philosophical natural history," he was by no means the first nor the only naturalist of a "philosophical" disposition in the early nineteenth century. Hence, I set out to determine the extent of that phenomenon.

In the conception, research, and writing of this work I have accumulated many debts. Above all my thanks go to Professor William Coleman of the University of Wisconsin, and to Professor Camille Limoges of the Université de Montréal. To Professor Coleman I am indebted for countless consultations on problems of conceptualization, style, and bibliography, and for his ever-wise counsel in matters administrative as well as academic. To Professor Limoges must go the credit for first suggesting that a closer look at Edward Forbes and his milieu was in order.

In the ecological aspects of the work I have been fortunate in having the patient assistance and encouragement of Professor Jeremy xiv Acknowledgments

B. C. Jackson of The Johns Hopkins University. I am also indebted
to Professors David Spring and Robert Kargon of Johns Hopkins for
their guidance in problems of British history, and to Professor Frank
Egerton of the University of Wisconsin–Parkside for information
and documents on the Forbes-Watson relationship. My treatment of
idealism in biology has benefitted immeasurably from the critiques
of my colleagues in Hawaii: Donald Worster, David Davis, Fred
Bender, and Robert McGlone. And the entire manuscript received a
careful scrutiny by Harold Burstyn and Alison Kay.

During two regrettably brief but memorable visits to the United
Kingdom I received many kindnesses and much assistance from a
number of people. At the British Museum (Natural History), the
pleasures of research were augmented by the congenial aid of Mr.
M. J. Rowlands, Miss Anne Twallin, Mr. Tony Rice and Mr. Al-
wyne Wheeler. The Archivist of Imperial College, Mrs. Jeanne Pin-
gree, was generous in both assistance and conviviality. Mr. John
Thackray was a most able assistant at the Geological Museum, and
Mr. James Friday gave valuable services at the Royal Institution.
Important aid was also provided by Mr. Gavin Bridson at the Linnean Society, Mr. L. P. Townsend at the Royal Society, Mr. Peter
Gautrey at the Cambridge University Library, and Miss J. H. Dring
of the British Association for the Advancement of Science.

At the Manx Museum, Miss A. M. Harrison and Miss Killip rendered friendly services during my short sojourn on Forbes's native
isle. And I am happy to express my special thanks, first to Forbes's
cousin, Miss F. Beatrice Kneen of Ballaugh, Isle of Man, for her gra-
cious hospitality and tour of Forbes's childhood haunts; and to Mlle.
Nora de Pianelli of Saint Jean de Luz, France, granddaughter of
Forbes, for information on surviving family documents.

For permission to quote from manuscripts in their possession I am
exceedingly grateful to the Librarian and Archivist of the Royal
Botanic Gardens, Kew (Hooker Papers); the Syndics of the Univer-
sity Library, Cambridge (Darwin Papers); the Librarian, Botany
School, Cambridge (Watson Papers); the Master and Fellows of
Trinity College, Cambridge (Owen-Whewell correspondence); the
Edinburgh University Library (Emerson-Brown correspondence);
the Trustees of the National Library of Scotland; the Manx

Museum, Douglas (Forbes Papers); and the American Philosophical Society (Lyell Papers, J. E. Gray Papers).

For the typing of this and so many other manuscripts, it is a real pleasure to thank Mrs. Barbara Hoshida and Mrs. Sandra Miyashiro of the General Science Department, University of Hawaii. Their patience and perseverance in wedging my work in amongst their more immediate responsibilities have been essential links in this production.

Finally, the greatest debt of all is to my wife, Karen, and my daughter, Maile, for their encouragement and tolerance of my academic habits. It is indeed miraculous that many families survive the demands of a career in academe during the present no-growth era.

A portion of this research was carried out with the financial support of the National Science Foundation.

Honolulu, Hawaii
Summer 1982

# The Philosophical Naturalists

# Introduction

In his first book—that tantalizing alloy of travel narrative and evolutionary anticipations, the *Journal of Researches* from the *Beagle* voyage—Charles Darwin wondered why the fossil skeletons of extinct species frequently bore a close resemblance to the skeletons of existing animals in the same geographic area. "The law of the succession of types," as Darwin called this phenomenon, "although subject to some remarkable exceptions, must possess the highest interest to every *philosophical* naturalist."[1]

During the same year that Darwin published his *Journal* (1839), the orotund Edinburgh anatomist Robert Knox translated Henri Marie DeBlainville's lectures on comparative anatomy for the London medical journal *Lancet*. Knox felt it necessary to explain to his readers that "the term 'signification of the skeleton' belongs peculiarly to the *philosophic* or *transcendental* anatomy."[2]

"Philosophical" naturalists? "Philosophic" anatomy? What did Darwin and Knox, two very different personalities of the early Victorian scientific world, mean by their use of the adjective "philosophical"? Could they have intended the same meaning? Is "philosophical" in these contexts merely a term of approbation, such as "thoughtful" or "penetrating"?

Darwin's sense of "philosophical" implied a preference for certain topics or questions in natural history; a "philosophical naturalist" was one particularly concerned with the history and distribution of species. Knox's usage, on the other hand, implied a distinct methodology for scientific practice, involving an a priori belief in the existence of ideal, or "transcendental," patterns in nature. For both men, however, a "philosophical" worker was one interested in discovering the *laws* of the living world, one who was not satisfied with the mere description of individual beings. It was precisely this search for laws or generalizations that, in the course of the nineteenth century, transformed the study of natural history into the science of biology.

Beyond their concern for the elucidation of nature's laws, Darwin and Knox had little in common. The scientist who bridged their worlds, who shared their belief in the need for laws, and who best exemplified their passions for species' history and distribution as well as ideal patterns, was the Manx naturalist Edward Forbes. A student in Knox's Edinburgh class at the height of the latter's career, Forbes subsequently moved to the front rank of Victorian naturalists as a result of his marine biological research and his engaging personality. When Darwin completed his 1844 essay on the transmutation theory, he named Forbes second only to Lyell as his preference for editor of the essay for publication in the event of his death.[3] The American transcendentalist Ralph Waldo Emerson met Forbes during a visit to Britain in 1848, and on the homeward voyage he wrote of Forbes as "one of the most remarkable men and one of the greatest promise in England."[4] And in 1851 the young T. H. Huxley ranked Forbes and Richard Owen as the two leaders of "Zoological Science in this country," reserving to Forbes the honor of having "more claims to the title of a Philosophical Naturalist than any man I know of in England."[5]

In Britain, natural history—the study of the earth's animal, vegetable, and mineral productions—first became a subject of serious scholarship in the latter half of the seventeenth century. The well-traveled John Ray and his friend Francis Willughby, Edward Lluyd and Robert Plot of Oxfordshire, and the naturalist fellows of the

Royal Society of London were among the earliest active researchers.[6] Their initial concerns were primarily taxonomic—how to identify, name, classify, display, and preserve the rapidly growing catalogue of nature's objects—and secondarily theological—how to comprehend and glorify a prolific Creator by the study of His Creation.

The accelerating pace of seventeenth-century research did not long survive in eighteenth-century Britain. Natural history entered into a relatively stationary phase, during which the discovery and classification of new species were the *ne plus ultra* of naturalists. To be sure there were striking exceptions: the studies of plant and animal respiration by Stephen Hales and Joseph Priestley, and the ecological and ethological observations of Gilbert White in the environs of his native village of Selborne, come to mind most quickly. But these brilliant beginnings remained isolated in a culture overwhelmingly devoted to collection and classification. The chemistry of plants and animals found most of its eighteenth-century contributors on the Continent; and White's *Natural History of Selborne* was largely ignored until well into the nineteenth century.

Events outside Britain, including the tremendous increase in knowledge of exotic species resulting from the voyages of exploration and the domination of natural history by the great classifier of Sweden Carl Linnaeus, dictated in great measure British research interests. And there were indigenous feelings which prevented the posing of new questions. Wasn't a knowledge of each of God's productions a sufficient goal for any naturalist? That in itself was a near impossible task for anyone in the eighteenth century. And weren't there impassable barriers to the solution of other questions, such as the first origins of plants and animals, the causes of their present distribution over the globe, and the relationships between present species and the fossilized forms found in the earth? Answers to these latter questions evolved only in the nineteenth century, when naturalists began to agree that nature herself *had* a history, that today's species and today's environments are different from those of the past. Few naturalists of the eighteenth century saw any reason to doubt the constancy of nature and its origin as described in Genesis. Consequently the science of natural history, with the exception of its taxonomic branch, remained largely devoid of theory. Without a body of theory it could not aspire to the level of respectability enjoyed by the physical sciences. And without theory there was little justification for regarding natural history as a legitimate academic subject.

The physical sciences shared to some extent in this eighteenth-century malaise. It continued into the early decades of the next century, until the 1830s, when a conscious, nationalistic outcry was heard about the "decline of science in England" from both established and aspiring scientists. The initial spokesman for this new concern was the mathematician Charles Babbage, who decried Britain's loss, primarily to France, of the hegemony in the physical sciences which she had enjoyed in Newton's time.[7] But the naturalists of early nineteeth-century Britain also had reason to feel inferior with respect to their Continental counterparts. From the time of Buffon in the mid-eighteenth century, French biological theory had grown steadily more sophisticated, and the Paris Muséum Nationale d'Histoire Naturelle had grown to be recognized as the leading center of biological research. Additionally, natural history scholars scattered through the German universities were contributing new ideas at a rate second only to the Muséum. It was no accident that the word *biology*—signifying a theoretical as well as a descriptive science of living things—was first used (about 1800) by German and French naturalists, not by an Englishman.

Recognizing the superiority of Continental biology and hoping to create a professional tradition of natural history research at home, British naturalists brought about a subtle but far-reaching transformation of their science during the period 1830–1860. These were the years of "philosophical" natural history. These were also the years of Darwin's voyage and his first publications. But Darwin was not yet the preeminent figure in the field. The "great Guns" of this era, as Darwin's botanical confidant Joseph Hooker called them,[8] were Charles Lyell, Richard Owen, William B. Carpenter, and Edward Forbes. The publication of *On the Origin of Species* in 1859, though typically treated as the commencement of a new epoch in the theory of natural history, was in fact the climax of half a century of searching for the philosophical foundations of the new science, "biology."

A great deal of recent scholarship has centered on Darwin,[9] but the topography of the pre-*Origin* period has not yet been fully mapped. There are important dimensions of natural history which remain in shadow, dimensions which bear directly on Darwin's achievement and are best subsumed under the contemporary phrase "philosophical natural history." Though frequently used, especially by Knox, Forbes, and Owen, the term *philosophical* was nowhere explicitly defined. It stood for an attitude, an approach to the study of natural history in which several features were characteristic.

First, the goal of philosophical natural history was the establishment of the laws of the living realm. No longer was God to be glorified by the mere description of His created species. Classification, that passion of the eighteenth-century naturalist, was of course still a major activity; but for the philosophical naturalist, it had become the most mundane of exercises. The old distinction between natural philosophy (the determination of principles operating in the physical world) and natural history (the description of the earth and its natural productions) had begun to break down. Naturalists began to view their endeavors as nomothetic—oriented toward the establishment of general laws—in contrast to the ideographic impulse (a concern for individual phenomena) which dominated their predecessors in the eighteenth century.

To contrast these two points of view, consider first the following statement by the Reverend James Grierson, an amateur naturalist writing on geology in the *Memoirs of the Wernerian Society* of Edinburgh in 1823. Reflecting the philosophy of his eighteenth-century forebears, Grierson was quite clear on the point that the naturalist must be contented with a description of what exists in nature, abjuring interpretations of the wheres, whens, and hows:

To know and distinguish [natural objects], to arrange or classify them; ascertain their properties and relations, so as that when we find one, we may in some degree know where to look for another; to ascertain their uses; to find whether there is any order in the structure of the earth on the great scale, and if so, what it is;—these, I should think, are subjects sufficiently attractive and interesting to any philosophic mind, and this is perhaps all the length we shall ever be able with certainty to go in the path of the science of which I now speak. For the subjects about which we reason are so hid from our view, and so completely beyond the reach of any thing like a thorough investigation, that it is nearly as unlikely we shall ever fully ascertain the manner of their formation, as it is unlikely we shall ascertain whether there are inhabitants in the moon or no. The subject, however, certainly has abundant interest without this, without any speculations and conjectures about the modes of original formation;—as much interest, I believe, as Botany has, or Zoology, or even Astronomy itself. Now, what botanist, or what zoologist, when he finds a new plant, or a new animal, puzzles himself and his readers, by endeavouring to ascertain how it was formed, or how it came to be in the place in which he found it? It is sufficient for him to know what place in his system the plant or the animal is to be referred to, what are its distinguishing properties, what are its uses, economical, medical, or ornamental.[10]

Now observe the new, nomothetic attitude expressed by the eloquent but forgotten anatomist Robert Knox near the end of the period of our study.

Zoology, to be esteemed a Science, must be based on philosophical principles. True, it is a science of observation and not of calculation; it has to deal with living bodies, and with the mysterious and hitherto undiscovered principle of life, whose laws are not to be explained by numbers, however multiplied, nor by geometry, however refined. Fluxions avail not here, nor the integral calculus. Nevertheless, some great minds have shown that Zoology has its laws, which, despite difficulties almost innumerable, may be so inquired into as to evolve some truths of more import to man that at first appears.

The observation of nature is no doubt the first duty of every candid observer; next comes the duty of the inquirer into her laws, for the mere observance of a fact is of no value whatever, unless that fact be placed in its relations with all others.[11]

The physiologist William B. Carpenter applauded the new approach more concisely in the opening paragraph of his popular *Principles of Comparative Physiology:*

There are few things more interesting to those who feel pleasure in watching the extraordinary advancement of knowledge at the present time, than the rapid progress of philosophical views in every department of Biological Science; the pursuit of which has until recently been made to consist, almost exclusively, in the mere collection and accumulation of *facts*, with scarcely any attempt at the discovery of the ideas of which they are but the expressions.[12]

The "philosophical" naturalist, therefore, was out to discover, not new species, but the laws of life itself.

For writers like Knox, "philosophical natural history" had a second, methodological meaning. It entailed an increasing dissatisfaction with traditional teleological arguments—arguments in which the existence of a particular organism or structure was accounted for in terms of its function or purpose—that had permeated British writings on natural history and natural theology throughout the eighteenth century and were brought to their peak of sophistication in the Bridgewater Treatises of the early 1830s.[13] No longer was it universally acceptable to argue that a certain organ or organism had a particular shape because of the physiological or ecological operation it was destined to perform. Biologists were not denying the existence of purpose and plan in the Creation; but they were rejecting the wholesale invocation of final (i.e., teleological) causes as the primary mode of explanation in their science. In the later nineteenth century they would turn, with Darwin, to genetic explanations, to efficient causation. But in the long transition from final causes to efficient causes came a period in which formal causes were in vogue. Organisms, in their morphology and in their distribution in space and time, were regarded as manifesting ideal patterns.[14] The ultimate goal of the naturalist was then to discover those patterns.

The method proper to this search for the patterns of the living realm was not always limited to the Baconian mode of inducing generalizations from facts previously amassed. In this instance *philosophical* was synonymous with *transcendental,* implying that the patterns to be discovered in nature might best be acquired by intuitive leaps of the imagination, rather than by coaxing from impersonal heaps of data. The great plan upon which nature had been built, the highest laws governing the appearance, the form, and the demise of organic beings, might be discovered a priori. These idealist "philosophical" naturalists took their inspiration, not from English philosophers like Francis Bacon or John Herschel, but from Plato, Kant, Goethe, the German idealist *Naturphilosophen,* and, in Britain, from William Whewell, Samuel Taylor Coleridge, and the earlier Cambridge Platonists.

This speculative methodology was severely denigrated by later positivistic scientists and historians, who viewed the results as, at best, over-hasty generalizing, and at worst muddle-headed or scientifically pathological. But no matter how the idealist or transcendental approach to science may have been judged by subsequent critics, it occupied the thoughts and governed the actions of major scientists in the early nineteenth century in Germany, France, and Britain. As such, it constitutes an undeniable case of the influence of metaphysical and epistemological theory upon science.

For naturalists like Darwin and Lyell, a third meaning of "philosophical" was uppermost. Their "philosophical naturalist" was one immersed, not in transcendentalizing, but in establishing the laws of the spatial and temporal distribution of organisms, laws whose comprehension might lead to a much larger understanding of the history, and perhaps the origins, of life than the ideographic activities of collectors and cataloguers ever could. This is clearly the meaning intended, for example, by Joseph Hooker when he wrote to Darwin in 1845 regarding the impending biogeographic dispute between Forbes and the phytogeographer Hewett Watson (see Chap. 5). Hooker hoped that Darwin could "offer some way or means of keeping these, almost the only 2 *philosophical* Brt. Botanists, out of a broil, at which all the dirty species-mongers will chuckle."[15]

Although there were hints of an interest in distribution studies in earlier British writings, such as those of John Ray, William Derham, and Richard Bradley, a conscious assault in this direction was initiated only in the early nineteenth century. "The distribution of organized beings in space and time" then became the typical phrase for referring to phenomena now treated by the sciences of ecology, biogeography, palentology, and stratigraphy. The discovery and relative dating of fossils—"distribution in time"—quickly became a visible and controversy-filled specialty, engaging much of the efforts of the fellows of the newly formed Geological Society of London, for example. Studies of the distribution of extant species "in space" gathered proponents rather more slowly. John Fleming, Hewett Watson, and Edward Forbes each began ecological studies in the 1820s and 1830s, but no scientific society sprang up to sponsor such investigations exclusively.[16] General recognition of the importance of ecological and biogeographic studies came only toward the close of the nineteenth century, under the expanding influence of evolutionary theory.

The exciting new hopes for early-nineteenth-century British biology were summed up in the adjective "philosophical." For some this meant an idealist approach; for others the key was in distribution studies. My goal in the present work will be to elaborate these two aspects of "philosophical" biology, in the belief that they are crucial to our vision of the intellectual landscape of that era. I shall begin, in Part I, by considering the idealist, pattern-seeking tendencies of British naturalists, because this aspect of their work is both fascinating, especially from the standpoint of the interaction between science and philosophy, and relatively little known.[17] Idealism among British biologists is usually associated only with Richard Owen, but we will find its appearance first in Robert Knox, and its applications most diverse in Knox's student, Edward Forbes. In our survey of the leading idealist naturalists, we will discover that they were predominantly Scottish or had an Edinburgh training, that they were far better known in their own time than they are to historians now, that manifestations of the tradition were most abundant in the early 1850s, and that by 1860 the movement had run its course.

In Part II, I turn to the "distribution" theme. Early nineteenth-century developments in ecology will be followed by an examination of the controversies which beset historical biogeography in its infancy. Here Forbes occupies a position of even greater centrality, as the precipitator of the priority conflict with Hewett Watson, the figurehead of the "extensionist" biogeographers, and the chief promoter of the biogeographic studies underwritten by the British Association.

The idealist and distributionist movements existed concurrently and, generally speaking, independently. The idealist methodology was usually confined to investigations in comparative anatomy and morphology, whereas distribution studies at this early stage appeared to rest inherently on a purely empirical, statistic-gathering foundation. On the few occasions when idealism and distribution studies were combined, most notably in Forbes's theory of "polarity" in the history of life, the results were confusion, derision, and/or oblivion. A discussion of the "polarity" case marks the transition from Part I to Part II.

These two contours of the scientific landscape, idealism and distribution studies, were essential components of "philosophical" natural history in the pre-*Origin* period. In retrospect it is now clear that Darwin's success was the result, among other things, of his belief in the significance of the distribution philosophy and his rejection of the idealist methodology.

# Part I
## The Idealist Approach to Nature

# 1

## *The Continental Background to Idealist Natural History*

Idealism, the metaphysical doctrine that ideas and minds are the fundamental realities and that matter—nature, the physical world—is secondary or dependent upon ideas, has had a long and fascinating career in the history of science. The notion that numerical ideas, such as certain whole numbers or geometric shapes, underlie specific physical phenomena, is generally associated with Pythagoras (582?–507? B.C.). Plato, a student of Pythagoreanism for a time, is credited with the more general "Theory of Forms," stating that Forms (ideas, essences) are the ultimate reality and that earthly phenomena are mere replicas of these ideas. Unlike material things, ideas do not come into or go out of existence; they do not exist in time at all. Accordingly, the task of the natural philosopher, in Platonic terms, was to discover the precise Forms which lay behind transient physical appearances. The goal of Ptolemaic astronomy, for example, was to determine the ideal geometry of uniform circular motions which was believed to determine the observed motions of the planets.

Medieval philosophers reinterpreted the theory of Forms in the light of Judeo-Christian theology, claiming that the Forms existed in God's mind. They were the models or patterns upon which He created the phenomena of nature. From this doctrine came the later assumption (which pervaded taxonomic thought through much of the nineteenth century) that every species of plant and animal consisted of a group of individuals, all of which adhered more or less closely to an ideal type in the mind of their Creator.[1]

Idealism in its Christianized form reemerged in the Renaissance, first as a fresh alternative to the established Aristotelian philosophy of Scholasticism, and later as a reaction to the materialistic aspects of the seventeenth-century mechanical philosophy. The astronomical innovations and geometric musings of Kepler were a conspicuous but hardly unique manifestation of the idealist mind of that era.[2] But when the mechanical philosophy, with its foundations in empiricism and materialism, prevailed as the successful metaphysical basis for science toward the end of the seventeenth centy, idealism was forced into the background. The Newtonian synthesis of mathematics, astronomy, and mechanics, buttressed by the empiricist arguments of Francis Bacon and John Locke, dominated scientific beliefs and aspirations for the next one hundred years, through the period of the Enlightenment.

### *Kant and* Naturphilosophie

The first major idealist challenge to the philosophical basis of Newtonian science was issued by Immanuel Kant (1724–1804) in the *Critique of Pure Reason* (1781). Kant's idealism was of a new stamp in that he emphasized the active participation of the human mind in the perception of phenomena. Sense experience alone is not a sufficient basis of knowledge of the external world, he insisted. Such knowledge is utterly dependent upon the organizing and interpreting functions of the mind. External objects in themselves (Kant's "noumena") are unknowable; only our mind-structured perceptions (his "phenomena") are knowable.

The fundamental truths of which we can be certain a priori are, according to Kant, the various concepts or patterns by which the mind organizes and interprets—the Categories of the Understanding, as he termed them. These Categories, such as cause and effect, space (including geometric shapes), time (chronological sequencing), and quantity, are arrived at by reasoning and hence transcend the world of physical appearances. Kant referred to his metaphysics, therefore, as transcendental idealism.

Kant went on to demonstrate the implications of transcendental idealism for the sciences in his *Metaphysical Foundations of Natural Science* (1786). In place of the Newtonian notions of matter and space, Kant founded his physics on the idea of force. We perceive the presence of matter, he explained, by the forces it exerts upon our senses—by its resistance to our efforts to move or divide it. The idea of force is itself a Category of the Understanding, a mental construct not subject to empirical verification. Once the a priori Categories are known, however, science then proceeds by experiment and observations to a detailed description of nature.[3]

To appreciate the full impact of Kant's critique, one must follow the idealist tradition through his successors. Most prominent among the German idealist philosophers of the period were Johann Gottfried Herder, Johann Gottlieb Fichte, Friedrich Wilhelm Joseph von Schelling, and Georg Wilhelm Friedrich Hegel, all of whom tended toward a more absolute form of idealism than Kant. Especially important in the context of science was the thought of Schelling (1775–1854), professor at the University of Jena (the early headquarters of romantic science and philosophy), whose writings also show a closer relationship to the Romantic movement than those of the other idealists. Schelling argued that the world of phenomena is a mind-ordered world and that knowledge of the mind's ordering principles is not to be gained empirically but through intellectual intuition. The deepest, most fundamental truths are won by speculative reasoning, from the attempt to grasp certain broad and irrefutable principles about reality, and to deduce logically other, less general principles from them. This constituted the way to knowledge for Schelling, including the way to knowledge of nature; thus, it was the proper method of science, both for Schelling and for the other thinkers in the tradition of *Naturphilosophie,* as the strain of scientific thought deriving from Kantian idealism came to be known.

Given this speculative conception of the scientific method, one might well ask if there were any fundamental principles of a priori knowledge upon which Schelling and the Naturphilosophen could agree. Generally they accepted the following premises:

(1) Since transcendental knowledge is foremost and since it is achieved by the operations of an acute intellectual intuition, it is essential that the mind be deeply and delicately sensitive— not only to the details of natural phenomena, but also to their overall beauty. Here we see most clearly the affinity of Natur- philosophie with the Romantic movement.

(2) Since the knowable reality is one of ideas, scientific explana- tions need not depend exclusively on materialistic or atomistic causes, as had been the pattern of Western science since the seventeenth century. Spiritual or nonmaterial causes were as acceptable as material ones.

(3) The existence of God was taken for granted, not because it could be proven through reason but because the alternative, the nonexistence of a First Cause, was neither palatable nor convenient. Faith in a divine being gave justification for faith in the ability of the human mind to arrive at true conceptions about Nature through speculative reason. The attempt to un- derstand the plan of Nature through a process of speculation was not a matter of guessing what was in God's mind but rather an act of participation in God's mind.

(4) Nature is purposive. Events can be accounted for in terms of the ends they achieve. Teleological arguments are thus accept- able in both the physical sciences (where they had been dis- allowed since the scientific revolution) and in the biological sciences (where they still enjoyed a vogue and would do so well into the nineteenth century).

(5) Nature is an organismic whole. It is more than merely the sum of its individual parts; hence it must be studied holistically, not analytically. (In this respect the Naturphilosophen antici- pated the perspective of nineteenth-century American tran- scendentalists like Thoreau, and the ecologists and environ- mentalists of the present day.)[4]

(6) Nature is composed of conflicting forces which are constantly in tension and may manifest themselves as polarities. In their

interaction these conflicting forces constantly give rise to new, higher forces and conflicts. Nature is thus a continually evolving progression, not a static, machinelike structure as pictured by Enlightenment science.[5]

The methods and attitudes of Naturphilosophie affected a great many German scientists in the late eighteenth and early nineteenth centuries. Among those working primarily in the physical sciences, we can include Hans Christian Oersted, Johann Ritter, and Christian Samuel Weiss. Outside Germany naturphilosophisch predelictions have been noted in Jakob Joseph Winterl, Jöns Jacob Berzelius, André-Marie Ampère, Humphrey Davy, and Michael Faraday.[6]

Idealism was no less prominent in the biological sciences, where Germany's great poet Johann Wolfgang von Goethe (1749–1832) was the seminal figure. He associated with Herder, adopted Kantianism, and was acquainted with Schelling and others at Jena, where, in the early 1780s he had studied anatomy under Just Christian Loder. Goethe's philosophy of nature was strongly neo-Platonic: he accepted as a priori principles the unity of all nature (including man), and the *scala naturae,* or chain of being.[7] He regarded as misdirected Linnaeus's efforts to classify all organisms by the analysis of minute differences; instead, naturalists should strive to find analogies between organisms which demonstrate the unity rather than the diversity in nature. Goethe's *Metamorphosis of Plants* (1790) has long been regarded as among the finest examples of scientific (or quasi-scientific) literature in the transcendental tradition, as well as an early classic in plant morphology. Elaborating on a theme suggested in Linneaus's *Philosophia Botanica,* Goethe interpreted each of the various parts of the flowering plant as successive modifications or metamorphoses of the basic form, an idealized, primal leaf. Beyond that, he regarded all the flowering plants as variations on an ideal plant archetype or *Urpflanze.*[8]

As we have seen, the highest principles of any field of scientific inquiry were, according to Naturphilosophie, to be discerned through reason, a priori, because they were a part of the reasoning process and hence transcended sense experience. Thus, transcendental anatomy and transcendental morphology were regarded as comprising the most profound principles of those sciences. As an example of such a principle, Goethe regarded the idea of *unity of plan* in the organic realm as one of the key principles of transcendental morphology,[9] and he was the first to insist upon its significance. According to this concept, the animal and the plant kingdoms are each built upon a single, general plan, or archetype, of which every species is a modification of one sort or another. Nature was thus "a vast musical symposium, in which the poverty of a solitary theme was enriched by an endless and expanding series of variations."[10] Because unity of plan is a transcendent pattern imposed by the mind, it does not depend on experimental observation for its validity. Rather it suggests to the observer how he is to interpret the phenomena. If a certain bone is found in the skeleton of one kind of vertebrate animal, unity of plan dictates that it will be found in other vertebrates, though perhaps in a modified form. After Goethe this concept became a theme in many treatises on comparative anatomy, morphology, and osteology. It was championed by Félix Vicq D'Azyr, Peter Camper, and especially Étienne Geoffroy Saint-Hilaire.

Unity of plan (usually synonymous with the "unity of design," "unity of structure," or "unity of organization" of later writers) was the most basic and enduring of the principles upheld by the transcendental morphologists. But there were other concepts which received much attention. The law of the *serial homology of parts,* which may have originated with Vicq D'Azyr, was promoted by Goethe and Lorenz Oken in Germany and by Geoffroy and Henri Marie DeBlainville in France, among others. This law stated that the morphology of every species is dictated in part by a repetition of certain basic structures, such as the vertebrae in mammals or the appendages in insects. One of the more extreme, yet popular arguments derived from this law was the vertebrate theory of the skull, i.e., the belief that the skull is composed of a number of vertebrae which are serially homologous with those of the spinal column. This theory was suggested by Goethe, J. H. F. von Autenrieth, and Jean-Pierre Frank; taught by Karl Friedrich Kielmeyer; and elaborated by Oken, André-Marie-Constant Dumeril, Jean-Baptiste von Spix, and many others.

Another of the transcendentalists' principles was the law of *parallelism,* stating that there is a parallel development between the embryonic states of higher animals and the permanent, adult states of lower animals; in other words, embryogeny repeats zoogeny.[11] This law was apparently first taught by Kielmeyer (1793), but expanded upon by many, including Oken, Johann Friedrich Meckel, Karl Gustav Carus, and Geoffroy's disciple Étienne Marcel de Serres. It has often been referred to as the Meckel-Serres Law.

These transcendental "laws," it should be emphasized, were *not* generalizations reached empirically from the careful consideration of experimental observation, for, as Naturphilosophie stressed, the central principles of every science must be intuitively, not empirically, founded. Accordingly, particular phenomena which appeared to follow these laws were not, strictly speaking, to be taken as evidence in support of the laws, but rather as illustrations of what was regarded as known a priori. And equally important, phenomena which appeared to violate the laws were not of great concern, since their inconsistency could be caused by inadequate interpretation, or by the incomplete state of the science.

### Transcendental Biology in France

In view of the early advocacy of transcendentalism in biology by the naturphilosophisch Kielmeyer, it is ironic that France's most prominent comparative anatomist, Georges Cuvier (1769–1832), who received early indoctrination in "philosophical natural history" under Kielmeyer at Stuttgart,[12] should have rejected the transcendentalist approach. It was, in fact, Cuvier's great contemporary and rival, Geoffroy Saint-Hilaire (1772–1844), who became the strongest proponent of transcendental biology among the French. Geoffroy studied under Buffon's collaborator L. J. M. Daubenton at the Jardin du Roi, and upon its reorganization as the Muséum d'Histoire Naturelle in 1793, he was appointed professor of vertebrates. He accompanied Napoleon as zoologist during the Egyptian campaign (1798–1801), securing important collections for the Muséum. But by the time Geoffroy returned to Paris, Cuvier (whom Geoffroy had sponsored for the Muséum's post of comparative anatomy in 1795) had risen to the position of supremacy among French naturalists.

The German transcendentalists both influenced and were influenced by Geoffroy. The unity-of-plan principle began to pervade

Geoffroy's thinking as early as 1796 and thereafter became the foundation of his philosophy of natural history. If every animal species is truly a modification of a single plan or archetype, then it should be possible to correlate the anatomy of every species with that of every other, that is, to establish for each organ of a particular species the counterpart or homologous organ in another, taxonomically quite distant species. Geoffroy attempted such a correlation of homologues in the higher vertebrates in 1807, and later in his *magnum opus,* the *Anatomical Philosophy* (1818–22),[13] sought to extend the principle to all vertebrates. To accomplish this end, Geoffroy introduced two further principles which are corollaries of the unity-of-plan concept, namely the *principle of connections,* and the *unity of composition.* The principle of connections alleges that organs may be increased or decreased in size or importance but never shifted in their spatial relations or sequence of attachment with one another. The principle of unity of composition, on the other hand, states that the same materials or building blocks are used for every vertebrate. By "materials," Geoffroy apparently meant not whole organs but parts of organs; in determining skeletal homologues, he used individual bones and, later, centers of ossification ascertained by embryological study.

The application of the unity-of-plan principle and its corollaries to vertebrate comparative anatomy implies that there must be an archetype or abstract generalized form against which all vertebrates may be compared. For Geoffroy this archetype was not man (as had been implicit in anatomical studies since Aristotle), but a type in which each part is taken from the species in which it appears at the maximum of development, that is, having the greatest number of subordinate parts, having all of its potential realized.

The insistence on a unity of plan in the animal kingdom would seem to require an explanation for the tremendous diversity that is actually observed in nature. Geoffroy's answer was to postulate, in 1807, a "principle of compensation" (*loi de balancement*). Diversity arises from modification of the archetype in which one organ is exaggerated at the expense of another. The materials constituting the organism being limited by unity of composition, the hypertrophy of any part must be compensated by the atrophy of another. In addition Geoffroy was forced to admit exceptions to the principles of transcendental morphology, but often did so by invoking additional ingenious rules. For example, the principle of connections was not inviolate, as he found in attempting to relate both fish and mammals to a single archetype. In this case it was necessary to introduce a "metastasis," or shift, of some organ groups with respect to others—for example, an attachment of the limbs to the spine further in the anterior or posterior direction as appropriate.

One might reasonably assume that the Naturphilosophen and adherents of transcendental morphology would tend to favor an evolutionary or transformist view of the history of life. In most cases, however, they did not. The German idealist philosophers followed a Platonic, idealist view of species as manifestations of abstract, immutable, Divine ideas. Unity of plan implied an intellectual, not a physical or genetic, continuity between species of successive ages, the result of the workings of a single super-rational mind.[14] In his later years, however, Geoffroy adopted an evolutionary conception of life in which some species might be transformed into others by sudden mutation. These transformations he thought to be environmentally caused—for example, the alteration of the respiratory apparatus by changes in the composition of the atmosphere. Transformation is possible because the species has a great potential for complexity; the environment then limits the manner in which that potential is realized. Transformation is thus a passive response of the species, not an active striving. Geoffroy did not have in mind the evolution of all species from a single archetype, but rather an evolution of limited extent. In positing environmentally produced transformations, he was clearly abandoning his pure morphological approach for a partially functional morphology.[15]

In subsequent works, Geoffroy extended the unity-of-plan principle to insects and crustaceans (*articulata*) by likening the skeletal segments and appendages of articulates to the vertebrae and ribs, respectively, in vertebrates. These two great groups of animals were completely homologous, Geoffroy claimed, the only difference being that vertebrates live *outside* their vertebral column while insects live *within* theirs. The ultimate application of unity of plan came in 1829, when two of Geoffroy's followers proclaimed that cephalopod mollusks were morphologically homologous to vertebrates. The cephalopod structure, they felt, was just a vertebrate structure (with all organs in the same order) bent back upon itself at the point of the umbilicus. Geoffroy's support of this hypothesis capped a growing controversy with Cuvier over the legitimacy of transcendental morphology and its assumptions, a controversy which acquired political and religious overtones.

Cuvier approached comparative anatomy from the functional or teleological rather than the formal standpoint; organs take on a particular structure because they must perform a specific task in the animal machine and must accord with the conditions of existence, not because they are modifications of an ideal, archetypal plan.[16] He had no difficulty in destroying the supposed cephalopod-vertebrate homology, and from then on Geoffroy's battle for the claims of transcendental morphology was an uphill one, though his position was supported by Goethe, who took great interest in the controversy in the last years of his life.[17]

### The Appearance and Reappearance of Idealism in England

In Great Britain idealism had always been very much a minority point of view among both philosophers and scientists. Its only prominence before the nineteenth century was among the Cambridge Platonists of the mid-seventeenth century, the most notable of whom were Henry More and Ralph Cudworth. More (1614–87), a fellow of Christ's College and a founding fellow of the Royal Society, authored several treatises in which he attempted to refute the increasingly popular mechanical philosophies of Descartes and Hobbes. Such materialistic thinking was, he felt, a threat to religion. His hope was to reestablish a belief in the active role of spiritual agents in nature, a hope which led him into an unfortunate conflict with Robert Boyle over the interpretation of the latter's hydrostatic experiments.

Ralph Cudworth (1617–88) also spent a long career at Christ's College, first as professor of Hebrew and later as master. Like More he was anxious to refute the materialism of Hobbes, but he viewed the mechanical philosophy as beneficial to theology as well as science. If matter is truly inert, as the mechanical philosophers insisted, then the universe itself would be inactive and lifeless were it not for the pervasiveness of a spiritual principle. For Cudworth this principle was not God but an unconscious agent of God, often referred to as "plastick nature" or "plastick virtue."[18]

Neither Cudworth nor More was well versed in seventeenth-century advances in natural philosophy. In general, the influence of the Cambridge Platonists upon their scientific contemporaries appears to have been momentary; little mention of them is to be found in eighteenth-century writings. When idealism finally reappeared in early-nineteenth-century Britain, it was the idealism of Kant and the Naturphilosophen that led the way. One of the first to visit Germany and return to England with an ardor for the new idealism was the poet Samuel Taylor Coleridge. After spending the better part of a year (1798–99) at the University of Göttingen, a center of naturphilosophisch thought,[19] Coleridge embarked on a lengthy program of Kantian and Schellingian studies. His enthusiasm for the new philosophy infected not only the poets of his era but also London's popular chemist Humphrey Davy, who passed it on to his assistant, Michael Faraday. In Faraday's hands the more moderate tenets of Naturphilosophie, especially the beliefs that nature is whole, interrelated, and dominated by forces and polarities rather than by atoms and collisions, contributed to the philosophical basis for what was probably the most inspired and influential career in nineteenth-century physics.

By the 1820s a second, separate German-inspired movement was taking root at Trinity College, Cambridge. A coterie of anti-materialist, anti-utilitarian academics led by the classics scholars Julius Charles Hare and Connop Thirlwall and the polymath William Whewell sought to modernize British scholarship and science by the introduction of German ideas and methods and to reduce the dominance of Lockean empiricism in the university's curriculum. Hare and Thirlwall translated the then-controversial *History of Rome* of Barthold Niebuhr, whose critical, antimythical analysis of classical source materials had helped revolutionize German historical methodology during the history-conscious Romantic era. Hare, in particular, was attracted to all things German and Romantic, including the thought of Kant, Goethe, and Schelling, the last of whom he visited in 1832.[20]

Both Hare and Thirlwall were teachers during the 1820s under Whewell, who was to become master of Trinity in 1841 shortly after the publication of his strongly Kantian *Philosophy of the Inductive Sciences*. The *Philosophy* centered on the search for the ideal principles (i.e., Kantian categories) of each of the sciences—"Fundamental Ideas," as Whewell called them. Among these a priori Ideas he included "number," "affinity," "polarity," and—expressly for the biological sciences—"symmetry," "likeness," and "final causes."[21] This outspoken promotion of a markedly idealist philosophy of science touched off a major debate with the more traditional, empiricist philosophers of science John Herschel and John Stuart Mill.[22] Idealist enthusiasm apparently did not penetrate the study of natural history at Cambridge in any significant way, however. John Stevens Henslow, then professor of botany, was largely a species man with an interest in geographical botany; and the University had no professor of zoology or comparative anatomy.

Thus far we have observed that idealism of the traditional Platonic form was urged by the Cambridge Platonists of the seventeenth century. And we have noted that a few enthusiastic devotees began to circulate praises of German idealism and to advocate its relevance to the natural sciences in London and Cambridge during the 1810s and after. In the 1820s there was a revival of idealism of the Platonic-Pythagorean type as well, brought about by the exertions of a group of taxonomy-minded naturalists known as the "quinarians." This earliest manifestation of idealism in nineteenth-century British natural history was instigated by William Sharp MacLeay (1792–1865). A highly regarded amateur entomologist, MacLeay was secretary of the Linnean Society of London from 1799 until 1825. In the latter year his responsibilities as a civil servant took him to Havana for a period of ten years. By 1839 he had retired and moved to Australia, where he spent the remaining years of his life.[23]

The "quinary" or "circular" system of classification, set forth in MacLeay's *Horae Entomologicae* (1819–21), elevated the number five and the geometric figure of the circle to preeminence in the natural world. MacLeay proclaimed that there were five primary groups in the animal kingdom: Vertebrata, Annulosa (insects), Mollusca, Radiata, and Acrita (polyps and worms). Each of these groups was alleged to be composed of five classes, the latter of five orders, and so on. Moreover, at each level of classification the five groups were ar-

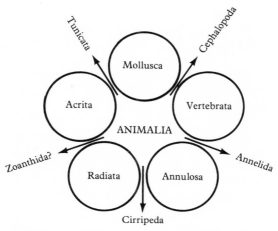

Fig. 1.1. MacLeay's quinary system. (From William Swainson, *A Treatise on the Geography and Classification of Animals* [London, 1835], p. 203.)

ranged in a circle, so that the taxonomist could begin at any point and progress through a series of forms, each having close affinities to the next, and eventually return to the starting point (Fig. 1.1).[24]

While the forms constituting any particular circle were arranged according to their gradually shifting *affinities* (i.e., adjacent forms having the greatest number of anatomical similarities), the forms at corresponding points on two different circles were related by their *analogies* (striking anatomical similarities present in forms that are otherwise distinctly different). Every circular series was thus linked in parallel to every other series. MacLeay believed this parallelism held even between the plant and animal kingdoms, as illustrated in Figure 1.2. This differentiation of the relations of affinity and analogy generated much discussion. It was also the probable source of Richard Owen's more clearly defined concepts of homology and analogy of the 1840s (see Chap. 3).

Although MacLeay graduated with a master of science degree from Trinity College in 1818, at precisely the time that Hare and Thirlwall were provoking interest in German thought, and although he met Geoffroy while attached to the embassy in Paris (1819), his writings show no obvious manifestations of the Naturphilosophie

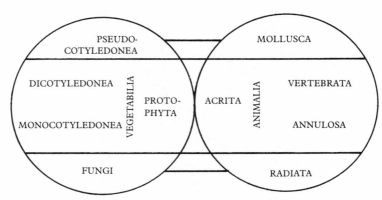

Fig. 1.2. Quinary arrangement of the plant and animal kingdoms. (From W. S. MacLeay, "Remarks on the Identity of Certain General Laws Which Have Been Lately Observed to Regulate the Natural Distribution of Insects and Fungi," *Transactions of the Linnean Society* 14 [1822]:65.)

tradition. The quinary system seems to have emerged from a purely empirical investigation of beetles. And MacLeay himself insisted that "naturalists have nothing to do with mysticism, and but little with *a priori* reasoning."[25] But once the system became clear to him, MacLeay was convinced that it was nothing less than the design God had conceived for His Creation on earth. It was too orderly, regular, and aesthetically neat to be a product of mere chance or human artifice. Just as Ptolemy had "saved the appearances" of the planets by reducing their apparently erratic motions to uniform circular motions, so MacLeay was "saving the appearances" here on earth by reducing the chaos of living beings to sets of circles within circles. The Platonic Form for the natural world had at last been grasped!

Quinarianism was debated at considerable length at the Zoological Club of the Linnean Society during the 1820s. A group of supporters, including Nicholas A. Vigors, William Kirby, Thomas Horsfield, and John Edward Gray, lent credence to the system by working out the taxonomy of various animal groups along quinarian lines.[26] And John Lindley, botanist at University College, London, subscribed to the theory, in part because it had been conceived independently by the Swedish mycologist E. M. Fries.[27] MacLeay's strongest backer was the prolific nature writer William Swainson.

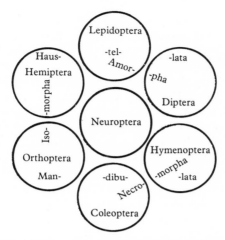

Fig. 1.3. Newman's septenary system. (From Edward Newman, "Further Observations on the Septenary System," *Entomological Magazine* 4 [1837]: opposite 236.)

The latter devoted the better part of several chapters of his 1835 *Treatise on the Geography and Classification of Animals* to an explication and defense of MacLeay's innovation (though he had decided that the primary ruling number was three, five being secondary).[28]

A different variation on the same Pythagorean theme was the septenary system of Edward Newman (1801–76). An amateur entomologist, Newman was a founding member of the Entomological Society and editor of several natural history journals during his lifetime. In 1832 he proposed that all major taxonomic groups could be divided into seven minor groups, one of which contained organisms "more perfect" than those of the other six. The proper pattern was achieved by placing the superior group in the center with the six inferior groups surrounding it in a definite sequence.[29] His chief illustration utilized the insects (Fig. 1.3). But septenarianism, even more complex than MacLeay's quinary system, was heavily criticized and won few if any followers.

In spite of Swainson's publicizing, the heyday of quinarianism had passed by the 1830s. Copies of MacLeay's original treatise became very rare owing to a bookseller's fire. More important, there was no consensus on the proper number of circular groups. Was it five? or three, or seven? Some support of the general concept of circular arrangements lingered as late as the mid-1850s: both Joseph Hooker and Thomas Huxley expressed the belief that there was "a great law" submerged in MacLeay's invention.[30] But the quinarian enthusiasm evidenced in the pages of the *Transactions of the Linnean Society* in the 1820s had disappeared.

Idealism in natural history was far from dead, however. Just as quinarianism was fading, the transcendentalism of Goethe, Geoffroy, and the Naturphilosophen began gradually to win converts across the Channel. The first beachhead to be established was at Edinburgh.

# 2

## *Robert Knox:*
## *Idealism Imported*

The Scottish Enlightenment, following its counterpart in France, made the city of Edinburgh perhaps the most intellectually exciting place in Britain between 1760 and 1830. Scientific associations began to flourish, led by the Edinburgh Philosophical Society and its longer-lived descendant, the Royal Society of Edinburgh. The social scene sparkled with some of Scotland's greatest luminaries: Adam Smith (economics); David Hume and the Common-Sense Philosophers: Thomas Reid, Dugald Stewart, Thomas Brown, and William Hamilton; John Playfair (mathematics); Robert Burns and Walter Scott (literature); James Hutton and Robert Jameson (geology); Joseph Black and Thomas Charles Hope (chemistry); William Cullen and Alexander Monro *secundus* (medicine); and the versatile Henry Home, Lord Kames.[1] "Athens of the North," as the city came to be called, was a well-deserved title in this period of Edinburgh's history.

Kantian idealism did not penetrate the ebullient atmosphere of Edinburgh until well into the nineteenth century. Britain's primary philosophical tradition had been one of realism and empiricism since the time of Bacon, Hobbes, and Locke. After the blow dealt to strict empiricism by the scepticism of Hume, the tradition was reestablished in the late eighteenth century by the Scottish Common-Sense Philosophers. The popularity of the Common-Sense school meant that the new idealism of Kant made headway only slowly. News of Kant's philosophy came into London and Edinburgh in the 1790s; Sir Walter Scott, for example, learned of Kant at this time as a student in the German classes of A. F. M. Willich. But the Scottish philosophers who tried to absorb Kant's reasonings, including Stewart and Brown, developed erroneous notions by depending on secondary sources or inadequate translations, and in general their attitude toward Kantian ideas was hostile. Assimilation came only in the 1830s, with William Hamilton's assumption of Edinburgh's chair of philosophy and logic (1836) and Francis Haywood's English translation of the *Critique of Pure Reason* (1838). Hamilton's attempt to reconcile Kantian thought with Common-Sense philosophy, though unsuccessful, was the initial event in the acceptance of Kant's ideas in British philosophical circles.[2]

But since the idealistic-transcendental approach to natural history was an application of Kantian precepts by Goethe, Geoffroy, and the Naturphilosophen, it is clear that these precepts began to make their way into British science before their assimilation into British philosophy. For at Edinburgh, the heartland of the empiricist Common-Sense Philosophers, idealism was promoted as essential to the study of comparative anatomy at least a decade before Hamilton's concessions to Kantianism. The promoter of this approach was the popular anatomy lecturer at the Edinburgh extra-academical school Robert Knox.

## Comparative Anatomy at Edinburgh

The medical school at the University of Edinburgh was at the peak of its eminence during the Scottish Enlightenment, with an international reputation which drew aspiring physicians not only from England and Ireland, but from the Continent and North America as well. Moreover, Edinburgh's curriculum included some of the only courses in natural history and related topics that were then available in Britain. Natural history was offered by Professors Robert Ramsay, John Walker, and Robert Jameson successively; botany by John Hope, Daniel Rutherford, and Robert Graham; *materia medica* by Francis Home and James Home; and anatomy by the Alexander Monros *secundus* and *tertius*.[3]

Although the courses in natural history at Edinburgh generally addressed the three principal branches of the subject (zoology, botany, and geology/mineralogy), comparative anatomy was not included. The latter subject, regarded as an aid to human anatomy and thus to medicine, was first taught by Alexander Monro *primus* (1697–1767) as a special summer course during the 1740s. A transcript of his lectures was published in 1744 as *Essay on Comparative Anatomy*.[4] His son, Monro *secundus* (1733–1817), shared this interest and published a work on the comparative anatomy of fishes in 1785.[5] But the subject apparently held no appeal for Monro *tertius* (1773–1859), so that when the latter assumed the chair of anatomy in 1808, students anxious for training in comparative anatomy sought out the Monros' rival in the extra-academic school, John Barclay (1758–1826).

Barclay, trained in the classics and theology at St. Andrews and Edinburgh, became a preacher and tutor, then turned to natural history.[6] By 1789 he had begun to study medicine, especially general and comparative anatomy. He was an assistant to John Bell (1763–1820), brother of Sir Charles Bell (1774–1842), and studied under both these distinguished anatomists. After receiving the doctorate in medicine at Edinburgh (1796), Barclay determined to become a teacher of anatomy. An additional year of study in London ensued, so that Barclay was nearly forty by the time he began formal teaching. His classes in anatomy, offered every winter from 1797 until 1825, were highly successful. When his competitor, Monro *secundus*, turned over the university chair of anatomy to his less illustrious son, Barclay's enrollments began to climb, reaching a peak of 300. This achievement may have been due, in part, to the fact that Barclay devoted all his time to teaching instead of dividing it with a medical or surgical practice, as was common with his predecessors and competitors.

Barclay's enthusiasm for comparative anatomy was evidently unusual in that time and place. He accumulated a museum of human and comparative anatomical specimens for lecture and study purposes, and during his last few years taught comparative anatomy in

Fig. 2.1. John Barclay and comparative anatomy: "The Craft in Danger." (From John Kay, *A Series of Original Portraits and Caricature Etchings,* new ed., 2 vols. [Edinburgh, 1877], 2:448.)

the summer months. Such was his reputation that in 1817 there was a move to create a chair of comparative anatomy at the university for him. Opposition from established colleagues was severe enough, however, to quash the proposal. The affair inspired an amusing and informative caricature (Fig. 2.1) in which Barclay is depicted as attempting to ride the skeleton of an elephant into the university. His progress is assisted by two friends (Dr. James Gregory and town council member Robert Johnston), but opposed by Professors Hope, Jameson, and Monro.

The period of Barclay's tenure in Edinburgh coincides precisely with the inception of transcendental morphology in Germany and France. Barclay is not known ever to have visited the Continent. He was cognizant of the overall unity of structure among vertebrates, however,[7] and it seems likely that the two British anatomists most noted for their idealist inclinations, Robert Knox and Richard Owen, received their first stimulus in this direction from Barclay. Because Knox's career is far less well known, I will deal with it here

Fig. 2.2. Robert Knox. (A sketch by Edward Forbes, appearing in Henry Lonsdale, *A Sketch of the Life and Writings of Robert Knox the Anatomist* [London, 1870], opposite 40.)

at length, leaving Owen (who was Knox's junior by eleven years and may even have been his student briefly) to a later chapter.

## The Tribulations of Robert Knox

Born in Edinburgh in 1793, Knox was allegedly related to the religious reformer John Knox and (on his mother's side) to German ancestors.[8] His father, a schoolmaster, sympathized with the French Revolution and most things French, which may account in part for his son's later Francophilism. After a solid training in the classics at Edinburgh High School, Knox entered the university as a medical student in 1810. Completing the course in the requisite three years, he stood for examinations but failed, ironically, in anatomy. The anatomy lectures of Monro *tertius* had been suffered through once, apparently to little avail, so Knox sought out the dedicated Barclay. The latter provided the intellectual inspiration which in Monro had been absent, and in 1814 Knox received his degree in medicine.

Probably at Barclay's suggestion, Knox then traveled to London to study surgery and physiology at St. Bartholomew's Hospital under the eccentric but popular John Abernethy (1764–1831),[9] student and successor of John Hunter, England's most famous comparative anatomist of the eighteenth century. Much of Hunter's career had been devoted to the assemblage of exhibits illustrating the principles of comparative anatomy.[10] For Knox, training with Abernethy as well as with Barclay meant exposure, early in his career, to the best traditions of comparative anatomy in both England and Scotland.

The following year (1815) Knox was sent to Brussels as an army surgeon in the aftermath of Waterloo. Despite the bloodshed and abominable conditions of army hospitals, Knox found the life of an army surgeon appealing enough to remain on active duty another six years. In 1817 he was sent to the Cape of Good Hope as surgeon-naturalist of the Seventy-second Highlanders Regiment. Natural history observations occupied his time during the voyage south, including thrice-daily temperature readings of atmosphere and ocean, and dissection of marine vertebrates.

Knox remained at the Cape colony until 1820. Bloody conflicts between Kaffir natives and Dutch and British colonials did not deter him from spending long periods on scientific pursuits. Observations of the character and habits of the South African natives presaged the fascination for ethnology of Knox's later years. They also led him to become a native sympathizer and anticolonialist—liberal views most unorthodox in his day. He skinned and dissected native animals, advancing his knowledge of comparative anatomy. His other investigations concerned physical geography, meteorology, and the influence of climate upon sanitation.

Back in Edinburgh by 1821, Knox began publishing articles on his South African research and experiences. He joined the prestigious Wernerian Natural History Society founded by Robert Jameson in 1808. Medical investigations were apparently still his first love, however, so to broaden his experience he traveled to Paris in the autumn of 1821. There he spent a year studying pathological anatomy and, by reason of his already established reputation, acquired lasting friendships with Cuvier, Geoffroy, DeBlainville, and other prominent figures of the French scientific establishment.[11] It was at this time that Knox absorbed the precepts of Naturphilosophie that he would later retail to his students and readers. Thus, his transcendentalism came principally from the Continental naturalists, not from reading Kant directly nor from studying purely philosophical sources of post-Kantian idealism.

The impact of the three leading French naturalists of the post-Napoleonic era upon Robert Knox cannot be too highly stressed. Extravagant praise of them, especially of Geoffroy, can be found in many of his writings, especially in those of his later years, such as the collection of biographical essays published in 1852 as *Great Artists and Great Anatomists.* "True descriptive anatomy," Knox claimed, had been founded by Xavier Bichat, but Bichat had limited his studies to man. Cuvier then carried this approach into zoology, thereby founding comparative anatomy, and then applied it to fossils, thus establishing vertebrate paleontology and providing a new "History of the Earth."[12] But Cuvier's scientific caution made him avoid "the philosophy of that history,"[13] made his work too ideographic, too little nomothetic:

Occupied with facts and details, that is, history,—eschewing principles, that is, philosophy,—[Cuvier's] view, even of the past, was limited and confined. That past he did not fully comprehend, or rather he avoided admitting that he did; of the future he said nothing. Simultaneously with him arose others, who valued facts merely as leading to principles; of those, Goethe and Geoffroy may be considered the type and the leaders. Other illustrious names must be conjoined to these. They did not discover the transcendental in anatomy, but they collected the facts in support of its principle. . . . Descriptive anatomy, which Cuvier and his followers called comparative anatomy, in his hands overturned all existing cosmogonies; [but] the transcendental went further; it developed the great plan of the creation of living forms; the scheme of Nature. It unfolded the secondary laws by which the transformations are made, the metamorphoses out of which variety springs from unity: the natural history of creation was for the first time explained to man.[14]

If there is to be a science of living things, Knox insisted, it must certainly go beyond individual phenomena and penetrate the larger questions of that realm:

Zoology is either a science or it is not. If it be a science, it ought to enable us to decide on some principles applicable to the zoological world. . . .

Zoology, if a science, should enable us to decide on the great questions of unity of organization, and of a serial unity of all that lives; and if of all that now lives, by the anatomy of the fossil world the unity of the past and present ought to be proved or disproved.[15]

The tremendous enthusiasm for comparative and transcendental anatomy Knox acquired in Paris he continued to preach for the next forty years. Always he looked to France and Germany as the source of transcendentalism.[16] Especially pronounced was his esteem for Goethe, who

by his discovery of the unity of the organization, had, long prior to Cuvier, laid the basis of a superstructure which will in all probability prove enduring; but his labours in the field of the transcendental remained unknown; men's minds were not prepared to comprehend them; it was as if a Newton had appeared in the fourth or fifth century of the Christian era; even to Humboldt the illustrious Goethe was incomprehensible; he had appeared before his age, a misfortune which has befallen many great men; and so, disgusted, he left that field, in which, had he persevered, he would no doubt have distanced all others.[17]

And always Knox denigrated the backwardness of the British for failing to understand transcendentalism. In his retrospective analyses published in the 1850s, Knox found several reasons for the degenerate state of British zoology. First, there was a general disinterest in science.[18] This apathy was compounded by a reluctance to adopt ideas from the Continent.[19] Science was thus left to the popularizers, who, more often than not, debased the writings of Continental naturalists.[20] Cuvier in particular had been greatly misunderstood. And transcendental biology had been first ignored, then later adopted in a diluted form, and finally accepted *in toto,* without criticism, long after Continental naturalists had become critical of its excesses. "A few years ago," Knox wrote in 1856,

the English transcendentalists proclaimed themselves to be low transcendentalists, and maintained [Lorenz] Oken and his followers to be decidedly insane—a remark I heard from an illustrious French savan [*sic*] in Paris so long ago as 1822. That the same opinion of the ingenious and gifted German prevailed in England until a very few years ago is a fact beyond all dispute. Since then—that is, since the translation of Oken's work [*Elements of Physio-Philosophy,* 1847]—the doctrines of this worthy and simple-minded enthusiast have been all the rage in England, taken up *con furore* on this side of the channel so soon as they had been laid down on the other.[21]

But in 1822 the young Knox's outlook about the prospects of philosophical natural history in Britain was not yet tarnished. His student and biographer, Henry Lonsdale, gave the following account of Knox's inspired attitude upon returning to Edinburgh from Paris:

Elated by the presence, and still more by the personal recognition, of these great masters Cuvier, Geoffroy and DeBlainville, whose bold inquiries had penetrated the arcana of science, and revealed to mankind fresh realms of thought, Knox longed to soar above the stereotyped formulas of medicine and to take part in the extension of the new philosophy. Amid the zoological treasures obtained by Napoleon, and the osteological collections of Cuvier, Knox became imbued with a great emulation for biological study. This spirit was manifested in all its freshness on his settling down in Edinburgh at Christmas 1822, and continued unabated through life.[22]

During the next two years Knox improved upon his knowledge of comparative anatomy by daily dissections and reading of foreign works. Election to the Royal Society of Edinburgh followed the presentation of papers there and elsewhere, including his important monograph "Observations on the Comparative Anatomy of the Eye" and shorter pieces on the anatomy and ethology of mammals, monotremes, reptiles, and fishes.[23] Much of his zoological research was conducted at the university museum of natural history, where a growing relationship with Robert Jameson gave Knox access to rare specimens from Africa and Australia. In return Knox provided editorial assitance in Jameson's *Edinburgh Philosophical Journal.*[24] These activities soon convinced Knox of the need for a bona fide museum of comparative anatomy in the Scottish capital. After some months of negotiations and preparations, the Royal College of Surgeons of Edinburgh appointed him assistant to the keeper of the existing pathological collections, with the responsibility of acquiring and maintaining a museum of comparative anatomy. Thus began seven years (1824–31) of collecting efforts, ranging from the purchase of marine specimens from fishwives on the Firth of Forth to the acquisition of a part of Sir Charles Bell's anatomical collection in London. The college recognized his acumen by electing him conservator of the museum in 1826.[25]

Concurrent with work at the museum, Knox entered into partnership with the aging John Barclay at the extra-academical school of anatomy. There he took over Barclay's lectures in the fall of 1825, and all other responsibilities of the partnership a year later when Barclay died. Barclay's annual student following of some 300 students was built up to more than 500 by Knox only three years later; this amounted to two-thirds of all Edinburgh medical students—the largest anatomical class in British history.[26] In addition to lecturing on human anatomy continuously until 1842, Knox gave lectures on comparative anatomy in 1825–1827.[27]

While Barclay has been referred to as "the first teacher in Britain to give direction to the study of Comparative Anatomy,"[28] his successor went a step further. Knox insisted that neither human nor comparative anatomy should be regarded as ends in themselves. Human anatomy should lead us to an understanding of comparative anatomy, which in turn can open our eyes to the larger philosophy of living beings, to the laws governing the morphology and history of all species. Thus, in his lectures Knox proceeded from descriptive anatomy, in the manner of Barclay, to transcendental anatomy and paleontology, *à la* Geoffroy and Cuvier.

"To some lecturers," Lonsdale recounted, "a bone was but a structure with certain physical features, and nothing more. Knox made it assume an historical position in the scale of organization; its size and form were patent enough, but he sought in the osteogenesis and type and homologues to fix its place in the general superstructure of the animal series: in short, he gave not the mere description, but the philosophy of the osseous form."[29] Knox's eloquence reputedly drew "barristers, scholars, clergymen, noblemen, artists and men of letters" [30] to his lecture rooms. Among his students were many of the leading lights of mid-century British science: the anatomists John Goodsir, William Fergusson, John Reid, John Hughes Bennett, Thomas Wharton Jones, and Henry Lonsdale; the zoologists Edward Forbes, Harry Goodsir, and possibly Richard Owen; and the geologist Hugh Falconer.[31] As we shall see, some of these "Knoxites"[32] were among Britain's principal exponents of transcendental natural history.

Despite the great popularity of Knox's Edinburgh lectures, it appears that they were never published, either in full or in syllabus form. From his own later references to this period, however, we know that he gave emphasis to such transcendental principles as the unity of plan and the law of compensation even in his earliest lectures: "Convinced of the soundness of the basis on which Autenrieth, Goethe, and Geoffroy had constructed the great theories of Transcendental Anatomy, I hesitated not applying them constantly in all my researches in zoology, from 1820 inclusive: these principles were fully explained by me in three courses of lectures on Comparative Anatomy delivered to distinguished classes in 1825–26–27."[33] Since Knox had then only recently returned from months of exposure to the intellects of the Paris Muséum, it seems probable that his students were treated to the transcendentalist views in all their freshness, a factor which certainly made Knox's courses unlike those of his rivals. Lonsdale confirms this interpretation, adding that Knox's presentation was well suited to his listeners, who were seldom prepared to accept all of the profundities advanced:

Knox imbibed the Germanic, or transcendental anatomy, as it was called, from [Geoffroy] St. Hilaire, and preached the new doctrines from his earliest career as a lecturer. While he spoke of the similarity of constitution traceable in the osseous formation of the vertebrae and cranium, the English student, fond of matter-of-fact principles, was disposed to smile at the "Transcendentalists." Knox rode no hobby in this matter, but gave a cautious exposition of both the data and the doctrines—the best precursor to further inquiry among men whose minds had to be prepared for a further insight into the Continental philosophy.[34]

Lonsdale stressed as well Knox's priority in introducing transcendental anatomy to Britain:

Knox appeared to have been among the foremost to make St. Hilaire's doctrines on the unity of organic structure known to large classes of British students. His lectures on osteology were all the more attractive that he indicated to the pupils the structural elements or essential parts of each bone in man, the developmental relations these bore to other vertebrated animals, the borrowing of elements, so to speak, here, the imparting of elements there; or what St. Hilaire called *balancement des organes*, and, as he further espressed, *"l'atrophie d'un organe tourne toujours au profit d'un autre."*[35]

Beyond these pronouncements on Knox's pedagogical approach, we should note his efforts to make available to his students what he regarded as the best of European anatomical texts. In 1828 he published an annotated translation of Hippolyte Cloquet's *System of Human Anatomy*. This was followed in 1829 by a reprinting of *The Anatomy of the Bones of the Human Body* by Jean Joseph Sue and Bernhard Siegfried Albinus (previously used by Barclay), and in 1830 a translation of Pierre Auguste Béclard's *Elements of General Anatomy*. The last was a compilation from the work of Meckel, prominent amongst the German transcendental anatomists and proponent of the law of parallelism.[36] A decade later, after the popularity of his lectures had fallen off, Knox published a serialized translation of his "constant correspondent"[37] DeBlainville's lectures on comparative anatomy.[38]

Apparently Knox felt that the British student of anatomy would be better served by annotated translations of the best Continental works than by a new text of his own composition. Despite frequent displays of egotism about his scientific career, Knox seems to have regarded himself primarily as the articulator of the best in French and German science to an ignorant Britain, rather than as the creator of original work. The last of the translations cited above, for example, shows Knox, as always, to be an admirer of DeBlainville, though not unwilling to correct what he regarded as errors of anatomical detail.

Knox's record of publications in scientific journals was an erratic one, to say the least. In the 1820s his articles numbered nearly thirty, mostly on vertebrate anatomy. Many concerned exotic species, such as the platypus, echidna, cassowary, dugong, and wombat. These articles appeared principally in Edinburgh journals, however, and evidently did not bring Knox the degree of national and international renown he thought should be forthcoming. During the next decade, which ought to have found him in the prime of his career, he authored only half as many articles, and these on more local topics, mainly the whale and the salmon. Between 1844 and 1850 his output consisted of two brief communications on fish to the British Association meeting at Southampton (1846).[39]

This record must be viewed in relation to the grave difficulties which befell Knox's career, beginning in 1828. As a dedicated teacher of anatomy he had insisted on an abundant supply of cadavers for the illustration of his lectures and for the practical dissection experiences of his students. Prior to the passage of the Warburton Anatomy Act in 1832, however, British law prohibited the dissection of human bodies except those of executed criminals. As a result, body-snatching from graveyards by students and professors' assistants had been common practice since the early eighteenth century. Like all of his competitors, Knox had to acquiesce to "resurrectionism." He was, in fact, in the habit of paying top prices to insure adequate numbers of subjects for his large classes. The shortage of cadavers became even more severe in 1826, when courses in practical anatomy, requiring dissections by every student, began to be compulsory. Unfortunately, fate dictated that it was Robert Knox who became the chief client of the infamous Edinburgh murderers William Burke and William Hare. Discovering that murder was a far simpler means of obtaining corpses for anatomy professors than grave-robbing, Burke and Hare sold their victims to the unknowing Knox and his student demonstrators for nearly a year. When they were found out, Hare turned King's evidence; his confession brought about the conviction of Burke. Shortly before his hanging in January of 1829, Burke exonerated Knox of any complicity in the murders, and several months later a committee of inquiry confirmed his innocence. Knox nevertheless had to bear, along with Hare, the public hysteria that followed. Moreover, his anatomical rivals, Monro *tertius,* James Syme, John Lizars, and John Aitkin, who but for chance might just as well have been the clients of Burke and Hare, responded to Knox's plight not with sympathy but with disdain. The stigma of this tragic association remained with Knox for the rest of his life.[40]

Despite mob violence and threats to his life, Knox maintained his schedule of lectures, becoming ever more popular with his students on that account. But outside the lecture hall things did not go well. At meetings of scientific societies he was no longer a welcome partic-ipant. His colleagues at the Royal College of Surgeons, taking the attitude of the public rather than that of the students, harassed Knox into resigning the position of museum conservator. Knox himself seems to have lost interest in his formerly active research on human anatomy; much of the next decade was spent on the dissection and skeletal reconstruction of beached whales.[41]

By the mid-1830s enrollment in Knox's classes had begun to de-cline, and with it his salary. This plight was not unique to Knox; Edinburgh was losing its hegemony among centers of medical train-ing. Schools in London and Dublin had undergone improvements, and new institutions were being established in the provinces. Mean-while, Edinburgh's medical program took longer for the student to complete, was more costly, and was under the direction of too many aging professors. Better training and a more abundant source of sub-jects for dissection were to be had elsewhere.[42] Knox struggled along, applying for various lectureships within the university, and in defeat, becoming increasingly cynical. Finally, in 1842 he was un-able to attract a class at all. Hopeful of employment elsewhere, he traveled to London. But there he was equally without welcome. He had indeed become the "surgeons' scapegoat"[43] throughout the country.

Thus began a period of itinerant lecturing and writing for London medical journals. He toured the provincial cities, lecturing on the subject of his newly revived interest: ethnology. He took a position in Glasgow briefly, teaching a small class "On the Brain and Ner-vous System."[44] No permanence was to be found in any of these ac-tivities; in little more than ten years Knox had fallen from a position of increasing wealth and prominence within the intellectual society of Edinburgh to homeless, borderline poverty. The Royal Society of Edinburgh, which had "looked upon Dr. Knox as its chief anatomist, by consulting him on all zoological questions, and entrusting him with the dissection of animals obtained from abroad,"[45] went beyond removing his name from the membership rolls; it revoked his original election.

In the midst of these trials, Knox became caught up in a second scandal, this one involving the certification of medical training. Mr. John Henry Osborne had fraudulently obtained a diploma from the Royal College of Surgeons of England by claiming a long apprenticeship to his father and producing certificates of attendance at various lectures in Edinburgh and Glasgow. As luck would have it, the most obviously questionable certificate was one for Knox's lectures during the winter of 1839–40. Knox had apparently signed the certificate himself, but other evidence indicated that Osborne had not been in Edinburgh during the alleged course of lectures. The College of Surgeons could, and perhaps should, have taken action against Osborne, but it did not. He was allowed to continue his practice and later held medical positions of considerable responsibility. The Edinburgh College of Surgeons stepped in, however, to determine Knox's role in the scandal. When requested by the college to justify his actions, Knox took the medical profession to task for the looseness of its licensing policies rather than giving a reasoned defense of himself. Always the champion of principles, Knox saw this occasion as an opportunity to air, once again, his conviction about the need for medical reform, when in fact he ought to have been looking after his own career. Not surprisingly, his replies were found to be unsatisfactory by the body that ten years before had turned him out of its museum. In the end the college withdrew its approval of Knox's lectures as qualifying toward the surgeon's diploma, notifying all other similar licensing boards in Britain of the action. Thus, in 1847 Robert Knox's career as a teacher of anatomy, the occupation at which he excelled, was effectively terminated.[46]

With the prospect of lecturing all but demolished, Knox turned his talents more fully toward writing. And it was during the 1850s that his powerful style of exposition, previously confined to lectures, became manifest in print. Between 1849 and his death in 1862, he authored or translated no less than eight books and at least a dozen articles. The larger works ranged in subject matter from zoology and fishing to ethnography and the relations between anatomy and art.[47] Some sold very well, fortunately, as they were at times his only source of income.

### Knox and Philosophical Anatomy

Knox's advocacy of the transcendental approach to biology is most evident in his writings of this later period, especially in a series of largely historical and philosophical papers published in *Lancet* and the *Zoologist*, and in his *Great Artists and Great Anatomists* (1852). The time had come, he seems to have felt, to promote in England the venerated Continental tradition of Goethe, and not coincidentally to reassert the credentials, exceptional among British anatomists, of the Scottish "friend" of Cuvier, Geoffroy, and DeBlainville.

Transcendental anatomy, "the only instrument of research at present known by which a correct basis can be laid for the philosophy of Zoology,"[48] entered Knox's consciousness as early as 1811, from the writings of Vicq d'Azyr.[49] There is little doubt that he discussed the doctrines of transcendentalism in his lectures of the 1820s and 1830s, and that he was the first in Britain to do so. Yet there is scant evidence of such views in his published writings prior to the 1840s. The only significant reference to his French colleagues during the earlier period, in fact, is a denunciation of Cuvier's principle of the functional correlation of parts.[50] Knox was utterly opposed to the a priori deduction of unknown fossil structures from known structures based on presumed functional necessity, the famous first anatomical rule of Cuvier and his followers. With a partial knowledge of the anatomy of a particular species it is possible to guess at the nature of the remaining organs, but such guesses, Knox insisted, are just that. As there are exceptions to every known correlation, the only way to be sure of the unknown structures is by empirical examination. "The quadruple stomach of the ox and sheep is said to compensate for the deficiency of the incisor teeth; [yet] the camel has teeth of this kind, and its stomach is quintuple."[51] *Func-*

*tion* cannot, therefore, be said to dictate or determine *structure*. Quite the opposite, Knox insisted:

The causes, then, of nearly all structures are concealed, as yet, by an impenetrable veil from human sight, leaving only a few great and general laws applicable to animal nature, but so loosely as greatly to diminish their value. It is not with animal machines as with a watch or other piece of human mechanism, wherein the purpose of its creation is expressly known and understood, and the reason, which, moreover, is purely a mechanical one, for the presence of each wheel and pivot, chain and box, made known to us by the mechanist, or discovered, on investigation. The animal machine abounds with structures, the reason for whose pressure he cannot guess at, neither can he calculate what might be the result of their absence or destruction. That design generally, in the complex machinery of animal bodies, is too obvious to require even a thought; but the attempts at particularizing the particular design connected with separate individual organs, seem to me hitherto to present a series of the most lamentable failures in human reasoning. I do not hesitate to declare nearly all the systems hitherto built on these opinions as so many systems of false philosophy, of which some are below criticism, and others of a pernicious tendency.[52]

Knox may well have been following the antifunctionalist lead of DeBlainville here. Precisely the same opinions were expressed by DeBlainville in his lectures on comparative osteography (translated by Knox):

Unquestionably there exists an appreciable harmony as to number, form, position, and proportions, between all the solid organs which enter into the composition of the skeleton of every vertebrate animal. . . . This observation could have escaped no one since the time of Galen to the present day; but to believe that the science of osteography is sufficiently advanced, or can ever be so, to enable us ever to reach such a degree of pre-vision . . . that a single bone, or a single facette of a bone, being examined, it would be possible for any person to re-construct or pourtray [*sic*] the whole skeleton, and afterwards add to it the remainder of the organization of the animal to which the bone had belonged, is to encourage a pretension which will appear the more exaggerated and the more extraordinary in proportion as any one may himself have studied the science, as well *à priori* as *à posteriori*.[53]

In the late 1830s, Knox was still harping on this point. British zoologists, in particular, had been easy victims of the fallacious reasoning of the Cuvierian functionalists, he complained. His own warnings to this effect had gone unheeded, to the detriment of the progress of philosophical natural history:

> As early as the year 1821, I denounced the pretensions . . . of the Cuvierian school and its followers, as being without any foundation in truth; being, in fact, absolutely absurd. Subsequently—in a series of lectures on comparative anatomy, delivered here to large and distinguished classes from the year 1825 to 1828 . . . —I endeavoured, to the utmost of my power, to stem the torrent of assertion, amounting to absolute nonsense, which had set in, in this country, on the subject. So many persons had studied, read, and got by rote the works of the great Cuvier, instead of the book of Nature—so many had translated, copied, and appropriated his views to themselves,—and so extensive, indeed, had the Cuvierian mania and party become in this country, that to doubt the correctness of any of the views of Cuvier amounted to a personal attack upon thousands of his satellites, who thought only through and by means of him, and who, in fact, placed him precisely in the same position as the Monkish writers of the middle ages placed Aristotle.[54]

For Knox, the form of every species was to be explained by reference to the transcendental archetype working through secondary laws as yet unknown, not by any sort of teleological or mechanical reasoning. He was consistently disdainful of the kinds of explanations based on final causes that the authors of the Bridgewater Treatises had employed.

> There are persons who believe that the blubber of the whale is placed in the animal by Nature, to render the animal buoyant; and that the rudiments of mammae are placed on the human male breast to warm and cherish the heart, and also for the sake of ornament. I feel, of course, that to persons whose physiology is of this cast, all my previous remarks must appear puzzling and contradictory; but they will not, I trust, appear the less unimportant that they are not fully understood by those whose habits of loose reasoning induce them to grasp at the first explanation of a phenomenon which presents itself to their minds.[55]

At the same time, however, Knox was cognizant that transcendental doctrines did not in themselves constitute the causes of phenomena; the causes were still not known. Rather, the purpose of transcendental interpretations was to help the anatomist or zoologist arrive at a correct *description* of the facts. The transcendental theory, he admitted, "gives us no insight, it is true, as to *why* these things should happen so, but it shows the *manner* of their taking place."[56]

Despite Knox's espousal of transcendentalism from the 1820s onward, the earliest *published* intimation of his position appears only in his translation of DeBlainville's lectures (1839). Here as elsewhere his attitude is positive yet cautious. In a footnote to DeBlainville's statement about having given a course on "the signification of the skeleton" at the Paris Muséum in 1835, Knox added: "The reader, perhaps, need not be told that the term *signification of the skeleton* belongs peculiarly to the philosophic or transcendental anatomy, and that with respect to this subject, almost as many different views are held, as there are distinguished comparative anatomists in Europe."[57] By 1843 Knox was willing to announce himself more fully in the transcendental camp. In a series of short essays for the *London Medical Gazette,* he made laudatory references to nearly the full range of principles of "German transcendental theory."[58] Like Goethe and Geoffroy he gave first place to the unity-of-plan (or unity-of-organization) doctrine. "A great plan or scheme of Nature exists, agreeably to which all organic forms are moulded."[59] The unity of organization in the animal kingdom had been discovered by Goethe, who had thereby "laid the basis of a superstructure which will in all probability prove enduring."[60] Unfortunately, Goethe's ingenious work was disregarded; it was ahead of its time. "His labours in the field of the transcendental remained unknown; men's minds were not prepared to comprehend them; it was as if a Newton had appeared in the fourth or fifth century of the Christian era."[61] Geoffroy also received his share of lionizing from Knox, who often compared Geoffroy's work in transcendental anatomy to Newton's laws of gravitation.[62]

Knox's philosophy of anatomy was very much an amalgam of ideas from various Continental naturalists. The unity of organization in nature, advocated by Geoffroy, Knox believed to be expressed in serial manner. Here he was subscribing to the traditional *scala naturae,* or "chain of being," doctrine, which, though discredited by Cuvier, was still supported by DeBlainville.[63] Knox did not accept the idea of a "temporalized" chain of being, according to which successive creations through geological time had populated the earth

with forms of increasing perfection.[64] Nor did he feel comfortable
with Lamarck's or Geoffroy's views of evolutionary descent, doctrines which he regarded as "altogether speculative, and positively
contradicted by all human experience and chronology."[65] There had
been but one Creation, Knox declared, and this had been a creation
of genera (or generic ideas), not of species or of individuals. "Species
perish, but not genera, and thus the past, present and future, form
but one."[66] In the young of each genus is present the potential for
manifesting the characteristics of all the species of that genus. "To
institute a species, all that is required is to omit or cause to disappear, or cease to grow, some parts of the organ or apparatus already existing in the generic being."[67] There is thus a community of
hereditary descent among all the species of a particular genus, but
this genetic connection, according to Knox, does not exist between
different genera: "Generic creation at least is universal, applicable to
countless generations. Specific appearances, on the contrary, are accidental chapters in the history of the globe; species perish, genera
persist."[68]

Knox seems to have been led to this conception of the permanence
and distinctness of genera by his studies of the Salmonidae (salmon,
trout, and sea trout), the group with whose anatomy and embryology
he was most intimate.[69] The theory raises a number of obvious questions, especially, What causes a new species to be "instituted"? Why
are some potential structures in the generic embryo actualized in the
adult and others not? Here Knox, like others of his era, was non-
committal, though certainly he was not thinking of an evolutionary
process. "The development of any species depends on its position in
time and space, and not on the transmutation of one species into another."[70] And "time, which means plan and circumstances, which
mean the geological changes on the earth, are, no doubt, the producing causes of species."[71] Thus, there is a hint that alterations in
the environment through geological time have some influence on the
process; this would seem to be the meaning of Knox's statement that
the development of the "transcendentally generic" young into "any
peculiar species must be dependent on physical causes at least, which
must have a direct relation to the existing order of things."[72] Yet the
generation of new species he also thought to be accomplished by a
process analogous to the development of an individual:

The embryo, the young, is perfect generically; the adult specifically. This is the law of species, and this is no doubt the law by which Nature provides for the extinction of certain species and the appearance of others in time and space. Were our observations sufficiently delicate I have no doubt that the principal species composing any natural family might be determined *à priori* by an inspection of the embryo and young: then and then only can Zoology be esteemed a Science.[73]

In one of his last writings on the subject (1857), Knox was still equivocal but favored the embryological analogy over environmental determinism as the cause of new species:

The influence which external circumstances are adequate to exercise on the living organic world, must at all times be small, imperceptible, as diffused through countless ages,—lost in the gulf,—the abyss of time. . . . The conversion of the *generic* product of all animals into the specific is thus a mystery, but it seems to be one which includes, could it be explained, the extinction of certain species and the appearance of others; in other words, it explains the fossil and the present organic world, and their relation to each other.[74]

Thus, just two years before Darwin's *Origin* appeared, Knox too was pondering the species question; his answers, however, were far removed from those Darwin would present.[75]

By his conception of the variable manifestations of characters within the genus, Knox was able to account (at least in his own mind) for the obvious paleontological evidence for the changing faunas of successive ages, without having to hypothesize either a theory of universal descent, or the numerous miraculous creations of Cuvier's followers and "the theo-geological school of England."[76] Knox explained that his theory derived from an "application of the transcendental."[77] By this he meant, presumably, that the theory rested upon the doctrine of the structural unity of the animal kingdom. This unity arose from a plan, a single archetypical idea upon which all species—past, present, and future—had been, or would be formed.[78]

The gaps evident in the animal series (which had led taxonomists like Cuvier to reject the scale-of-nature concept) are only apparent, said Knox; they result from our temporal bias in favor of the present. Many former species are unknown to us because they were not fossilizable. Other species have not yet appeared on earth. If all past and future species could be known, we would see a complete series without gaps. Even the distinctions between species would disappear, the "species" being an artifice anyway.[79] This would apply equally to the hiatus between the apes and man; from our present knowledge of primates, "the inference is, that a class or natural family between man and animal is wanting, or they never have appeared. Anthropomorphous apes there are none, nor pithecian men; but as there unquestionably exists a *serial unity* of all that lives, or has lived, or may hereafter, so no such gap can be as that alluded to. This serial unity implies one origin of all things, which, for want of a more suitable term, we call a Creation."[80]

Besides the doctrines of the unity of organization and the scale of nature, we find in Knox's writings a form of the belief, so common to Naturphilosophie, that phenomena arise from the meeting of conflicting forces.[81] According to Knox, the final form of the individual organism is the outcome of an antagonism between the "law of species" which produces diversity and specialization, and the "deformating powers or laws" which sustain the unity of organization.[82]

The laws regulating the growth of *specific* forms are the antithesis of the laws presiding over *transcendental forms;* the one bestows individuality on the species, the other struggles to reduce all to one type; as the one prevails, the specific form is preserved; with the predominance of the other, a destruction of all *speciality* exists: we call these laws of type deformating laws, because they are opposed to our ideas of species, and to the obvious endeavours of nature to maintain this struggle and to perpetuate species.[83]

Knox's concept of life phenomena arising from conflicting, polar forces was probably adapted from the writings of the arch-Naturphilosoph Lorenz Oken. As early as 1809, Oken had written, for example: "Polarity is the first force which appears in the world. If time is eternal, polarity must also be eternal. There is no world, and in general nothing at all without polar forces." And, "galvanism is the principle of life. There is no other vital force than the galvanic polarity."[84] Varying forms of the idea of a conflict of morphological forces were later expressed by Richard Owen and, in America, by J. B. Stallo.[85]

In advocating a conflict between the law of species and the law of the archetype, Knox was subscribing concurrently to two distinct forms of biological idealism: essentialism and transcendentalism. Essentialism, the doctrine that each species (or genus) is a physical manifestation of an idea, or essence, in the mind of the Creator, was (as noted above) widely held among eighteenth- and early-nine-teenth-century naturalists, and can be traced to Plato.[86] Transcendentalism, the belief in a single or a few ideal patterns behind all the varied forms, was, as we have seen, a more recent product, largely of German origin.

Knox's biological philosophy was, thus, an eclectic one, containing ideas drawn primarily from French and German anatomists. Although his ideas show greatest affinity with those of DeBlainville, it is clear that he did not simply adopt DeBlainville's doctrines wholesale, but modified them on the basis of his own experience. He rarely had a good word for any of his own countrymen. Occasionally he would acknowledge the brilliance of John Hunter,[87] but as a rule he seemed to prefer denouncing the foibles of co-workers in England and Scotland. Knox perceived these deficiencies to have an ethnic basis. From his ethnological studies he concluded that the most high-minded, philosophical thinkers were of south German, or "Slavonian," origin: Kant, Goethe, and Oken, for example. By comparison, Anglo-Saxon peoples and other "Northern Europeans" were far down the scale; accordingly, not much in the way of philosophic truth could be expected from them:

As early, then, as 1820–21 I became convinced that the element of mind to which the German owes his vast reputation as the most philosophical of all men; the most abstract in reasoning; the most metaphysical; the most original; and, in a word, the most transcendental; the element of mind which produced Kant, and Goethe, and Gall, Leibnitz and Oken, Carus and Spix, and a thousand others whom I could easily name, is not, cannot be Saxon—cannot be Scandinavian.[88]

## Conclusion

In his last years, Knox did finally settle into a situation of tranquility. The Cancer Hospital of London appointed him to the position of pathological anatomist in 1856. Working in both the hospital and its museum, Knox was devoted to the institution until his death in 1862. Concurrently he took up a practice, principally in obstetrics, in the vicinity of his home in Hackney. His former fascination with anthropological questions was continued through the activities of the Ethnological Society of London, which made him an Honorary Fellow and honorary curator of its museum in 1860. These associations were apparently altogether amicable, suggesting that after twenty-five years of social exile Dr. Knox had begun to regain the respectability withdrawn by his public in the wake of Burke and Hare. Surely, however, the life of Robert Knox should rank as one of the conspicuous tragedies in the history of science.

The neglect of Knox by historians of science in this century is matched by, and may be a consequence of, the scant attention paid him by his own contemporaries. Why was his influence on early-nineteenth-century biologists not more potent? Clearly there was eloquence in his style of expression, evident today in his published writings and testified to by those who heard him lecture. He was an exceedingly competent anatomist and an exciting teacher of anatomy. And he was in touch with the leading issues of biology of his time, having studied with the recognized masters in Paris, and having comprehended the works of the Germans. Why then was his own work so seldom acknowledged?

The solution to this perplexity is not a simple one. First, many of his contemporaries, especially those who did not know him intimately, might well have found him offensive. He was openly critical of established politics, without favoritism to any party. He was also disdainful of organized religion. An abrasive anticlerical attitude cannot have endeared him to the many naturalists in Britain who had official ties with the Church. Knox's anti-British attitudes cannot have helped him either. He was a sympathizer with the French Revolution at just the time that the British were most paranoid about the possibility of a revolt at home. Testimony to these misanthropies is to be found in an unsigned review of Knox's *Great Artists and Great Anatomists*. While admitting that Knox was "a man of great ability," "a *piquant,* vigorous writer," and "a very good practical anatomist," the reviewer was highly critical of the man whose "difference from the rest of mankind is something really overpowering."

We are sorry to have had to find so much fault with Dr. Knox. We are sure he would find a public ever ready to listen to him, if he approached them as reasonable beings, and not as Saxon dolts and boors,—if he would freely admit the merits of his countrymen and contemporaries, though they may not be so tall as himself by some head and shoulders. Abuse never carries with it conviction; and if Dr. Knox would calmly reflect on his own career and productions, he would feel that he has lived in a house of a kind of glass that would not bear the return of such very large stones as he has been freely throwing at the houses of others.[89]

The concluding sentence of the above quotation alludes to another fundamental fact of Knox's career. Because of the stigma attached to his name by the Burke and Hare and the Osborne incidents, scientists may have been reluctant to cite him as an authority, just as in a court of law a witness of questionable morality is seldom a great advantage to the defense. Lonsdale's biography was in part an attempt to rectify Knox's public image so that his scientific accomplishments might receive just treatment.

Knox's record of publication and choice of journals raises many questions. Why was much of his original zoological material published in *medical* journals, where naturalists were unlikely to encounter it, or in the *Transactions of the Royal Society of Edinburgh* which at that time were seldom read by persons interested in anatomy?[90] Moreover, why did he wait until the last phase of his career to elaborate in print his transcendental philosophy of natural history? Was this because he felt that British naturalists were then more receptive to such ideas than they had been èarlier? Had his editors in the 1820s and 1830s perhaps been unwilling to publish "philosophical" considerations of an unempirical, un-British cast? For the present these possibilities must remain conjectural.

If Knox's written works did not attract a following among scientists, the same cannot be said of his anatomy classes. In the chapter to follow we will trace the fortunes of a number of naturalists who were first introduced to transcendental natural history through the *"piquant"* lectures of *"Knox, primus et incomparabilis."*[91]

# 3

# *The Specific and the Transcendental*

Although Robert Knox was the earliest and most outspoken proponent of idealism in British natural history, the actual application of that philosophy to scientific practice was carried out by others. Knox was magnificent and effective as a teacher and critic, but his research achievements in anatomy and zoology were not of the first rank. The expansion of idealism in comparative anatomy and its extension to other branches of natural history were accomplished by men many of whom were Knox's students in the 1830s. Moreover, there was at least one other early, respected source of idealist doctrines in British biology independent of Knox, namely the Bridgewater Treatise of Peter Mark Roget (1779–1869).

### *The Laws of Variety and Conformity to Type*

Considering Knox's great disdain for the teleological form of argumentation epitomized by the "Bilgewater Treatises," as he called them,[1] it may seem paradoxical that one of the earliest British works to treat approvingly the unity-of-plan doctrine and other transcendental concepts should have been Roget's *Animal and Vegetable Physiology Considered With Reference to Natural Theology* (1834). This anomaly is reduced, however, when we recognize that the unity of plan in anatomy and other ideal patterns could easily be interpreted as evidence of the "Power, Wisdom, and Goodness of God," which it was the purpose of the treatises to expound. Evidence for *purposeful* design was certainly abundant in nature, but many natural phenomena seemed to manifest a design based on an abstract *form* rather than on a function to be performed. How much greater does God's wisdom appear when we recognize His ability to combine, in the same organism, perfect efficiency of function with simple beauty of form!

Such was Roget's understanding of the matter. A graduate of the Edinburgh medical school in 1798, Roget subsequently held a variety of posts—tutor, lecturer, physician—principally in Manchester and London. Like Knox he studied for a time under John Abernethy. In 1833 he was appointed the first Fullerian Professor of Physiology at the Royal Institution. He later took an active part in the founding of the University of London and, in the 1840s, retired from medical practice to compile his famous *Thesaurus.*[2]

As one expects of the Bridgewater Treatises, *Animal and Vegetable Physiology* opens with a chapter on final causes. But in the second chapter, Roget asserted that there was more to animal and vegetable structure than simply adaptation to function. There were also two morphological laws at work. The first he called the law of variety:

In every department of nature it cannot fail to strike us that boundless variety is a characteristic and predominant feature of her productions. . . . Not only is this tendency to variety exemplified in the general appearance and form of the body, but it also prevails in each individual organ, however minute and insignificant that organ may seem. Even when the purpose to be answered is identical, the means which are employed are infinitely diversified in different instances, as if a design had existed of displaying to the astonished eyes of mortals the unbounded resources of creative power. While the elements of structure are the same, there is presented to us in succession every possible combination of organs, as if it had been the object to exhaust all the admissible permutations in the order of their union.

Some wise purpose, though dimly perceptible to our imperfect understandings, is no doubt answered by this great law of organic formation, the *law of variety.*[3]

Keeping in check this great diversity was the second law, of unity of type:

That [the law of variety] is not blindly or indiscriminately followed is apparent from its being circumscribed within certain limits, and controlled by another law, . . . that of *conformity to a definite type.*

The most superficial survey of nature is sufficient to show that there are certain general resemblances among great multitudes of species, which lead us to class them into more or less comprehensive groups. Thus in the animal kingdom, Quadrupeds, Birds, Fishes, Reptiles, Shell-fish, and Insects, compose natural assemblages or classes, and each of these is readily divisible into subordinate groups or families. Now it results from a closer examination of the structure and economy of plants and animals, that the formation of all the individual species comprehended in the same class, has been conducted in conformity with a certain ideal model or *type*, as it is called. Of this general type all the existing forms appear as so many separate copies, differing, indeed, as to particulars, but agreeing as to general characters.[4]

The phenomena of animal morphology were thus the outcome of two laws acting concurrently: a law of variety which explained the marvelous diversity of earthly beings, and a law of conformity or unity which explained the general similarities among all species of a particular class. The abundant evidence for these laws of variety and unity convinced Roget that the Creation was governed by more than utilitarian adaptation.

The bulk of Roget's 1,200-page treatise was an explication of the physiological mechanisms manifested by each of the animal classes (arranged according to Cuvier's system of classification), followed by discussions of the major organ systems (nutritive, sensory, reproductive) as they are manifested throughout the animal kingdom. But in the final chapter, entitled "Unity of Design," he returned to the law of conformity to type. While certain of its importance, Roget felt that the law must yet be treated as tentative. He described several of the many "numerous and striking" lines of evidence which seemed to support the law, but concluded that "great care should be taken not to carry it farther than the just interpretation of the facts themselves may warrant. It should be borne in mind that these facts are few, compared with the entire history of animal development; and that the resemblances which have been so ingeniously traced, are partial only, and fall very short of that universality, which alone constitutes the solid basis of a strictly philosophical theory."[5] Roget was aware that some of the transcendentalists had carried the search for unity to "unwarrantable and extravagant" extremes. This was clear warning that a careful rein must be kept on the imagination in research of this sort, lest "seductive speculations" lead us "far away from the path of philosophical induction."[6] Yet, in addition to the laws of variety and type, Roget referred with varying approval to a multilinear chain of being (the "law of *Gradation*"), the law of parallelism, and William MacLeay's taxonomy of circular arrangements. Evidently he felt that all of these theories could be correct; at any rate each was invoked when appropriate to account for particular observations. *Animal and Vegetable Physiology* was clearly an assemblage of ideas from British, French, and German authors of the first three decades of the nineteenth century.

In short, Roget's work was a positive but cautious presentation of the leading themes of transcendental biology, circulated and at least partially legitimized through the vehicle of a Bridgewater Treatise. These themes received a second, brief airing four years later in an article on physiology for the *Encyclopaedia Britannica*.[7] For some English readers, Roget's writings were a first introduction to the ideas of Geoffroy, DeBlainville, and the German transcendental anatomists.[8] For others already aware of these Continental developments, Roget's treatment of the laws as hypotheses was a stimulus for new research. Among those so inspired were Martin Barry (1802–55) and William B. Carpenter (1813–85).

Barry is chiefly remembered for his contributions to embryology, including the discovery of spermatozoa inside the ovum in 1843 and the introduction of Karl Ernst Von Baer's embryological theories to Britain.[9] Though born in Hampshire, he spent most of his career in Edinburgh, having received his M.D. degree there in 1833. He also studied on the Continent for several extended periods (both before and after taking the degree), working with many of the most prominent German scientists of the period: Friedrich Tiedemann, Theodor Schwann, J. E. Purkinje, and Justus von Liebig, among others. Barry's attitude toward transcendental anatomy was, like

Roget's, one of guarded interest; his principal contribution was a developmental interpretation of the law of "conformity to type" (i.e., unity of plan) based on careful embryological description.

In 1834, just after receiving his medical degree, Barry traveled to Heidelberg to study under Tiedemann. Tiedemann, one of Germany's pioneer embryologists and an early advocate of the law of parallelism, seems to have imparted to Barry the passion for embryological studies. From 1835 onward, Barry carried on a program of meticulous research which earned him the Royal Society's Medal in 1839.

Among his earliest publications was the 1837 essay "On the Unity of Structure in the Animal Kingdom." The essay opens and closes with themes from Roget's Bridgewater Treatise: the evidence for divine design to be found in both structure and function in the animal kingdom, and the need for caution when generalizing upon "the idea of a subjective unity."[10] The greater part of the article is a qualification of the law of unity of plan by the invocation of Von Baer's embryological law, that "a heterogeneous or special structure, shall arise only out of one more homogeneous or general; and this by a gradual change."[11] The unity that exists among all animals, Barry explained, has its origin in the earliest stage of development, when the germs of every species, from infusoria to man, are essentially identical. As the germs metamorphose, they do so in an identical manner—i.e., from a homogeneous to a heterogeneous structure—but in different directions, vertebrates, arthropods, and mollusks diverging from one another. The divergence along nearly parallel lines to end points of varying complexity accounts for the "resemblances between some of the embryonal phases of very different animals."[12] Thus, Von Baer's law accounts for all of the phenomena subsumed under the laws of unity of plan, variety, and parallelism.

When Barry concluded that "all the varieties of structure in the animal kingdom, are but modifications of, essentially, one and the same fundamental form,"[13] the "form" he had in mind was not an archetype of adult forms, but rather a homogeneous germ or cell. In this germinal stage the law of unity of plan is manifest, but in the subsequent development of the embryo into an adult the law of variety holds sway. The law of variety produces a gradual divergence of form during the process of development in such a way that class differences appear first, followed successively by order, family, genus, species, and varietal differences. The last characteristics to become evident in embryonic development are sexual and individual differences.[14] Because development is a process of divergence from the very beginning, Barry insisted that the law of parallelism, in its literal sense, is false; "no animal absolutely *repeats* in its development, the structure of any part of any other animal." The law is true only in the sense that there occurs "in the development of a single organism, a *modified* reappearance of structures common to other animals."[15]

Barry's embryological interpretation of the doctrines of transcendental morphology in 1837 was a prelude to his later, more intense research published in the *Philosophical Transactions of the Royal Society*.[16] Highly regarded as these works were, they did not immediately generate a larger assault on embryological questions in Britain. The inherent difficulties of such research given the rudimentary state of microscopy at that time (Barry's eyesight had become seriously impaired by the early 1840s, necessitating periodic cessations in his research), coupled with the requirement for study abroad (or at least a fluency in German) in order to be at the frontier of research, may have been responsible. Thus, Barry's associate in the medical and other scientific societies of Edinburgh, William B. Carpenter, when influenced by Roget's discussion of design, turned to physiology rather than embryology. His contribution was the concept of unity of function.

## Unity of Plan and Unity of Function

Another graduate of the Edinburgh University medical school in the 1830s, Carpenter was first a physician in his native Bristol and later lecturer at several London institutions and, from 1856 to 1879, registrar of London University. His earliest research specialty was the nervous system, but he became equally well known for his contributions to microscopy and marine zoology, including extensive studies of Foraminifera. His importance as an original researcher was surpassed, however, by his successes in organizing the knowledge of biology of the mid-Victorian period in several popular texts and in promoting large-scale scientific pursuits such as the oceano-

Fig. 3.1. William Benjamin Carpenter. (From Carpenter, *Nature and Man* [New York, 1889], frontispiece.)

graphic voyage of H.M.S. *Challenger* and the marine biological laboratory at Plymouth.[17]

Carpenter's formal medical studies began in 1834 at University College London, where he was especially intrigued by the course on comparative anatomy given by the Lamarckian Robert Edmond Grant.[18] In his early years, perhaps more than in later life, Carpenter's curiosity was attracted to the possibility of large, general principles governing the entire organic realm. By 1835, when he left London for Edinburgh, he was already entertaining plans to publish a work on "the philosophical study of natural history."[19] His philosophy of scientific method at this point appears to have followed traditional English empiricism, for he mentions John Herschel and Charles Lyell as leading influences. Nevertheless, he was favorably disposed toward Goethe's transcendental morphology.[20]

Among Carpenter's earliest scientific papers were two which manifested a concern for ideal principles in the living realm. The first (1835–36) contains a survey of the various structures by which respiration is carried out in the animal and vegetable kingdoms. Despite the apparent diversity among the organs of respiration, Carpenter found clear evidence of a unity of function:

> The organs appropriated to the performance of the function of respiration appear, at first sight, so very different, that a superficial observer would hardly trace any analogy between them. There would seem, for instance, but little resemblance between the gills of a fish, and the lungs of a quadruped; or between the beautiful tufts on the body of a sand-worm, and the air tubes of an insect: but a little consideration will show that all these forms are reducible, as in vegetables, to one simple element—an extension of the external surface, specially modified by its permeability and its vascularity for the aeration of the blood.[21]

Thus, the unity of physiological function arises from a fundamental similarity of organ structure.

Elsewhere in the same article Carpenter accepted other transcendental laws, including "the great law of unity of type in the development of organs, which has few apparent and perhaps no real exceptions,"[22] the law of parallelism, and the then aging concept of the chain of being. The article was indeed a compilation of ideas from a number of published sources, most notably Roget's Bridgewater

Treatise. Carpenter closed his discussion, in fact, with a quotation from Roget's last chapter, citing the "unity of design and identity of operation" in nature as evidence for a benevolent, omniscient Creator.[23]

The second paper was stimulated by his friend Martin Barry's "Unity of Structure" article of 1836. "On Unity of Function in Organized Beings"[24] appeared in the same journal only a few months after Barry's article. Carpenter's chief object was to extend to biological function the principles Barry had stated for biological structure and to do so more thoroughly and emphatically than he had done in the previous article. Von Baer's law, that "a heterogeneous or special structure, shall arise only out of one more homogeneous or general; and this by a gradual change," was modified by Carpenter to read "a special function arises only out of one more general and this by a gradual change."[25] And the theme of the first paper—that a particular function (e.g., respiration) is accomplished in a series of increasingly complex organisms by a single organ (e.g., a respiratory surface with a connecting circulatory surface) modified to perform in increasingly complex ways—was reiterated and extended to the functions of nutrition, excretion, and reproduction.

The respiratory organs are found specially developed both in plants and animals, as soon as a particular part of the surface [of the organism] is set apart for absorption; and the fluid is brought to them by the circulating system before being applied to the general purposes of nutrition. In plants we always find them formed by expansions of the external surface, beneath which the fluid is exposed to the influence of the air; and this is the type on which the brancheae of aquatic animals are construed, whatever may be the modifications of their form and situation. In air-breathing animals, on the other hand, the prolongation of the surfaces takes place internally, so that the air comes to meet the blood, instead of the blood being sent to meet the air.[26]

An ideal unity is thus behind the multiplicity of manifestations. "I think," Carpenter concluded, "that the structure of the respiratory organs affords a beautiful illustration of the argument which might be raised on *a priori* considerations in favour of the doctrine of the 'fundamental unity of structure.'"[27] The latter doctrine, propounded by Barry, was itself a corollary of the central law of Divine design, or as Carpenter put it, "the law, which everywhere prevails throughout creation, of the attainment of every *end* by the best adapted *means.*"[28]

This last statement suggests that Carpenter regarded function as the dictator of structure (not the reverse, as we might have expected), and accordingly thought that final causes must prevail over formal causes, purpose over plan. At the time he may not have fully thought through these implications. But the appearance of William Whewell's three-volume *History of the Inductive Sciences* a few months later gave Carpenter the stimulus to do so. Whewell discussed the morphological doctrines of Goethe and Geoffroy with considerable respect but was highly critical of Geoffroy's rejection of the teleological method in biology. "Whether we judge," Whewell said, "from the arguments, the results, the practice of physiologists, their speculative opinions, or those of the philosophers of a wider field, we are led to the same conviction, that in the organized world we may and must adopt the belief, that organization exists for its purpose, and that the apprehension of the purpose may guide us in seeing the meaning of the organization."[29] Whewell's espousal of final causes in physiology (an attitude he did not countenance for the physical sciences) was for Carpenter a major flaw in an otherwise commendable treatise. In an essay for the *British and Foreign Medical Review,* Carpenter defended Geoffroy and insisted that "whilst the study of final causes is of great value in leading to the *discovery of facts,* the search after general laws to be based on these facts must be totally independent of them."[30] There is no "distinct line between physics and physiology" which warrants the exclusion of final causes from the one but not from the other.

Carpenter had written all of the above essays while still a medical student. In 1839 he completed the doctorate in medicine at Edinburgh and published the first edition of the *Principles of General and Comparative Physiology,* the widely used textbook which first brought him into prominence.[31] Here he repeated his opposition to teleological reasoning in biology and expounded the laws of pure morphology: unity of plan, Von Baer's law of development, laws of eccentric development and arrest of development, the principle of compensation, and especially the unity of function.[32] Thus, as early as 1840 Carpenter was becoming a leading expositor of transcendental doctrines in Britain. But he was more effective in circulating

Fig. 3.2. Edward Forbes, 1852. (Courtesy of Ipswich Museums and Galleries.)

Photo-engraved by Walker & Boutall from a Daguerreotype.

*Richard Owen*

Fig. 3.3. Richard Owen. (From the Reverend Richard Owen, *The Life of Richard Owen*, 2 vols. [London, 1894], 1: opposite 319.)

these earlier ideas than in developing new ones. His own concept of the unity of function, emphasized even more heavily in later editions of his *Principles* (see below), was largely ignored by his contemporaries.

### Analogies, Homologies, and Polarities

The tentative support of, and modest additions to idealist biology in the 1830s by Roget, Barry, and Carpenter grew into a movement during the 1840s through the advocacy of Edward Forbes and Richard Owen. This was the decade of greatest innovation.

Of all the idealist naturalists Forbes evokes the greatest fascination, as much for the unusual breadth of his interests as for the great esteem in which his contemporaries held him. As professor of botany at King's College, London, paleontologist of the Geological Survey, and finally Regius Professor of Natural History at Edinburgh, he lectured and published abundantly on marine zoology, botany, biogeography, geology, and literary topics.[33] And in all the branches of natural history he invoked, at least intermittently, the methodology of ideal patterns. That Forbes failed to maintain a stature comparable to Owen's, that he was little remembered by the end of the nineteenth century and is now rarely mentioned by historians of science, is largely due to his unfortunate death in 1854 at the age of thirty-nine. "Poor Edward Forbes," Owen lamented upon hearing of Forbes's passing; "there was never a scientific man whose unexpected death caused a more general or sincere regret."[34]

Forbes was a native of the Isle of Man, whose biota he knew intimately when at age sixteen he left the island for medical studies at Edinburgh. But when the time arrived for his final examination (1836), he failed to show up: his interest had been diverted elsewhere. The subject matter of Robert Jameson's course on natural history, attended during the spring and summer of 1832, had consumed him, with the result that the years of medical study saw him apply his energies increasingly to the collection of Scottish plants and invertebrates.

For subject matter Jameson's course may have been the most influential for Forbes, but for philosophy and methodology the anatomy lectures of Robert Knox were undoubtedly more important.

Forbes encountered Knox's course during his first term at Edinburgh, when Knox's popularity among students was at its peak. Human anatomy held no appeal for Forbes (and Knox by this time had dropped his own anatomical research in favor of zoology), but Knox's lectures, with their enthusiastic invocations of the transcendental doctrines of Geoffroy *et alii,* marked the beginning of Forbes's lifelong fascination with the possibility that abstract patterns governed the manifestation of natural history phenomena. These doctrines were undoubtedly the topic of conversations among Forbes, Barry, Carpenter, and others who were all members of the Royal Physical Society, the Botanical Society, and other Edinburgh associations in the mid-1830s. Moreover, Forbes's particular fascination was reinforced in the winter of 1836 when he traveled to Paris and attended the course of the aging Geoffroy himself.

The first hint of Forbes's interest in what he called the "philosophy of natural history" is to be found in the prospectus to a series of public lectures given in Edinburgh (1840–41) with his close friend Samuel Brown, the chemist. These "Popular Lectures on the Philosophy of the Sciences" were intended (impudently, as Forbes later reflected)[35] to raise the level of popular scientific lecturing in the city and to spread "more *philosophical,* and therein more *intelligible,* ideas than are commonly prevalent, of the great principles and central facts of natural science."[36] Forbes's half of the lectures, uniquely titled "On Zoo-geology and Psycho-zoology," focussed on the embryonic science of paleoecology (to which he would make his most innovative contributions) and on the relations of "life and intellect" in the animal kingdom. The latter portion has an unmistakably idealistic cast, evident in such subheadings as "Threefold constitution of the animal organism—Substance, Form and Intellect"; "Distinctions between the analogies and affinities of animal forms—Regularity and irregularity—Parity and imparity—Polarity—Metamorphosis —Number considered as an element of form"; and "View of Naturalists, Metaphysicians, and Physiologists on Psycho-zoology— Metaphysical Natural History systems."[37] Unfortunately, no details were given that would indicate precisely what Forbes taught or believed respecting each of these themes. But clearly, even at this early stage in his career he was entertaining a priori notions in natural history.

Curiously, these lectures came just months after the publication of William Whewell's *Philosophy of the Inductive Sciences*, with its idealist program of "Fundamental Ideas." Thus, there is the distinct possibility that the idealistic tone of the Forbes-Brown lectures was stimulated or reinforced by the Whewellian philosophy of science.[38] In any event, by 1840 the idealistic philosophy of biology had acquired strong advocates in Edinburgh as well as in Cambridge. And when Forbes assumed the professorship of botany at King's College in 1842, the movement began to work its way in London.

In his inaugural lecture at King's, Forbes anticipated one trend of his future research when he called attention to Goethe's doctrine of the ideal metamorphosis in plants: "The great moving ideal of modern botanical philosophy is that of the origin of all the appendages of the vegetable axis in the transformation of the leaf, their normal type."[39] The following year, in the first of a series of papers all of which displayed a marked transcendental orientation, Forbes presented a morphological comparison of the reproductive systems in the hydroid coelenterates *Sertularia* and *Plumularia* with that of flowering plants. From close observation of these hydroids during their entire life history, he noted that the reproductive structure appeared as an "urn-shaped" or "pod-shaped" vesicle on the axis or branches of the organism, by a process precisely analogous to the formation of floral buds:

The vesicle [in the coelenterate] is formed from a branch or pinna, through an arrest of individual development, by a shortening of the spiral axis, and by a transformation of the stomachs (individuals) into egg-producing membranes, the dermato-skeletons (or cells) uniting to form the protecting capsule or germen; which metamorphosis is exactly comparable to that which we find in the reproductive organs of flowering plants in which the floral bud (normally a branch clothed with spirally arranged leaves, an assemblage of respiratory individuals) is constituted through the contraction of the axis and the whorling of the individuals borne on that axis, and by their transformation into the several parts of the flower.[40]

In this description, and in his reference to the developmental process in the hydroids as an "*ideal* metamorphosis,"[41] Forbes was interpreting the phenomenon of morphological change as conforming to a preconceived, geometrically idealized pattern. The pattern involved two opposing axes: a "vertical" growth axis and a "spiral" reproductive axis.[42] The life-cycle stage determined which of the axes the developmental tendency would follow. Forbes regarded this metamorphosis of zoophytes as "exactly comparable to that which Linnaeus first, and Goethe afterwards, demonstrated in the flowers of vegetables."[43]

The idealistic nature of this brief paper on hydroid morphology, presented at the 1844 meeting of the British Association, did not go unnoticed by his listeners. In the discussion following, Richard Owen (who had not yet published his own transcendental treatises) commented that Forbes's work was "a beautiful application of the principles of transcendental anatomy." And he did not miss the opportunity to point out that biology need not be limited to strict inductivism:

The idea of morphological change could not be derived from inductive science alone. It was something different from induction, and hence, as it were, became a new handle for science. The idea of resemblance as a guide in our researches had been applied with great success in the study of vertebrate animals, and the great invertebrate kingdom of animals was now [through Forbes's researches] made to connect the vegetable kingdom, and the higher forms of vertebrate animals by the same great laws of morphological change. By the application of this principle the apparently confused details supplied by our countrymen [John] Ellis, on the corallines were reduced to order.[44]

After Owen, Carpenter and the ethnologist R. G. Latham added their praise of the transcendental approach. And in a later communication the naturalist R. Q. Couch confirmed that he had reached similar conclusions about the growth of zoophytes from observations on the Cornish coast.[45]

Forbes was evidently encouraged by these responses to his first advocacy of transcendental views before a scientific body.[46] The following year, in a Friday evening lecture at the Royal Institution, he discussed two idealistic conceptions which he regarded as central to biology: the relations of analogy and polarity. By analogy he, like Owen, meant the existence of morphological resemblances between different groups of organisms. He cited numerous instances of analogy, including that of hydroids and flowering plants which he had previously demonstrated. The relation of polarity, on the other hand, was a matter of "opposition or divergence" of the organisms of the two kingdoms. Plants and animals stand in a polar relationship to each other, Forbes observed, because they share similar morphologies in their simplest forms but become increasingly unlike as they become more complex: "Thus, instead of finding, as we might expect *a priori*, the most perfectly developed vegetable bearing the closest resemblance to the lowest animal form [as required by the eighteenth-century chain of being concept], we find, on the contrary, that it is at the lowest points of both systems (the sponges, &c, in the one, and the marine fuci in the other) that the closest resemblance exists."[47]

Forbes's use of "polarity" in a biological context was not new. The Swedish naturalist E. M. Fries had used the term to describe the divergence of the plant and animal kingdoms from a common morphological center (as Forbes later noted).[48] The London botanist John Lindley regarded the upward growth of the stem and downward growth of the roots as a case of polarity in plant morphology. And Whewell had discussed polarity at length in the *Philosophy of the Inductive Sciences;* for him it was one of the "Fundamental Ideas" of the "Mechanico-Chemical Sciences," having specific applications in optics (light polarization), magnetism (including terrestial magnetism), electrical induction, galvanism, chemical composition, crystal formation, and elsewhere.[49]

At the outset of the lecture Forbes pointed out that British naturalists still looked upon "speculation on the analogies of animated beings" with distrust. He insisted, nevertheless, that "the transcendental philosophy of natural history [is] one of the most important developments of that science."[50] The appearance the following year of Owen's memoir "Archetype and Homologies" (discussed below) was a further positive sign.

In subsequent years Forbes became increasingly intrigued by the possibility of polarities in nature (see below) but lost interest in the unity of plan. The most important level of abstraction, he felt, was the genus. He explained this conception in a highly theoretical lecture at the Royal Institution in 1852.[51] Although the theme of the lecture was the alleged analogy between the life stages of an individual organism and the duration of a species[52] (an analogy that Forbes discounted), the principal attraction of the lecture lies in the definitions of "individual," "species," and "genus" that Forbes provided.

The individual is simply the single organism; it occupies a series of points in time, but only a single point in space. Forbes referred to it as a "positive reality." The species is an assemblage of individuals having "certain constant characters" and the relationship of common descent. The species has spatial and temporal extension. Like the individual, it occupies a single, continuous series of points in time; "once destroyed, it never reappears."[53]

The genus for Forbes was not simply a collection of closely related species. It was an abstraction created by God, "an idea impressed on nature and not arbitrarily dependent on man's conceptions."[54] All the species of a particular genus were the partial, worldly representations of a Divine idea. Forbes's concept of the genus was thus a strongly Platonic one: his generic ideas are Plato's ideal forms, of which all observable manifestations are but imperfect copies. In regarding the genus, rather than the species, as the "permanent and original"[55] idea, Forbes concurred with his mentor, Knox, but was at variance with most other naturalists of his era.

His belief in the supremacy of ideas in general was expressed in eloquent terms in a letter to A. C. Ramsay in 1848: "In truth *ideas* & *principles* are independent of men—the application of them & their illustration is man's duty & merit. The time will come when the author of a view shall be set aside & the view only taken cognizance of. This will be the millenium of science."[56] This affirmation, taken with his other transcendental writings, indicates that Forbes's idealism was at least as much Platonic as Kantian or Whewellian. Most likely it originated not only in Knox's lectures but in Forbes's reading of Plato (as part of the traditional, classics-based education) and especially the Cambridge Platonists, probably during medical school years. On more than one occasion he evinced a fondness for the writings of Henry More, most prominent of the Cambridge Platonists.[57] It is interesting to note, though, that Whewell's name stands at the head of a list of Forbes's associates which he prepared in connection with the 1852 lecture (see Fig. 3.4 and the transcription in Table 3.1). This list probably represents those of his associates whom Forbes thought would be interested in this "chapter" of his transcendental philosophy of natural history; perhaps it was a list to whom copies were to be sent.

Prominent in the center of the list is the name of Britain's most

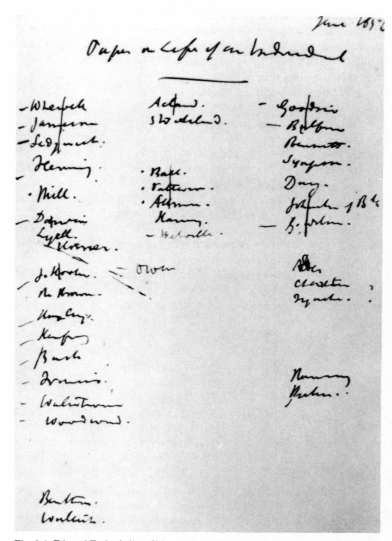

Fig. 3.4. Edward Forbes's list of his associates, from a notebook ca. 1852. (From British Museum [Natural History] Library, Forbes Notebooks [#2], ca. p. [18]. Courtesy of the British Museum [Natural History].)

famous transcendental naturalist, Richard Owen. A native of Lancaster and classmate of Whewell at grammar school, Owen was apprenticed to several surgeons in his home town in the early 1820s. Matriculating at Edinburgh in 1824, he attended the lectures of

Table 3.1. Transcription of Forbes's List of His Associates, June 1852

| Paper on Life of an Individual | | |
|---|---|---|
| [William] Whewell | [H. W.] Acland [?] | [John] Goodsir |
| [Robert] Jameson | [H. E.] Strickland [?] | [J. H.] Balfour |
| [Adam] Sedgwick | | [J. H.] Bennett |
| [John] Fleming | [Robert] Ball | [J. Y.] Simpson |
| [John Stuart] Mill | [Robert] Patterson | [G. E.] Day |
| [Charles] Darwin | [George] Allman | [George] Johnston |
| [Charles] Lyell | [W. H.] Harvey | G[eorge] Wilson |
|   [Leonard] Horner | [A. G.] Melville | |
|   [Richard] Owen | | |
| J[oseph] Hooker | | [?] |
| R[obert] Brown | | [?] |
| [T. H.] Huxley | | [Nicholas] Tyacke [?] |
| [Arthur] Henfrey | | |
| [George] Busk | | |
| [John F.] Francis [?] | | [A. C.] Ramsay |
| [George Robert] | | |
| Waterhouse | | [J. Beete] Jukes |
| [S. P.] Woodward | | |
| | | |
| [George] Bentham | | |
| [George Charles] Wallich | | |

Note: The manuscript reproduced in Fig. 3.4. and transcribed here is apparently a checklist of scientists to whom Forbes sent (or intended to send) copies or announcements of his paper "On the Supposed Analogy Between the Life of an Individual and the Duration of a Species." The list has been transcribed with first names or initials added. Question marks in brackets indicate indecipherable or uncertain entries.

In the center and right-hand columns are the names of Forbes's naturalist friends in Ireland and Scotland and at the Geological Survey. The left-hand column is the most interesting, however, as it includes nearly all of the naturalists who were concerned with biogeographic theory at that time: Fleming, Darwin, Lyell, Hooker, and Henfrey. The name of Forbes's archrival, Hewett Watson, is noticeably absent— probably a calculated omission. In general, the list gives an indication of those members of the scientific community most closely associated with Forbes's research, particularly those likely to have an interest in the more theoretical and speculative aspects of his work.

Hope, Home, Duncan, Jameson, and Monro *tertius,* but most importantly those of John Barclay and Robert Knox. Owen's grandson and biographer claimed that "of all his teachers at Edinburgh it was John Barclay that he owed the most."[58] And according to Knox's biographer, Owen "truly received zoological inspiration from 'lectures the most brilliant ever delivered on anatomy,' and today speaks of Knox's influence in prompting him to visit the Jardin des Plantes, and seek the teachings of the French *savans.*"[59] Barclay sent Owen on to London to study (as had Knox) with John Abernethy. Soon qualifying as a member of the Royal College of Surgeons of England, Owen obtained a position as assistant to the conservator of the college's Hunterian Collection. In this capacity he guided Cuvier through the college museum when the French celebrity visited London in 1830. The following year Owen visited Paris at Cuvier's invitation. By 1836 he had secured both the positions of Hunterian Professor and museum conservator at the College of Surgeons.

The impact of Cuvier and the fossil vertebrates of the Paris Museum upon Owen's intellectual development was equaled, if not exceeded, by the transcendental *philosophie anatomique* of Geoffroy and the Naturphilosophen.[60] A preference for formal, as opposed to final, causes was expressed by Owen in lectures as early as 1837.[61] And in an 1838 paper before the Geological Society, he gave the first indication of what would become a long-standing interest, the abstract form of the vertebra. A recently discovered specimen of *Plesiosaurus* had, he said, given him the impetus to utilize "the views and nomenclature of M. Geoffroy St. Hilaire" regarding "a vertebra in the abstract."[62] Surprisingly, Owen added in passing that Geoffroy's views had been "generally adopted in this country." Perhaps they were "generally adopted" for discussion among British biologists, but the published record gives very little evidence of their acceptance before the 1840s.[63] On the other hand, it may be that Owen was overstating the degree of their acceptance in order to erect a straw man, because one of the purposes of the paper was to show the inadequacies of Geoffroy's interpretation and to set forth a new interpretation of his own. It was in this paper that Owen's diagram of an ideal vertebral segment (Fig. 3.5), often repeated in his later works, first appeared.

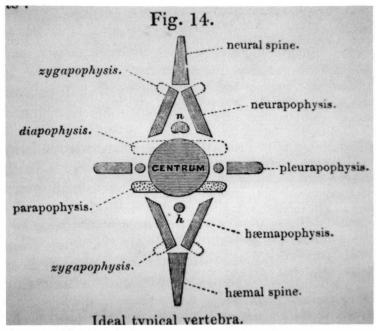

Fig. 3.5. Owen's "ideal typical vertebra." (From Richard Owen, *On the Archetype and Homologies of the Vertebrate Skeleton* [London, 1848], p. 81.)

After this initial announcement of his interest in vertebral abstractions, Owen published nothing further in the transcendental vein until his 1843 Hunterian Lectures on invertebrates.[64] Paying tribute to Goethe, Lorenz Oken, and the "Unity of Organization" in the last of these lectures, Owen wondered if the law of unity of organization extended to invertebrates as well as to vertebrates. He concluded (as Barry had in 1837, following Von Baer) that in the invertebrates the unity was evident only in the earliest stages of embryological development. There was a unity in the *germs* of individuals of different classes, when they all resemble the "infusorial Monad"; but with growth came divergence and dissimilarity. Thus, "the fulness of the unity of organization which prevails through the Polyps and larval

Acalephs, is diminished as the latter acquire maturity and assume their special form." And in general, "the extent to which the resemblance, expressed by the term 'Unity of Organization,' may be traced between the higher and lower organized animals, bears an inverse ratio to their approximation to maturity."[65]

Most important was Owen's clear differentiation of the terms *analogy* and *homology*. Analogous structures are organs of different species which perform similar functions but may have differing forms or embryological origins—for example, the leg of a human being and the leg of a crab. Homologous structures, on the other hand, are organs which are identical or similar in form, have similar embryological origins, and have the same position and connections with respect to other parts, but may differ in their functions; the human arm and the bat's wing are thus homologous.[66]

What impact did these particular Hunterian Lectures have? It is curious that Robert Knox should have first announced his support of transcendentalism in print in this year of 1843. Knox, it will be remembered, had given up his position in Edinburgh and, late in 1842, had moved to London, where he remained until early 1844. It is possible that the downtrodden Knox attended some of the lectures of, or otherwise communicated with, his now successful student during this time, and that some reinforcement of his transcendental enthusiasm resulted.[67] Such an interaction would explain in part why Knox, in June and July of 1843, published the series of "Contributions to Anatomy and Physiology" which included arguments in support of the laws of unity of organization and of parallelism.

If Knox and Owen did meet, it is clear that they did not agree on all points. In his "Contributions" Knox denounced vehemently the teleological arguments of traditional British natural theology in a way which Owen (who regarded functional adaptation as well as ideal archetype to be evidence for divine design) would never have countenanced. For example, after describing certain anomalies in the structure of the human humerus and the sternum, Knox declared:

Whatever may be the ultimate determination in respect to the real nature of these bones, it is surely more philosophic to suppose them "rudimentary" of some structure more highly developed in some other class of animals, than to adopt the "Bridgewater" and "Guy's Hospital" physiology, which argues that every animal is made for itself alone, stands alone, and has nothing to do with any other, and that the individual organs of man and animals are to be explained by a physiology whose highest stretch of generalization is to represent the mammae of the human female as having been purposely created double, that the accidental loss of one, by milk abscess, or otherwise, might occasion no interruption to their function! Profound philosophy! But proving, at the same time, to how little purpose Mr. John Hunter lived and laboured, and bequeathed to Britain his immortal museum, seeing that into the educational institutions of his adopted city he failed to introduce a single spark of his philosophy.[68]

The stated target of this attack was Sir Astley Cooper of Guy's Hospital. But the final sentence is a veiled criticism of Owen—Hunterian lecturer and heir to the philosophy of Hunter, who, as noted above, advocated the study of comparative anatomy as a basis for the philosophy of natural history. Knox, it seems, was a more thoroughgoing idealist than Owen, rejecting all explanations which would account for form in terms of function. For Knox, transcendental views "are the only views which, in the present state of science, can be adopted, and . . . what has been written against them in France, and more especially in England, is simply, and, to use the mildest phrase, ingenious nonsense; sometimes very pompous and imposing, as in the Bridgewater Treatises, but still downright nonsense, and not meriting the smallest attention from any philosophic mind."[69]

Owen's eclecticism allowed for both teleology and transcendentalism. As early as 1837 he had written Whewell of the desirability of achieving, in comparative anatomy, "a harmonious theory combining the transcendental and teleological views."[70] As a model for this approach Owen looked to John Hunter:

This first great step in comparative anatomy was undoubtedly the consideration of an organ under its most general conditions, comparing all its known modifications and educing the law or amount of its variations, with reference to the general plan or pattern adhered to on the one hand, and the exigencies of the species to which deviations related on the other—or in other words its transcendental and teleological relations. The writer in whose works I find the animal organs treated of in this comprehensive spirit, with reference to physiology more especially, is Hunter.[71]

Precisely the same form of eclecticism was adopted by Whewell in the *Philosophy of the Inductive Sciences* three years later. And Owen, for his part, may well have regarded Whewell's Fundamental Ideas as philosophical justification for his own "ideal vertebra" and later vertebrate archetype, though the evidence suggests that his idealism was more akin to the traditional, Platonic version than to the newer Kantian one: abstractions like the ideal vertebra originate as Divine Ideas of the Creator, not as inherent categories of human understanding.[72] At any rate he was certainly familiar with Whewell's *Philosophy* at an early date, having read portions of the first edition while it was still in proof.[73] And his own contributions to anatomy, in turn, were adopted by Whewell.[74]

Despite Knox's opposition to Owen's teleological tendencies, he must have been pleased by the advancing transcendentalism of Owen's subsequent writings. In the lectures on vertebrates, published in 1846,[75] Owen began to set forth the concepts and terminology which would make him the British exemplar of transcendental anatomy. He distinguished three sorts of homologies: a *special* homology, a relationship of similarity between particular organs of two different species; a *general* homology, a relationship of similarity between the organ of an actual species and that of the ideal, generalized form of the group to which the species belongs; and a *serial* homology, a relationship of similarity among the repeated structures (e.g., vertebral segments) within a particular species. Philosophical anatomy, for Owen, was largely the elaboration of these homologies, as far as they could justifiably be extended, throughout the animal kingdom; in fact, he often referred to it as "homological anatomy."[76]

Had there been any previous doubts about Owen's supremacy among British anatomists, the 1846 *Lectures* dispelled them. No less an authority than Carpenter announced that "for comprehensive knowledge of the comparative anatomy of the vertebrate series, alike exact in its details and philosophical in its generalizations, [Owen] is certainly second to none, either living or dead."[77] Carpenter was especially supportive of Owen's transcendental efforts, against those critics who would not trouble themselves to treat philosophical anatomy seriously. After describing Owen's interpretation of the upper limbs as appendages of the "occipital vertebra," Carpenter warned:

We can well anticipate the ridicule with which this determination will be received by those who delight in laughing at what they are pleased to call the outrageous absurdities of the philosophical anatomists—merely because they cannot comprehend them. That the hands and arms of man are nothing else than "diverging appendages" to his occipital bone, will be doubtless in their eyes to stamp the whole system as a tissue of dreamy transcendentalism. But if such persons will go to Nature, and interrogate her by a careful and candid scrutiny of the various forms and combinations which she presents, with the real desire to ascertain whether there be a guiding plan, a unity of design, throughout the whole, or whether each organism is built up for itself alone without reference to the rest,—we are confident that they will find the former doctrine to be irresistibly forced upon them.[78]

Transcendental anatomy gained additional supporters at the 1846 meeting of the British Association, when Owen presented his system in its most complete form.[79] "On the Archetype and Homologies of the Vertebrate Skeleton" provided the history of and justification for homological anatomy, followed by a thorough analysis of the homologies to be found in the spinal column and skull of the various classes of vertebrate animals. Owen gave new evidence and interpretations in support of the laws of unity of plan and repetition of parts; all vertebrate forms, he was convinced, were variations of a single, ideal "archetypus," which he boldly depicted in a foldout appendix (Fig. 3.6). A system of numerical notation was introduced whereby homologous bones in every animal were assigned the same number. (As Owen pointed out, years before Goethe had recommended the creation of a system of "signs and ciphers" that would show "the mutual relations and secret affinities of the bones.")[80] And he restated Oken's view of life as resulting from a conflict between a "polarizing force" which produces unity and repetition, and an organizing principle which results in diversity and teleological adaptation.[81] Every organism is, thus, the outcome of both formal and final causes.

There can be no doubt that Owen regarded himself as both the defender and interpreter of the German transcendental biologists, whose work had received little recognition in Britain because of the frequent errors and obscure language which had characterized it. In his discussion of serial homologies, for example, Owen was apologetic but firm:

It must be confessed that the expressions by which the philosophical anatomists of the school of Schelling have endeavoured to illustrate in the animal structures the transcendental idea of "the repetition of the whole in every

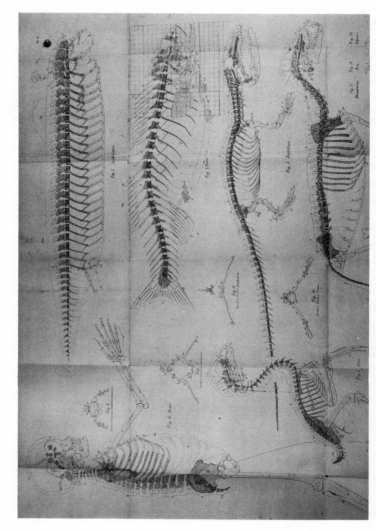

Fig. 3.6. Owen's "archetypus" of vertebrate osteology. (A fold-out insert in Richard Owen, *On the Archetype and Homologies of the Vertebrate Skeleton* [London, 1848].)

part," have operated most disadvantageously and discouragingly to the progress of calm and dispassionate inductive inquiry into that higher law or condition upon which the power of determining the special homologies of the bones of the skeleton depends. Nevertheless the utterances of gifted spirits to whom the common intellectual storehouses is indebted for such original and suggestive generalizations . . . are entitled to respectful consideration, even when they happen to be least intelligible or most counter to the conventional expressions of the current anatomical knowledge of the day; and, for my own part, I must acknowledge that reiterated attempts to detect their latent meaning have not been wholly unproductive.[82]

In the sequel to this treatise, presented to the Royal Institution in 1849, Owen began by explaining that the English language lacked the vocabulary for expressing the leading ideas of transcendental anatomy. German audiences would have no difficulty with a lecture on the "signification" (*Bedeutung*) of the limbs of man and animals because of the long tradition of idealism in German philosophy. By contrast, "how foreign to our English philosophy were those ideas or trains of thought concerned in the discovery of the[se] anatomical truths":

A German anatomist, addressing an audience of his countrymen, would feel none of the difficulty which I experienced. His language, rich in the precise expressions of philosophic abstractions, would instantly supply him with the word for the idea he meant to convey; and that word would be "Bedeutung." . . .

The "Bedeutung," or signification of a part in an animal body, may be explained as the essential nature of such part—as being that essentiality which it retains under every modification of size and form, and for whatever office such modifications may adapt it. I have used therefore the word "Nature" in the sense of the German "Bedeutung," as signifying that essential character of a part which belongs to it in its relation to a predetermined pattern, answering to the "idea" of the Archetypal World in the Platonic cosmogony, which archetype or primal pattern is the basis supporting all the modifications of such part for specific powers and actions in all animals possessing it, and to which archetypal form we come, in the course of our comparison of those modifications, finally to reduce their subject.[83]

No longer need British anatomical science be hampered by old philosophical prejudices or ignorance of the ingenious contributions made by Germans over the past fifty years. Owen would act as intermediary.

The growing vogue of transcendental anatomy fostered by Owen and Forbes was evidenced in the third and fourth editions of Carpenter's *Principles* (1851 and 1854). Carpenter now raised his doctrine of the unity of function to the rank of a major organizing theme of the work. But even more prominent in the *Principles* were the older themes of transcendental anatomy, the unity of plan ("conformity to an ideal 'archetype' "),[84] and the principle of connections. Drawing heavily from Owen's research on vertebrate morphology, Carpenter gave special attention to the concepts of homology and analogy. The study of analogies may lead us to a knowledge of Nature's diverse ways of accomplishing her basic functions, but to arrive at the true affinities among organs and organisms, one must attend to homologies.

The Philosophical Anatomist, who seeks to determine the *organic relation* of these parts, must first consider their internal conformation, and examine into the *structural elements* of which they are composed. . . . The next step . . . is to trace the *connections* of the organs compared, which frequently enables the real nature of parts to be recognized, which would be otherwise obscure. For it is a principle of very extensive application that similar parts are connected with similar parts, in different animals of the same type.[85]

The transcendental methodology was essential to understanding relationships *within* the major animal and plant groups, Carpenter insisted; but attempts to apply it *between* groups were unwarranted.

By some who have clearly recognized *organic identity* as the basis of their reasoning, it has been attempted to show that the law of *Unity of Composition* has an unlimited application; it having been maintained that the same elementary parts exist alike throughout the Vegetable and Animal Kingdoms, and that the difference between the several classes of each lies solely in the respective development of these parts. Such a doctrine, however, can only be supported by assertion, since Nature affords no sanction to it; as the most cursory survey of these two of her kingdoms will at once make obvious.[86]

Unity of composition thus had its limitations.

Passing from Owen to Von Baer, Carpenter stressed again the significance of embryology, the most potent weapon in the arsenal of philosophical anatomy. By the study of development, "the Philosophic Naturalist can press forward with the most assured prospect of success, in the search of that *general plan* of Organization, which it is his highest object to discover."[87] Embryological studies had already demonstrated, first, that Von Baer's law of progression (from the general to the special in the development of the individual) must replace the Meckel-Serres law of parallelism; and second, that the same law of progression applies whether one is seeking a taxonomic means for ordering the diversity of Nature's present-day species or examining a sequence of specimens from the fossil record.

Carpenter upheld the law of progression as the underlying " 'idea' of [the] combined unity and diversity of organization"[88] in the animal and vegetable kingdoms. His emphasis of the word "idea" may have been a reference to Whewell's Fundamental Ideas, the a priori concepts by which the mind apprehends and organizes knowledge of external things. In any case, elucidation of the law of progression, "the general principle of Von Baer," was central to biology as Carpenter conceived it: "In watching the history of the development of any one of the higher forms of organized structure, we find the realization of that ideal evolution of *the more special characters from the more general,* which is the object of the Philosophic Naturalist to bring into view by the [embryological] methods of proceeding already pointed out."[89]

Carpenter never worked out his idealist philosophy of science in a thorough and sophisticated manner. According to his son and biographer, "he had not had a metaphysician's training; and could not think in his language, or dwell at ease with his abstractions."[90] His idealism surfaced from time to time throughout his long career, including the presidential address to the British Association in 1872,[91] but most often it was expressed in writings intended for nonscientific audiences. One suspects that, in this connection, his influence was much more extensive among laymen than among his scientific colleagues.

The treatise of 1846 and the address of 1849 remained Owen's primary contributions to idealist anatomy. In his presidential address to the British Association in 1858, he reiterated the main themes of the discipline and called for new research in two directions. Whereas the skeletal system had previously dominated the search for homologies, that search should now focus on other systems: the nervous, muscular, respiratory, digestive, secretory, and generative organs were prime candidates. And whereas the vertebrate subkingdom had received nearly all of the attention of homological anatomists to date, the articulates and the mollusks should now be studied.[92] Ironically, in this same address Owen made references to the transmutationist papers which Darwin and Wallace had just submitted to the Linnean Society. In a few short years Darwinian theory would provide an utterly different interpretation of the formal similarities among organisms, eviscerating the program of the philosophical anatomists.

Owen's prominence in the community of nineteenth-century naturalists and his outspoken exploitation of transcendentalism in anatomy made him, not Knox, the British symbol of Naturphilosophie. T. H. Huxley cemented this impression for posterity in his appraisal of Owen, written in 1894. Although a follower of idealism to a limmited extent during the early years of his career,[93] Huxley had by 1860 abandoned the approach, regarding it as unscientific and errorprone. Hence Owen's less cautious and longer-lived association with idealism was, to Huxley, an association with "pseudo-philosophical word-play," an alliance with "metaphorical mystifications; for which, so far as they are to be taken seriously, no empirical justification ever existed."[94] Huxley acknowledged that some good had come of Owen's speculative writings; as was true of Goethe and Oken, Owen's work in "philosophical anatomy"[95] though not conclusive was certainly suggestive.

> It would be a great mistake . . . to conclude that Owen's labours in the field of morphology were lost, because they have yielded little fruit of the kind he looked for. On the contrary, they not only did a great deal of good by awakening attention to the higher problems of morphology in this country; but they were of much service in clarifying and improving anatomical nomenclature, especially in respect of the vertebral region.[96]

But all too often, Huxley lamented, Owen's writings manifested the excesses of "Okenism" and the divine organizing principles of the earlier Cambridge Platonists: "That [Owen] was deeply influenced by the philosophy of Oken, bringing it, apparently, in his own mind into harmony with that of the English Platonists, especially that of [Ralph] Cudworth, is a conclusion which can hardly be avoided."[97] As a result, Huxley felt that much of Owen's "great capacity, extensive learning and tireless industry"[98] had been for naught.

Owen proved to be the major spokesman for the idealist approach in natural history. Nevertheless, his idealist contributions were confined to comparative anatomy and paleontology. We can gain a better grasp of the true scope of the idealist tradition by examining the writings of two of Edward Forbes's close friends, Samuel Brown and John Goodsir. Brown tried to extend the concept of unity of plan to the science of matter in the hope of creating "transcendental chemistry." Goodsir remained with anatomy but sought to establish it on geometrical principles.

## The Unity of Matter

Samuel Morrison Brown (1817–56) hailed from Haddington in East Lothian. His father had been the founder of "itinerating libraries" in Scotland—a system instituted in 1817 whereby whole collections of books (primarily religious and practical scientific works) would be rotated biannually among the village libraries of East Lothian.[99] The elder Brown was also something of a practical chemist and set Samuel to work on experiments, igniting an enthusiasm which carried through his years of study for the medical degree at Edinburgh (1832–39). In the midst of this period of life Brown traveled to Berlin, hoping to study with Eilhard Mitscherlich (1794–1863), professor of chemistry and discoverer of the law of isomorphism.[100] This plan was foiled however, when, on a visit to his brother in St. Petersburg, Brown contracted typhus. This illness damaged his health permanently and may have contributed to his dying at the age of thirty-nine, as Forbes had.

Brown had sought out Mitscherlich because even at this early stage in his career he was already committed to a belief in the unity of matter, a sort of chemical idealism (or as he referred to it, "transcendental chemistry"),[101] and presumably he saw in Mitscherlich's discoveries support for this belief. If God is one, and if matter is the direct result of God's will, then, Brown deduced, matter must also be ultimately of one kind only. "The Will that matter be," Brown's cousin and obituarist explained,

> as it must partake of the absolute unity of its Author, resulting in an external world, and, indeed, in all things visible and invisible, is, in any essence which it may be said to possess, itself necessarily ONE, and is by the same infinite Will made what we find it to be, multiform and yet one; in a word, matter, when first willed, must have the unity of its Author:—"One God,—one law,—one *element*."[102]

From this a priori basis that all atoms are the same, Brown concluded that the fifty-five known elements owed their differences strictly to differing configurations of identical atoms; and that the rearrangement of atoms by chemical procedures could, accordingly, bring about the transmutation of elements.[103] The experimental demonstration of this conclusion, and with it the legitimation of his "atomic theory," became literally Brown's life work.

Brown's chemical philosophy bears a strong resemblance to that of one of Knox's early students, the Scottish parson-naturalist John Gibson MacVicar (1801–84). Born in Dundee, MacVicar took prizes in mathematics and natural philosophy at St. Andrews, then moved on to Edinburgh, where he found chemistry, natural history, and Knox's anatomy to be most to his liking. After receiving his license to preach, he acquired the lectureship (later professorship) in natural history at St. Andrews (1827). During the next twelve years he began a museum, lectured (stressing, like Knox, the recent contributions of the French), and traveled to northern Europe, establishing a close relationship with the naturphilosophisch physicist H. C. Oersted. A hiatus in his scientific work, occasioned by the acceptance of a pastorate in Ceylon, lasted until his return to the parish of Moffat (Dumfriesshire) in 1853.[104]

MacVicar's major publication during the pre-Ceylon period was his *Elements of the Economy of Nature; or, The Principles of Physics, Chemistry, and Physiology* (1830). The *Elements* propounded a theory of chemistry based on the principle of the unity of matter: every atom is identical to every other atom. As to the nature of the atom, MacVicar was more explicit than Brown; every atom consists of a hard, tetrahedral nucleus, surrounded by a subtle elastic sphere. The traditional chemical elements are then various multiples of these tetrahedral atoms: hydrogen is formed of two tetrahedrons united at their bases; carbon consists of five tetrahedrons; and so on.[105] MacVicar took his cue for these Pythagorean notions from the pyramidal form of fire described by Plato in the *Timaeus,* and added to it conceptions of electromagnetism acquired from Oersted, Faraday, and others.[106] The result was a unique union of the Newtonian theory of imponderable fluids of the eighteenth century with the nascent field theory of the early nineteenth century. At least one prominent Victorian chemist, Lyon Playfair, regarded MacVicar's chemical philosophy as being far in advance of the times.[107]

The *Elements* may well have been a guide to Samuel Brown's chemical thinking, especially in the later 1830s, when Brown became a close friend of John Goodsir, whom MacVicar had taught at St. Andrews. It is equally likely, however, that both Brown and MacVicar had become attached to the chemical philosophy of Sir Humphrey Davy, and in particular to Davy's suggestion, in the *Elements of Chemical Philosophy,* that "there is only one species of matter, the different chemical, as well as mechanical, forms of which are owing to the different arrangements of its particles."[108] MacVicar referred to this passage from Davy and stated explicitly in his own *Elements* that the "principal object" of the book was "to attempt the analysis here anticipated by this great philosopher and chemist, to show that there is only one kind of impenetrable matter."[109] Brown also was a great admirer of Davy; he later wrote an anonymous tribute to Davy for the *North British Review.*[110] Davy, for his part, had been influenced by the transcendental outpourings of the post-Kantian Coleridge, his close friend as early as 1800. And in Brown (and, one suspects, in MacVicar) we find, too, a great admiration for Coleridge. [111]

As with Forbes, Brown had no intention of practicing medicine, though he wrote a prize thesis and received the medical degree in 1839. (Carpenter was the other prize-winner that year.)[112] His hope was to attain a professorship of chemistry. It was undoubtedly with an eye to publicity and lecturing experience, as much as to monetary return, that he and Forbes offered their course "Popular Lectures on the Philosophy of the Sciences" in the winter of 1840–41. Brown's portion, entitled "On the Art of Natural Inquiry," contains many points of agreement with Whewell's *Philosophy of the Inductive Sci-*

*ences,* which had appeared earlier in the year. For example, on the subordination of facts to ideas, Whewell's Aphorism IV states:

> Facts are the materials of science, but all Facts involve Ideas. Since, in observing Facts, we cannot exclude Ideas, we must, for the purposes of science, take care that the Ideas are clear and rigorously applied.[113]

And Brown's syllabus includes the following notes:

> Facts not Science, but *one* of the elements of Science—Facts to be arranged according to Relations that are Natural—known facts methodized constitute Science, which again is an *Ideal* of known Nature.[114]

Other similarities to Whewell's philosophy include Brown's attention to the "abstract facts of space, number, time," and his great interest in founding scientific philosophy on an extensive knowledge of the history of science.[115] Judging from these resemblances and others (including even the titles of the two), it seems quite possible that Brown's and Forbes's encounter with Whewell's *Philosophy* may have provided the initial stimulus for their lectures.

During these years Brown carried out experiments to establish the transmutability of chemical elements. According to Goodsir's biographer, Brown

> joined in the poetic exaltations of Shelley, the erudite and metaphysical views of Coleridge, and the transcendentalisms of Goethe. Versed in the abstract, the abstruse, and the alchemical past of the Bacons and Van Helmonts, and daily sifting the current doctrines of Lavoisier and Dalton, he longed for a higher analysis than had been obtained by Cavendish, Priestley, or Davy and the laying of a more permanent foundation for his glorious science. . . . He was a profound thinker, with the hopes of a theoretical seer, heralding the time when the composite organic and inorganic worlds would be resolved by man to a simple element, and the subtle agencies of light, caloric, and magnetism to one entity.[116]

By 1841 he was convinced that he had succeeded in transmuting carbon (in the form of cyanide of lead) into silicon by carefully regulated heating, and also iron into rhodium. These revolutionary findings were published by the Royal Society of Edinburgh, with Brown's impassioned appeal to fellow chemists that the experiments be repeated.[117] And in 1843, though unconfirmed, they were the keystone of his bid for the chair of chemistry at Edinburgh vacated by

Thomas Charles Hope. A "transmutation war"[118] ensued, with numerous testimonials in favor of Brown being presented.[119] Brown gave a series of four "Critical Lectures on the Atomic Theory,"[120] which were heavily attended and praised by the metaphysician William Hamilton and the "Germano-Coleridgeans" Julius Hare and Thomas Carlyle.[121] Eventually experiments were performed by others[122] but without consistently positive results, and in the end Brown withdrew his candidacy for the chair. He continued his transmutation experiments privately, when health permitted, for the remaining thirteen years of his life but published nothing further on the subject. His later writings on chemistry were confined to its history. The tiny flowering of "transcendental chemistry" was, like Bacon's final causes, "barren of fruits." Nevertheless, Brown's case demonstrates (as does MacVicar's) that idealism penetrated even into Scottish chemistry and permeated the careers of highly respected chemists.

### *Triangular Morphology and the Inverse Cube Law*

More widely publicized were the transcendental ventures of Forbes's closest friend, John Goodsir (1814–67). The son of a Fifeshire surgeon, Goodsir's ancestry included several prominent doctors, Monro *primus* among them.[123] In his studies for the humanities degree at St. Andrews, Goodsir acquired a taste for Coleridge and was introduced to the "views of the French school *quoad* biology"[124] through the course in natural history offered by John MacVicar. Goodsir and his brother Harry (1816?–47) shared a fondness for examining the marine animals of the Fifeshire coast, an interest which they later exploited with Forbes.[125]

Goodsir was apprenticed to a dentist in 1828 and began medical studies in Edinburgh two years later. Upon attending Knox's anatomy lectures during his first session, he soon gave up thoughts of practicing dentistry or medicine in favor of surgery. The influence of Knox was powerful: he became both teacher and friend to Goodsir, who responded by quickly establishing a reputation for artful dissections and accurate plaster models of skeletal parts.[126] He was licensed by the Royal College of Surgeons of Edinburgh in 1835 and became its museum conservator in 1841.

Fig. 3.7. John Goodsir. (From William Turner, ed., *The Anatomical Memoirs of John Goodsir*, 2 vols. [Edinburgh, 1868], vol. 1, frontispiece.)

The early exposure to dentistry showed up in Goodsir's first British Association paper (1838), on the embryological development of the teeth, perhaps his best work.[127] This interest led him to the more general study of the anatomy of the human cranium, discussed in an unpublished lecture of 1840, "On the Cephalic Termination of the Sympathetic Nerve." Though the details of this lecture are unknown, this was his entree into transcendental anatomy. His biographer relates only that this was "the first marked indication of his study of the higher anatomy of Goethe, ably extended by Geoffroy St. Hilaire, and the subject of much comment and interpretation by Knox."[128]

Goodsir's publications over the next twenty years showed great diversity. He took up the study of cells soon after Schleiden and Schwann announced their cell theory, and his observations of the pathology of cells were sufficiently distinguished for Rudolph Virchow to dedicate the first edition of his famed *Die Cellularpathologie* to Goodsir.[129] Later papers contributed to the anatomy of the human digestive, reproductive, endocrine, and nervous systems, as well as to the biology of marine mammals, fish, and invertebrates.[130] In 1850 he founded and edited the quarterly *Annals of Anatomy and Physiology,* which terminated with volume 3 in 1853.

Goodsir's brilliance was soon recognized: Monro *tertius* took him on as demonstrator in 1844, and two years later he was appointed to the chair of anatomy, ending the 125-year reign of the Monros. By merging the approaches of the Monros, Barclay, and Knox, he revitalized the teaching of anatomy, which had declined under the last Monro. In 1847 he began a summer course of lectures on the comparative anatomy of the invertebrates, and in 1853 took over the natural history class of another of his mentors, the ailing Robert Jameson. These double duties led to the impairment of his own health, however, and from that time on he traveled frequently to the Continent for treatment, as well as for study and for the collection of anatomical instruments and models.

A pronounced interest in ideal morphology became evident in Goodsir's publications only in the 1850s, though it was presaged in his closing lectures on comparative anatomy in 1849. A future line of extremely significant research, he announced in these lectures, would be the establishment of the mathematical relationships and causal forces governing animal form. In the past, the "wonderful progress of biology" had been largely dependent on the study of final causes. The physical sciences, on the other hand, had not advanced until "the introduction of the inductive philosophy, and till final causes had been laid aside."[131] While granting that final causes "pervaded all nature," Goodsir suggested that the science of anatomy might benefit from the experience of the physical sciences. Final causes should be ignored, and instead, anatomists should seek out the geometrical regularities of animal morphology, in the same spirit that Kepler had sought the geometrical form of the planetary orbits:

> Suppose the anatomist gave the exact curvature of the surface, the volume and proportions which different parts of the organs might bear—what their formal geometry was might become [a] matter of calculation. He might begin, by the lengths, and breadths, and volumes of the different parts, by ascertaining whether they have a correspondency, and exhibit a mathematical relation, spherical or spheroidal curves, etc. These once ascertained, he would become certain of the geometrical construction, and could reason as to the probable forms of other parts.[132]

If this geometrical understanding could be achieved, the next step would be for an anatomical Newton to determine the laws of force responsible for the geometrical regularities. Whereas in the inorganic realm the force law (gravity) involved an inverse-square relationship, Goodsir imagined that the organic world might depend on an inverse-cube law:

> Newton had shown in his *Principia* that if attraction had generally varied as the inverse cube instead of as the inverse square of the distance, the heavenly bodies would revolve, not in ellipses but in logarithmic spirals, rapidly diffuse themselves, and rush off into space. It would be curious that if the law of the square were the law of attraction, the law of the cube might therefore prove to be the law of production. . . . If this law of force were admitted, and cellules grew by a certain law, we could thereby explain how all cellules passed off from one another, and how all form was produced—namely, in a rapidly-increasing geometrical ratio, instead of revolving round an axis. Probably the logarithmic spiral would be found to be the law at work in the increase of organic bodies.[133]

It was high time, Goodsir seems to have felt, that naturalists adopted the *modus operandi* of the astronomers, beginning with the search for the Pythagorean harmonies of animal bodies. Their previous neglect of this approach was due, he suggested, to their lack of mathematical education (although elsewhere he proposed that the poverty of ideal morphological studies stemmed from the difficulty of imagining that phenomena could be the result of two kinds of causes, i.e., formal and teleological, acting simultaneously).[134] This appeal that biologists take up the methods and concepts of physical science was no mere lip service. Goodsir sustained a curiosity about animal electricity, for example, which (with other interests) drove him to Berlin in 1857 to work with the "organic physicist," Emil DuBois-Reymond.[135]

In illustration of the possible fruits of this approach, he pointed to the geometrical studies of mollusk shell coiling by Henry Moseley (1801–72) and the analysis of the human figure just published by the painter and art theorist David Ramsay Hay.[136] It seems likely, however, that Goodsir's morphological interests were based on an idealism which had its origin in discussions of Forbes's circle in the late 1830s (Forbes and the Goodsir brothers were not only co-workers in marine zoology, but also shared an attic apartment in Edinburgh in 1839–41),[137] and from his reading of the semi-Kantian philosophy of his colleague William Hamilton. In an 1856 essay we find Goodsir espousing a theory of knowledge taken explicitly from Hamilton's *Discussions on Philosophy:*[138] information received through the senses is "conditioned by the laws of the consciousness," so that knowledge is necessarily relative. As Goodsir understood it, "All scientific, or other inquiry is . . . fundamentally regulated by the laws of thought. For these laws, as they are the conditions under which the Human Intellect works, cannot be dispensed with, and consequently constitute the logical process in every train of inquiry. Every sound intellect is necessarily—that is, is instinctively regulated, more or less, by the Laws of Thought."[139] Scientific "facts" are therefore mediated by the senses and regulated by the mind; "they are apparent, not real, they are phenomena, not noumena."[140]

John Goodsir was the Richard Owen of Scotland. Though his career was shorter and his renown narrower than Owen's, and though they disagreed on many details, Goodsir's approach to anatomy and zoology, employing a mixture of the ideal and the teleological, was identical to Owen's.[141] When, in 1858, Owen called for the advancement of idealist anatomy by the study of organ systems other than the skeletal, and by the study of animal groups other than the vertebrates, he was describing precisely the kind of work Goodsir had already begun. In a British Association paper of 1856, for example, Goodsir pursued both of these goals simultaneously by comparing the morphology of the nervous system of annulose (wormlike) animals with that of the vertebrates. These two types of organization, he found, were distinguishable primarily by the position of the mouth: the vertebrate mouth opened into the haemal (or ventral) side of the body, while in annulose animals the mouth was on the neural (dorsal) side. Otherwise, vertebrate and annulose animals "present parallel forms of structure, and must consequently be closely linked together in morphological inquiry."[142] To simplify this inquiry Goodsir introduced a system of nomenclature in which homologous parts in the two groups were given the same name. In other papers read at this 1856 meeting, he then applied the new nomenclature to the analysis of two questions which had so exercised earlier transcendental anatomists: the construction of the vertebrate skull and the nature of limbs.[143]

Goodsir's most extreme transcendentalizing came in his last years, when he began to contemplate a theory of triangular morphology. The triangle (and for solid figures, the tetrahedron) seemed to be the fundamental principle of form in both the organic and inorganic realms. The form of the human body, for example, could be inscribed within a triangle; and when this triangle was subdivided by "transverse, vertical and oblique lines,"[144] the lines intersected at such key points as the ribs, navel, and knees. Other animals and plants could be similarly analyzed. And there seemed to be multitudinous instances where internal organs too were constructed of triangular elements.

Goodsir's division of the human body into triangles probably arose from his association with the artist Hay, to whom he had given anatomical assistance. But curiously, the triangle had played a symbolic role during his student days with Forbes. The latter had instituted a small fraternal organization in 1835, later known as the Universal Brotherhood of Friends of Truth, which survived at least until the 1850s. The emblem of the brotherhood was a silver triangle (Fig. 3.8), and new members were initiated, after a period of probation,

## The Universal Brotherhood of Friends of Truth.

Fig. 3.8. Symbol of the Universal Brotherhood of Friends of Truth, heading for the organization's "Principles," printed in 1841. (From William Turner, ed., *The Anatomical Memoirs of John Goodsir*, 2 vols. [Edinburgh, 1868], 1: following 60.)

into the order of the "mystic triangle." Forbes's fascination with the triangle extended to its use in drawings of the naturalist's dredge and may have had its origin in the triangular shield of his native Isle of Man.[145] It is thus entirely possible that Goodsir's theory of triangular morphology received its initial stimulus from the "mystical triangle" of the Universal Brotherhood; perhaps it was reinforced by his intuition that organic forms might depend upon a *third*-power "law of production."

These speculations on triangularity came just before Goodsir's death in 1867 and were never published (or even committed to manuscript, so far as is known). They may be discounted as having arisen from the "growing metamorphosis of age,"[146] but they are also representative of the ultimate aspirations of the pre-Darwinian philosophic naturalist.

### Idealism Legitimized

By the early 1850s idealism in British biology was in full flower. After its hesitant beginnings in the writings of Roget and Barry, the leading younger naturalists of the 1840s—Owen, Forbes, and Carpenter—bolstered by the philosophical authority if Henry More, Coleridge, Whewell, and Hamilton, brought the idealistic impulse into fashion. Toward the end of the decade, translations of key German works began to appear. Oken's *Lehrbuch der Naturphilosophie* (a work so mystical that some members of the sponsoring Ray Society objected to its publication under the society's seal) was translated, appropriately, by Alfred Tulk, whose father, an intimate friend of Coleridge, had been instrumental in introducing into England the ideas of the scientific mystic of an earlier period Emanuel Swedenborg. And Von Baer's contributions to embryology, which had been so suggestive to Barry and Carpenter in the 1830s, were finally translated by Huxley in 1853.[147] By then Knox and Goodsir had begun to publish their views. Even lesser lights of the era like MacVicar found themselves delving into the ideal forms of plants and animals.[148]

As the idealist tradition was reaching its maximum vogue, the Scottish natural theologian James M'Cosh (1811–94) set forth the clearest enunciation of the movement's goals and the fullest account of its achievements. M'Cosh had received the M.A. degree from Edinburgh in 1834 with a prize essay in philosophy which earned the praise of Hamilton. After fifteen years in the Presbyterian ministry, he was appointed professor of logic at Queen's College, Belfast. He remained there until 1868, when the opportunity to become president of the College of New Jersey (later Princeton) drew him permanently to America.[149]

M'Cosh was no Kantian, but an idealist of the Platonic strain. Shortly after taking up his academic position at Belfast, he became fascinated by the study of the ideal morphology of plants. In addition to the short British Association papers which ensued,[150] he pub-

lished in 1851 an anonymous essay reviewing the recent developments in idealist botany and zoology as represented in the works of
Balfour, Schleiden, and Owen.[151] The Goethian doctrine of the leaf
archetype and its metamorphosis to produce the various organs of
the plant was at last widely accepted, M'Cosh announced with approval:

> Under some modifications [Goethe's views] have now commanded the assent
> of the most sagacious and practical of British naturalists, men slow to admit
> German theories in any case, and who never do admit them till they have
> accommodated them to their own common-sense type. . . .
>     . . . The doctrine of the metamorphosis of plants is now acknowledged by
> all the great doctors, and has been sanctioned by the great councils of sci-
> ence.[152]

Similarly in zoology, Owen's reworking of the naturphilosophisch
doctrine of the vertebrate archetype had been followed by its "almost
universal adoption."[153] These events, M'Cosh proclaimed, would
finally resolve the battle between Geoffroy and Cuvier over the unity
of plan versus final causes: *both* were essential in man's understanding of Nature. "The old controversy should now cease in the adoption of both doctrines, that of a general homology and that of a special adaption of parts; and the former properly interpreted will be
found, we are convinced, to yield as rich a contribution to the cause
of natural theology as the latter."[154] Moreover, in accepting these
two modes of explanation M'Cosh saw the possibility of their complete reconciliation. The archetypal plans of the animal and plant
kingdoms, and other formal relations in nature, have their own *final*
cause, in that they make nature comprehensible to man: "Without
the repetition and correspondence of parts, man would have felt himself lost in the midst of God's works, and this because of their very
profusion. It is by means of points of analogy that man is enabled
practically to recognise, and scientifically to classify, the objects by
which he is surrounded."[155] In this light, M'Cosh concluded, it
becomes apparent that Owen had (unconsciously) established a "teleology of a higher and more archetypal order than Cuvier."[156]
    Over the next five years M'Cosh elaborated this natural theology
of formal and final causes into the 500-plus pages of *Typical Forms
and Special Ends in Creation* (1856). He was assisted by his colleague

George Dickie (1812–82), Belfast's professor of natural history. This work deserves to rank as the Bridgewater Treatise of the 1850s and, as such, forms a fitting conclusion to a chapter which began with Roget's treatise of 1834. The differences between these two works highlight the transformation that occurred in British natural history during the intervening period. Roget's concern was with physiological function as evidence of the purposiveness of the Creator; his references to ideal plans were limited and cautious. M'Cosh had no such reservations; formal causes ("typical forms") were on an equal par with final causes ("special ends").

*Typical Forms* opens with a proclamation of the formal-teleological thesis: there are "two great principles or methods of procedure" in the constitution of the material universe. "The one is the PRINCIPLE OF ORDER, or a General Plan, Pattern, or Type, to which every given object is made to conform with more or less precision. The other is the PRINCIPLE OF SPECIAL ADAPTATION, or Particular End, by which each object, while constructed after a general model, is, at the same time, accommodated to the situation which it has to occupy, and a purpose which it is intended to serve."[157] Natural theology had been greatly advanced with respect to the former principle, M'Cosh said, through the recent "discovery of homologies by the sciences of comparative anatomy and morphological botany." The effects of these two causes in nature are not contradictory but parallel, and M'Cosh organized his treatise accordingly. Beginning with the plants and proceeding through the vertebrate and invertebrate groups (fossil as well as recent) to inorganic objects, he divided each chapter into two parts: the first recited evidences of pattern and order ("typical forms"), and the second gave the more traditional instances of function and purpose ("special adaptations").

Together, M'Cosh observed, the evidences of order and purpose provide man with a far greater understanding of God than was previously possible. We find that although He had adhered to a typical plan for all organisms, He has never sacrificed their functional well-being to that plan. "The general often gives way to the special, but the special never gives way to the general."[158] Hence for M'Cosh there was, after all, not a complete parity between formal and final causes. When necessary, utility must take precedence over form. And, as he had explained in the earlier essay, even formal order has its final cause. "The general order pervading nature is just a final cause of a higher and more archetypical character. In the special principle, we have every organ suited to its function; in the more general principle, we find all the objects in nature suited to man, who has to study and to use them."[159]

M'Cosh did not claim to have revolutionized natural theology by this two-pronged approach. He was merely returning to the wider views of philosophers of antiquity such as Plato, in contrast to the works of "British authors for the last age or two,"[160] which have been too narrowly confined to teleology. But a major difference separated the thought of the ancients from that of the mid-nineteenth century, he argued. "What was at first guess and vatication has become demonstration; . . . what was at first a mixture of fact and speculation has become, by the inductive methods of weighing and measuring every phenomenon, unadulterated truth."[161] Obscure intuitions have, through science, become firm knowledge.

## Ideal Patterns in Space and Time

Thus far we have surveyed the prominent aspects of idealism in early-nineteenth-century British anatomy, physiology, and taxonomy. One might wonder if idealism found its way into other branches of biology, such as biogeography or paleontology. To put the question more explicitly, were animal and plant distribution patterns ever taken to be manifestations of ideal plans, either divine or human? The answer is yes, in at least two cases: Swainson's geographic extrapolation of MacLeay's quinary system and Forbes's theory of polarity in the history of life.

The widely traveled naturalist and talented illustrator William Swainson (1789–1855) was the most avid promoter of MacLeay's quinary taxonomic system.[162] His *Treatise on the Geography and Classification of Animals* (1835) was the first book in English to treat the subject of animal distribution at length. Noting, as Buffon had, that different places have different species, Swainson set forth two questions which he regarded as central to the student of distribution: "What are the causes that have produced this dissimilarity of creatures? and, secondly, is there *method* in all this amazing diversity?"[163] The first question presented no difficulty to Swainson: the distribution of every species had been set in the beginning "by an Almighty fiat."[164] Obviating thereby any further consideration of the historical questions of origin and dispersal, Swainson moved on to the description of present-day animal distribution. The earth could be divided, he thought, into five major zoological provinces: Europe, Asia, America, Africa, and Australia. Each of these provinces was the home of one of the five races of mankind and a distinctive assemblage of animal races. Moreover, the races of these five regions were not totally separated; rather, they blended into each other at the boundaries between provinces. He supported these propositions with ornithological data and a smattering of observations from other animal groups. Finally, Swainson claimed that the five provinces could be connected in a circle. By so doing, he had achieved the biogeographic analogue of MacLeay's taxonomic system—a circular arrangement with five major segments.[165] This discovery he naturally offered as a new confirmation of the essential correctness of the original quinary system.

With the lapse of interest in MacLeay's system in the 1840s, Swainson's quinary biogeography was forgotten. Subsequent biogeographers have been much concerned with the division of the globe into provinces, but they have seldom attached special meaning to the actual *number* of regions or their geographic arrangement, as Swainson did. For a more influential instance of the merger of idealism and distributionism, we must turn from spatial to temporal distribution, and thus to paleontology.

Many geologists of the early nineteenth century looked upon the history of life as one of progression from simple to complex (or imperfect to perfect) forms. Although this progression of forms was usually regarded as having resulted from directional changes in the earth's environment such as a gradually cooling climate, some naturalists believed that progress was intrinsic to God's plan of creation and thus separate from any utilitarian necessity. Varying versions of this "transcendental progressionism"[166] were advocated in the 1840s by Louis Agassiz, Hugh Miller, and Robert Chambers. But opposition to progressionism in all its forms by influential geologists such as Lyell, Gideon Mantell, and Edward Forbes prevented any wide diffusion of idealist progressionism. The antiprogressionists emphasized the hazards inherent in any theory based on negative evidence

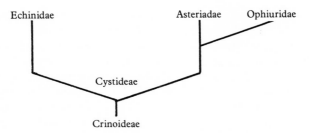

Fig. 3.9. The position of the Cystideae in the animal series. (Adapted from Edward Forbes, "On the *Cystideae* of the Silurian Rocks of the British Islands," *Memoirs of the Geological Survey of Great Britain* 2 [1848]:526.)

and the unlikely preservation of the higher (vertebrate) forms in older strata.[167]

In the late 1840s Forbes began to have other thoughts about the overall sequence of forms in the fossil record. During 1847–48 he spent considerable time on the identification and classification of British fossil echinoderms at the Geological Survey, including specimens of the recently established class the Cystoidea. At the time there was considerable disagreement as to the affinities of the Cystoidea with other fossil echinoderm groups—crinoids, starfish, urchins, and brittle-stars. Forbes's solution, shown in Figure 3.9, was to place the cystoids (which have been extinct since the late Paleozoic era) midway in a diverging hierarchy, with crinoids at the bottom and the other echinoderm classes at the top (all of which are still extant).[168] While this diagram appears to represent a phylogeny, Forbes undoubtedly regarded it as an atemporal plan for echinoderm taxonomy, showing morphological complexity, not genetic history (although the language used in these kinds of analyses was often deceiving).

The cause of this arrangement, according to Forbes's "abstract view," was "polarity." The cystoids were in the midst of a "perpetual struggle" between the "unquestionable progression towards a higher type" (which terminates in the echinoid-asteroid-ophiuroid pole) and the "negative or vegetative polar influence"[169] (terminating in the crinoids). He recognized that his interpretation was at odds with that of other paleontologists, notably Leopold von Buch, upon whose work he claimed to be building.[170] But, Forbes insisted, "without the recognition of the influence of the relation of polarity among the Echinodermata, it is impossible to understand the true position of the Cystideae in the series. To understand their variety and serial parallelism among themselves, we must have recourse to a relation equally mysterious."[171]

In the closing paragraph of the "Cystideae" memoir, Forbes foresaw objections to his speculations. "The view which I have here taken . . . will appear to those unaccustomed to look upon natural history questions in the abstract, fanciful and perhaps obscure."[172] Most notable among the sceptics was Charles Darwin, who found the polarity arguments "absolutely unintelligible" and was "not at all convinced"[173] by the paper as a whole. A phylogenetic interpretation made much more sense than "mysterious" polar forces.

The cool response to polarity in the fossil record apparently arrested Forbes's enthusiasm for the idea, but only temporarily. In 1854 he came back to it, proposing this time the polar distribution of all organic beings throughout geologic time. He introduced the theory briefly in the conclusion of his presidential address to the Geological Society, presenting it as a suggestion in need of additional confirmatory data. Two months later he gave a more thorough explication of polarity in a lecture at the Royal Institution. These were the only explicit statements of the concept in his published works, although his biographers state that polarity was discussed the following November in one of his last lectures at the University of Edinburgh.[174]

If the existing fossil record is viewed in its entirety, Forbes explained, with special attention paid to the number and variety of "generic ideas," it will be noticed immediately that the maxima of these ideas occur at opposite ends of the geological column, with a marked paucity of generic variation in the middle. Hence, genera seem to bloom out at the beginning of the Paleolzoic era, to decrease gradually to a minimum between the Paleozoic and Mesozoic eras, and then to expand again in Cretaceous, Tertiary, and modern times. On the basis of this polar distribution, Forbes suggested in his Royal Institution lecture that the accepted tripartite division of strata—Paleozoic, Mesozoic, and Tertiary—be replaced with a two-era system, using only the Paleozoic and the "Neozoic."[175] The Paleozoic would include the Silurian, Devonian, Carboniferous, and Permian

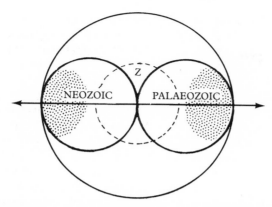

Fig. 3.10. Polarity in time. (From Edward Forbes, "On the Manifestation of Polarity in the Distribution of Organized Beings in Time," *Proceedings of the Royal Institution of Great Britain* 1 [1854]:428–33.)

periods, with the Neozoic covering the Triassic, Jurassic, Cretaceous, Tertiary, and modern periods. Forbes then presented the diagram shown in Figure 3.10, and remarked: "By a diagram such as the above we may fairly express this view, the shaded portions of the circles included within the great circle of the system of nature representing the maxima of development of generic ideas, and the dotted area, Z, the region of their minimum productions."[176] This interpretation, Forbes felt, correctly characterized the entire range of the fossiliferous strata then known.

Before the Silurian and after the *commencement* of the present, no special creations of generic types have as yet been shewn to be manifested. In the system of life of which all known creatures living or extinct as yet described, so far as our knowledge extends—and there is a consistency in its coordination that suggests the probability of our being acquainted with its extreme [a critical assumption]—the creation of the fauna and flora of the oldest Palaeozoic epoch would seem to be the primordial and the appearance of man the closing biological events.[177]

The polar distribution of fossils was demonstrated by contrasting certain groups of marine organisms representative of the Paleozoic and Neozoic eras, such as the abundance of the Crinoidea and octacorals ("4-starred corals") in the Paleozoic, as opposed to the

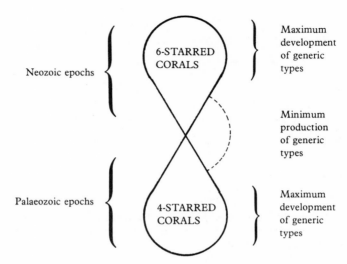

Fig. 3.11. Polarity of generic types. (From Edward Forbes, "On the Manifestation of Polarity in the Distribution of Organized Beings in Time," *Proceedings of the Royal Institution of Great Britain* 1 [1854]:428–33.)

Echinoidea and hexcorals ("6-starred corals") in the Neozoic. A second polar diagram illustrated this comparison (Fig. 3.11).

Forbes's vision of polarity was not as contrived an interpretation of the fossil record as it might now appear, since the Ordovician period was unknown in his time and the Cambrian was little explored. If we consider modern diagrams of the diversity of life through the geologic time scale, and delete those first two periods of the Paleozoic era during which metazoans first appeared, we obtain an approximation of the distribution he envisioned.[178]

A number of objections to the theory were anticipated by Forbes. One objection he attempted to resolve was the apparent contradiction in speaking of polarity *in time*. Since time indicates a unidirectional sequence of events, what would be the meaning of a multidirectional development dependent on, or occurring in, time? "How can we connect with time an arrangement that involves the notion of progression in opposite directions, proceeding from a median zero?"[179] He countered this objection by replying that unidirectional time is only a mental construct which the humble human being unconsciously superimposes on his experience to render it more coherent. Time need not be regarded as an essential attribute of reality.

> Time is an attribute with which man's mind invests creation; a mode of regarding Divine ideas, necessary for the conception of time by our limited faculties and forming in itself no part or essence of the Divine scheme of organized nature. We speak of Polarity in Time, for want of a better phrase: but this polarity, or arrangement in opposite directions with a development of intensity towards the extremes of each, is itself, if I am right in my speculations, an attribute or regulating law of the divinely originating scheme of creation, therefore strictly speaking independent of the notion of time, though perceptible by our minds only in connection with it.[180]

In stressing the subjective nature of time, Forbes was invoking a Kantian or Whewellian interpretation.[181] Polarity was a noumenal model which accounted for the phenomena or paleontology.

Earlier usages of "polarity" had referred only to spatial or morphological characteristics. Forbes's new usage extended the concept to a temporal phenomenon. He pointed out that there were four primary relationships between biological entities: analogy, affinity (or homology), representation (the substitution of one species for another in spatially or temporally separated but ecologically similar environments), and polarity. The first three of these relations had always been regarded as applicable to both spatial and temporal situations, but polarity had previously been thought of only as a spatial relation. By now positing its existence as a temporal relation, Forbes believed he had made the four relations totally symmetrical, undoubtedly a satisfying result for any naturalist of transcendental predilections.[182]

The theory of fossil polarity provokes other questions, equally interesting if not as profound philosophically, which Forbes did not address in his lectures. What led him to extrapolate from the earlier "polarity" of the Cystoidea to this new polar distribution of the entire fossil record? And what natural causes or mechanisms, if any, did he think might have produced this phenomenon?

As early as 1852 Forbes had spoken of the contrast between the Paleozoic and later fossil assemblages, noting that the former exhibited "differences in detail so great that on superficial consideration we might almost be inclined to regard them as belonging to some other world than our own."[183] At that time he had not yet re-

garded the distribution as a polar one, but by 1854 new paleontological work clarified the pattern for him. His summary of the year's
progress, in the anniversary address before the Geological Society,
included mention of Thomas Davidson's investigations of fossil
brachiopods:

Regarding the Present and the Lower Palaeozoic epoch as opposite poles of
time, we find the generic types among the Brachiopods concentrate as it
were around or towards each [pole], whilst they depauperate towards the
equatorial region of the scheme, about which indeed no generic types originate. The loop-armed types are regnant, as it were, anteally, the spiral-
armed types posteally; and the latter are in the main so dominant, that the
Brachiopoda, as a great assemblage of types, has its major development
towards the past, its minor towards the present, and its zero in the parting
epoch between the palaeozoic and after-ages.[184]

The idea that generic diversity was not constant through time but
was greatest at the opposite ends of the fossil record was thus suggested, according to Forbes, by the growing fossil record itself.

Although polarity was a key concept in Forbes's transcendental
philosophy of natural history, it was not his final answer to the problem of fossil diversity. It was, rather, the *key* to finding that answer.
Polarity was not a law but simply a manifestation of a law yet to be
discovered. It was not a solution to the changes in species from one
geological formation to the next; it was a useful way of viewing the
fossil record as a whole: "In the demonstration of this relation [of
polarity] it seems to me that we shall in all probability, discover the
secret of the difference between the life anterior to the Trias and the
life afterwards."[185] This same reservation about the meaning of
polarity, wherever it might occur in nature, had been expressed by
Whewell:

The general conclusion to which we are led on this subject is, that the per-
suasion of the existence and connexion or identity of various polarities in
nature, although very naturally admitted, and in many cases interpreted and
confirmed by observed facts, is of itself, so far as we at present possess it, a
very insecure guide to scientific doctrines. When it is allowed to dictate our
theories, instead of animating and extending our experimental researchers, it
leads only to errour, confusion, obscurity, and mysticism.[186]

If, then, polarity was not a final answer but rather a route to discovering "the secret of the difference" between Paleozoic and Neo-

zoic fossils, what sort of final answer did Forbes have in mind? Was the polar pattern a transcendent ideal and therefore metaphysically "caused"? Or could it have resulted from natural (i.e., environmental) causes? And if the latter, was it part of the Divine Plan to produce the polar pattern by a specific sequence of environmental events? Evidence to document Forbes's thinking here is scant, to say the least. To reach even a tentative solution to this problem, we must first pose several other, subordinate questions: What had caused the great generic diversity at the "poles"? Why did this diversity decrease in the transition between Paleozoic and Neozoic eras? And what had occurred, or would occur, beyond the poles, that is, before the Paleozoic and after the Neozoic?

Forbes believed that the variation in species from one epoch to the next was a matter of substitution of types for comparable ("representative") but not identical types, in the same way that present species seemed to vary from one geographic region to the next. These substitutions were accomplished by special creations. The particular nature of each special creation was dependent only upon terrestrial conditions: "Suitable conditions have been met by the creation of suitable types."[187] Thus, to account for a great diversity of life in any particular geological period, Forbes would have required only extensive, "suitable" environments and a large number of specific creations. Each species would continue to exist "so long as conditions favourable to the production and sustenance of the individual representatives or elements are continued."[188]

The relative dearth of generic ideas toward the middle of the geologic time scale implies the extinction of a great many genera and the absence of any immediate substitution of other genera. According to Forbes, this paucity meant an absence of "suitable conditions." At the time of his two polarity addresses, he apparently had no specific ideas as to the nature of this environmental decline. Within a few months, however, a possible explanation was supplied by his longtime colleague at the Geological Survey, Andrew Ramsay. In the course of fieldwork for the survey in 1852, Ramsay had noticed certain unusual Permian strata in the counties of Shropshire and Worcestershire. Upon reexamining the area two years later, he concluded that it had been the site of extensive glaciers during the Permian period. He communicated these findings to Forbes in July of 1854 and to the British Association the following September. A thorough exposition of Permian glaciation was presented to the Geological Society the next year.[189]

Both Ramsay and Forbes were quick to make the connection between these glacial phenomena and the disjunction of life between Paleozoic and Neozoic times. Ramsay recounted his discovery as follows:

> There is one point of resemblance between these Permian breccias with their associated strata and the Pleistocene drift deposits worthy of note. In the latter fossils are much scattered, and in most of the beds of rare occurrence. They are still more scarce in that part of the Permian series with which the breccias are associated. I have thought, that, in like manner, this paucity of life may be connected in these latitudes with the glacial phenomena of the Permian and Bunter [Pleistocene] periods, and I no sooner mentioned this to Professor E. Forbes than he suggested that it might also be connected with the great break in life that has taken place between Palaeozoic and Secondary times.[190]

Throughout his career, Ramsay maintained a belief in the existence of a frigid Permian period, despite the opposition of many fellow geologists. Lyell was the most notable adherent to the idea, though he regarded the evidence as pointing to river ice, rather than to glaciers and icebergs, as the agent behind the structures Ramsay had observed. For Forbes, the occurrence of widespread glacial conditions similar to, but of far longer duration than, those known to have occurred during the Pleistocene could account for the decline in Paleozoic genera. Thereafter, the retreat of the Permian glaciers and a moderating of climate had permitted a gradual repopulating of vacant lands and seas with new genera.

If this sort of environmental degradation could explain the decline in generic diversity in the middle of the geologic spectrum, did it also explain events *beyond* Forbes's Paleozoic and Neozoic poles? Did polarity, in fact, imply that generic diversity would increase indefinitely in each direction from the central minimum? Or would that diversity reach some maximum and then remain constant or decrease again? On this point the evidence in Forbes's work is ambiguous. For the Paleozoic pole he seems to have thought that life commenced with maximum diversity in the Silurian period, a belief certainly in accord with the fossil data existing in his time. He conceded to the progressionists that life forms might have undergone an increase in complexity prior to the Silurian, but the complete absence of fossil evidence for that early period placed all such theories in the realm of pure speculation: "For us, the arks that bore the primaeval types, and those that succeeded again, had foundered in the seas of protozoic time long before the earliest creatures, of which we now find remains in the crust of our globe, flourished. If there were transformations and transmutations, and progressions among genera, it was during the dark and impenetrable ages of pre-geologic time."[191]

At the Neozoic pole, Forbes thought that maximum diversity had again been reached, but that physical conditions might cause another great decline to set in, followed possibly by a third pole. This interpretation was noted by Lyell in his journals on the species question: "E. Forbes, says H[ooker], had supposed certain waves of poverty and richness of Creative Power wh. his Polarity doctrine favoured, & tho' no creation has taken place since Man, yet he looked forward to periods when the Creative Power w.$^{\mathrm{d}}$ be active again as at certain past times."[192]

From this analysis of the stages in the polar scheme, a clearer comprehension of Forbes's thinking emerges. "Polarity" was for him a Divine Idea made manifest through the interaction of a periodic life-creating force ("Creative Power") and a fluctuating environmental force ("suitable conditions"). Both forces were part of "the divinely originating scheme of creation," that is to say, both were God's handiwork. But by introducing the concept of polarity, Forbes was attempting to treat the phenomena of the origin and diversity of life as *law-governed* phenomena, and thus as phenomena amenable to scientific investigation. Accordingly, though we may now find polarity to be a dissatisfying, even obscurantist explanation, we can readily imagine that it might have held considerable appeal for the philosophical, law-seeking naturalists of the post–Bridgewater Treatise era of the 1850s.

A few naturalists did, in fact, take seriously Forbes's exhortations to seek out evidence in support of polarity. In the 1854 edition of *Siluria,* Roderick Murchison considered the theory an "ingenious speculation" of some merit, especially insofar as it accorded with his own belief that life had first appeared in a fully developed state in the

Silurian period. He added the qualification that polarity seemed to apply to plants and to invertebrates, but not to vertebrates, "whose main direction of development of generic ideas is . . . towards the newer or Neozoic pole."[193] When Forbes later reviewed Murchison's work, he disputed the latter's claim of the absence of vertebrates at the Paleozoic pole, insisting that Murchison had based his opinion on negative evidence.[194] However "ingenious" polarity seemed in 1854, Murchison deleted any mention of it in subsequent editions of *Siluria*.

Two years later the malacologist S. P. Woodward stated in his *A Manual of the Mollusca* (1856) that the numbers of brachiopod genera did show "'polarity' or excessive development at the ends of the [stratigraphic] series." Woodward added, however, that the polarity hypothesis was a result of its author's concentration on the fossils of England, where the Permian and Triassic strata "separate, like a desert, the palaeozoic from the 'neozoic' formations."[195] This may indeed have been the case, since the bulk of Forbes's stratigraphic work had been performed in Britain. But modern paleontology has vindicated his theory to the limited extent of showing that the decrease in the diversity of life in the Permo-Triassic transition was a worldwide phenomenon.

By far the most significant response to polarity came from Alfred Russel Wallace, for it was in reply to Forbes's presidential address that Wallace composed his important Sarawak essay of 1855.[196] In that essay he dismissed polarity as "quite unnecessary" and dependent on Forbes's assumption that the knowledge of the fossil record was complete and reliable; this was a "fatal objection," according to Wallace.[197]

There can be no doubt that Wallace held Forbes in high regard. In a footnote later appended to his 1855 essay, Wallace wrote: "Since the above was written, the author has heard with sincere regret of the death of this eminent naturalist, from whom so much important work was expected. His remarks on the present paper,—a subject on which no man was more competent to decide,—were looked for with the greatest interest. Who shall supply his place?"[198] Wallace found his critic in Darwin. And it was the efforts of Darwin and Wallace that obviated any further development of the concept of fossil polarity. "The great name of Edward Forbes," Wallace wrote in 1873, "did not prevent his theory of 'Polarity in the Distribution of Organic beings in Time' from dying a natural death."[199] Forbes had in fact concluded his Royal Institution address on polarity with the comment, "If [polarity] be true, as I believe it to be, then the truth that it contains is most important; if it prove in the end to be a misinterpretation, it will at least have served the good purpose of stimulating inquiry in a fresh direction."[200] The latter alternative proved to be the correct one.

Polarity, Forbes's final venture in transcendental natural history, was symbolic of the aspirations and preconceptions of philosophical naturalists. From the practical standpoint "polarity" represented years of examining the temporal distribution of fossils. On the philosophical side, it exemplified the penchant for seeing ideal, transcendental relationships among natural phenomena. The ultimate goal of the philosophic naturalist was to discover and explain patterns in nature. To do so he had to rise above the cataloguing of species to the observation of distributions in space and time. Transcendental ideas like polarity were, as the Whewellian philosophy stressed, fundamental instruments at the disposal of the philosophic naturalist for the interpretation of observations.

## Conclusion

The publication of M'Cosh and Dickie's *Typical Forms and Special Ends* in 1856 may have appeared, to many naturalists, to signal the legitimation of idealism in British natural history. In fact, however, it was the final triumph of a tradition about to be swept away. Forbes's hypothesis of paleontological polarity, proposed two years earlier, was the last strikingly new contribution to the idealist movement. Before the decade was out, the *Origin of Species* began to reorient the thinking of biologists and redirect the efforts of natural theologians. The brief era of biological idealism which began with a Kantian impulse and evolved into a more familiar Platonism, would be superseded by the era of Darwinism. In Chapter 6 we will return to this event.

The naturalists we have surveyed, from Knox to M'Cosh, were among the key advocates of the idealist approach. In their hands transcendental doctrines such as the unity of plan passed from anatomy into physiology and embryology, from plants to vertebrates and invertebrates, from recent to fossil forms, and even into chemistry. Additional study of a number of contributors, such as Huxley, Robert Chambers, Thomas Laycock, Robert Edmond Grant, and Thomas Rymer Jones (to mention only those on the zoological side), might well prove fruitful. But since the purpose here has been only to demonstrate the prevalence of idealism and the diversity of its manifestations, not to provide an exhaustive account of every naturalist's idealistic leanings, the further multiplication of instances is unnecessary.

For all the naturalists we have examined, idealism was an imported product, something non-British in its origins except insofar as it could be traced back to the Cambridge Platonists (a connection only Forbes seems to have emphasized). The factor of importation had both positive and negative aspects. On the one hand, French (and to a lesser extent German) science was held in high esteem during this period, while Britain was in the throes of reorganizing and reforming her scientific establishment. Thus, Continental ideas represented the leading edge of science, a commodity worthy of importation. On the other hand, idealism was decidedly foreign to the mainstream of traditional British philosophy and was therefore suspect. One senses that many of the naturalists who accepted the idealist approach still did not feel altogether comfortable with it, especially in its Kantian form.

By contrast, the investigation of the distribution of organisms, our theme in Part II, was an innovation indigenous to British as well as Continental naturalists. And in this case there was no ambivalence.

# Part II
## Organisms in Space and Time

# 4

# *Zonation, Provinces,*
# *and Biogeographic Statistics*

In recent years the science of ecology has achieved a prominence in both academic and political circles that is rare for any scientific specialty. Our concern with a deteriorating environment has made us more cognizant than ever before of the interrelations among ourselves, other organisms, and the physical world. Although writings of an ecological nature date back at least to the time of Hippocrates, the idea of a distinct branch of biology treating the relationships of organisms to each other and to their physical surroundings is scarcely more than a century old.[1] Prior to the *Origin of Species,* itself a landmark in ecological thought, only a handful of naturalists had given any attention to the external relations of organisms.

Important first steps toward an ecological outlook were taken in the mid-eighteenth century by Linnaeus. Elementary interactions of the animal, plant, and mineral kingdoms and their geographic distributions, for example, were set forth in a series of Linnean dissertations collected under the title *Amoenitates Academicae.*[2] Linnaeus popularized the concept of the "economy of nature," in which the relationships of the three kingdoms, and of all their included species, were permanently fixed at the Creation. The perfect balance that had since been maintained was a reflection of the perfection of the Creator's original plan. This conception of a static balance of nature became a widely accepted dogma of British natural history in the late eighteenth and early nineteenth centuries. Most of Linnaeus's ideas were treated favorably in Britain, in fact, because the pervasiveness of natural theology in his writings matched the spirit in which natural history had been pursued in Britain since John Ray's *The Wisdom of God Manifested in the Works of the Creation* (1691). So accepted was the "economy of nature" theme that few naturalists before Darwin cared either to contest it or elaborate upon it.[3] The only aspect of ecology to attract a significant following, even through the late nineteenth century, was the study of plant and animal distribution.

Distribution patterns have usually been regarded by twentieth-century ecologists as being of two kinds: small-scale, or local, patterns (including vertical zonation, or variation with elevation), the study of which constitutes a part of descriptive ecology; and large-scale (regional or global) patterns, which are the domain of biogeographers. The separate study of these two types of patterns derives from the assumption that they are regulated by different processes. Local distribution is assumed to be a function of the immediate physical and biological circumstances confronting the organism, while large-scale patterns require, in addition, the consideration of historical factors such as speciation (or creation), isolation, migration, and, more recently, continental drift. Opinions about the validity of this assumption are currently in a state of flux, but as the distinction was implicit in most nineteenth-century writings on distribution, the traditional interpretation will be followed here. Unfortunately no distinct terminology was employed in early-nineteenth-century discussions of the two types of phenomena. Studies of both local and regional distributions of plants, for example, were referred to as "plant distribution," or sometimes as "plant geography," "phytogeography," or "topographical botany." The terms *station* and *habitation* survived from the eighteenth century, referring approximately to the modern *habitat* and *geographic range,* respectively, but they were not used consistently. In the present chapter we shall be concerned principally with small-scale distribution patterns and ecological factors, reserving the larger-scale, historically determined phenomena for Chapter 5.

For the beginnings of descriptive biogeography we must again look to Continental authors. On the botanical side, studies of distribution received their first major impetus from Alexander von Humboldt (1769–1859). Among the publications resulting from his travels in South America with Aimé Bonpland was the fundamental *Essai sur la Géographie des Plantes*. The work marked the beginning of Humboldt's efforts to found a science of plant distribution, in which zonation patterns would eventually be correlated to environmental factors such as temperature, elevation, and barometric pressure.[4] He was also an advocate of "botanical arithmetic," which comprised, *inter alia*, the assemblage of statistics on the distribution of plant families, permitting the computation of ratios or fractions of species of particular families to the total number of species in a given region; changes in these fractions from one region to another were then expected to show patterns. Mathematics was for Humboldt the key to transforming distribution research into a science: "He who thinks that it is not yet time to search the *numerical elements* of the geography of plants, forgets the progressive march by which the physical sciences have elevated themselves to determinate results."[5]

The study of animal distribution was far less advanced by comparison. By the end of the eighteenth century two notable works had appeared: E. A. W. Zimmermann's study of man and the quadrupeds and J. C. Fabricius's work on the distribution of insects in Europe. Finally in 1803 came the second volume of G. R. Treviranus's *Biologie; oder, Philosophie der Lebenden Natur für Naturforscher und Aerzte,* which contained a comprehensive survey of existing knowledge of the distribution and external conditions of plants and "zoophytes" as well as animals. Humboldt regarded Treviranus's work as a forerunner of his own research.[6]

### Early Distribution Studies in Britain

A useful index of the condition of British distribution studies at the opening of the nineteenth century is *The Botanist's Guide through England and Wales* compiled in 1805 by Dawson Turner and L. W.

Dillwyn.[7] *The Botanist's Guide* was a practical manual in two volumes which provided its user with lists of the species to be found in each county, followed by their "situations" (localities and/or habitats). The local collector in search of a particular species could direct himself thereby to the location of its probable occurrence. Turner and Dillwyn had, in effect, accumulated the necessary data for an initial survey of the botanical geography of England and Wales. But their treatment of the data was strictly ideographic; they had no thought of deriving laws or generalizations, of producing a "philosophical" study. The *Botanist's Guide* was simply a new manifestation (albeit a valuable one) of the British preoccupation with identification and classification of species. The situation among zoologists was little different.[8]

A conscious interest in ecological and biogeographic considerations for their own sake began to appear in Britain by the 1820s. Humboldt's work was regarded approvingly by the botanist Robert Brown, who attempted a comparison of the vegetation of Australia with that of other continents.[9] But the entomologists William Kirby and William Spence looked upon Humboldt's ideas of correlation as erroneous in method.[10] Probably the most important contributions to British ecological thought during the first three decades of the nineteenth century were those of the Scottish zoologist and natural theologian John Fleming (1785–1857).

Fleming, a Church of Scotland minister, served small parishes in the north of Scotland from 1806 until 1834, by which time his avid study of zoology and geology earned him the professorship of natural history at Aberdeen.[11] In 1843 he advanced to the natural science professorship at New College in Edinburgh. This was not his first connection with the Scottish capital, for he had studied at the University of Edinburgh from 1802 to 1805, had been a founding member of the Wernerian Society in 1808, and a fellow of the Royal Society of Edinburgh since 1814.

Fleming's best-known contributions to natural history appeared in the 1820s. *The Philosophy of Zoology* (1822) was an attempt to treat the principles of the subject in a modestly priced textbook. In his preface Fleming complained that British zoologists had been too eager to limit themselves to animal taxonomy and to accept "the twelfth edition of [Linnaeus's] 'Systema Naturae' as the standard of all excellence."[12] His remarks were aimed particularly at the natural history establishment in London, dominated by the Linnean Society and its founder, James Edward Smith. Fleming felt that British zoology had declined since the golden age, or "physiological" era, of John Ray. The era of the artificial method had followed, led by the naturalists who ignored physiology, such as Thomas Pennant (1726–98). This second era was a period of "retrograde movement"[13] resulting from excessive emphasis on Linnaeus's artificial method of classification and too little attention to the spirit, and to other aspects, of his work.

Fleming advised that Linnaeus's *Systema Naturae* be set aside and the more philosophical Linnean essays of the *Amoenitates Academicae* be taken up in its place. This was clearly a call to the study of organisms in their environmental context. In a chapter entitled "On the Polity of Nature," Fleming took up the Linnean theme of the relationships of the three kingdoms. He concluded that the plant kingdom is dependent on the mineral kingdom, that animals in turn are dependent on plants,[14] and that the entire system functioned smoothly because God had so created it. "Judging from the mode of action peculiar to the species of each kingdom, we are led to conclude, that vegetables are superior in the scale of being to minerals; that animals are superior to plants; and that they constitute a harmonious whole, in which the marks of power, wisdom and goodness, are everywhere conspicuous."[15] With this emphasis on the interrelatedness of species, Fleming concluded (as had Linnaeus) that *all* species, not just the larger, more obvious, or more beautiful ones, were essential to the system of nature, and thus that even the most repulsive insect or parasite merited study. The earlier preoccupation with birds and quadrupeds was inappropriate to both the philosophical understanding of nature and the proper appreciation of God's works.

The Animal Kingdom is considered by many persons as furnishing a delightful field of rational enquiry, but they feel disposed to bestow all their praise on certain subjects of that kingdom which happen to be favourites, and they are ready to stigmatize the remainder as comparatively worthless. They would applaud the student inclined to investigate the instincts of the elephant, but would censure him, as engaging in degrading pursuits, were he detected in examining the habits of a spider, or the structure of a worm. Do such persons consider the wisdom of the plan of Providence as discoverable without an acquaintance with the relation of the particular parts, or a partial view as sufficient to enable them to comprehend the whole? . . . Know, that He, who, in the beginning, created the Heaven and the Earth, said, 'Let the earth bring forth the living creature after his kind, cattle, and creeping thing, and beast of the earth after his kind: and it was so.' Is it, then, to be considered as a degrading employment for man to examine those creatures which were formed by God?[16]

Fleming concerned himself not only with the general harmoniousness of the three kingdoms but with the specific circumstances of animal existence. Animals being limited in their distribution, what are the conditions which cause this limitation? Fleming regarded temperature, food, "situation" (habitat in the most general sense, i.e., land, fresh water, and salt water), and foes to be the principal factors governing animal distribution.[17] Temperature, food, and situation, he thought, placed absolute limitations on distribution, while "the presence of rapacious tribes" acted only to reduce the total number of individuals which might occupy a region; when the prey is sufficiently reduced, the predator must move elsewhere for its food, leaving "the defenseless kind to multiply in its absence."[18]

With some knowledge of these limiting conditions, naturalists would be in a better position to advance the neglected study of distribution: "Among British writers, at least, little or no attention is paid to the geographical distribution of the species."[19] Fifteen years later, in an article for the seventh edition of the *Encyclopaedia Britannica,* Fleming reiterated this deficiency, this time in regard to the Mollusca:

The effect of temperature in regulating the distribution of molluscous animals, has not been investigated with any degree of care or success. Over the terrestrial and fluviatile species, it probably exercises a very powerful control, greatly limiting their geographical range. . . . But, among the marine mollusca, the influence of climate is not felt in the same degree. Living in an element, the bulk and motions of which guard it equally from the extremes of heat or cold, these animals, like the sea-weeds, have a very extensive latitudinal and longitudinal range. . . . But as there have been few cultivators of this branch of science, the geographical distribution of the species has been but imperfectly explored. Few parts of either England or Scotland have been surveyed by the eye of the helminthologist, so that many species the range of which is considered as limited, may soon be found to be extensive.[20]

To Fleming, the study of distribution was coincident with the establishment of an accurate fauna of a particular country; this meant separating the truly native animals from those which migrated seasonally into the country ("periodic visitants"), those driven in by storms or foes ("irregular visitants or stragglers"), those brought in by man, either purposely or accidentally ("naturalized"), and those no longer surviving in the country ("extirpated") or on the globe ("extinct").[21]

Fleming's second major zoological work, the *History of British Animals,* was first intended to be a part of the earlier *Philosophy,* but limitations of size required its publication as a separate work.[22] The *History* was more traditional in approach, giving descriptions and systematic arrangement of all known British genera and species of quadrupeds, birds, reptiles, fish, Mollusca, and Radiata. Although Fleming did attempt to segregate the permanently resident species from other types, he did not describe the distribution of species within Britain nor the kinds of habitats they occupied. This kind of information had not yet been collected, and Fleming had not found the time nor devised a method for doing so. His own goal was a more limited and more practical one: to prepare a meticulous study of the ecology and behavior of the species of his native Linlithgowshire on the scale of Gilbert White's famed *Natural History of Selborne* of the late eighteenth century.[23] Two other naturalists, however, did embark upon studies of British animal and plant distribution within a decade of the publication of Fleming's *Philosophy.* They were Edward Forbes and Hewett Watson.

### Forbes and Watson in the 1830s

According to a notebook Forbes kept during his early student years, his initial contact with studies in which distribution was discussed occurred in 1831, via the *Introduction to Entomology* of Kirby and Spence, the *Elements of the Philosophy of Plants* of A. P. DeCandolle and K. Sprengel, and Fleming's *Philosophy of Zoology.*[24]

And sometime in the 1830s he must have read Charles Lyell's *Principles of Geology,* which included an important discussion of ecological concepts contained in Continental works of that time.[25]

The ecological portions of the *Principles* depended heavily on the work of the Swiss phytogeographer Augustin-Pyramus DeCandolle (1778–1841). In his article "Géographie botanique" (1820), DeCandolle had synthesized the earlier contributions of Linnaeus, Humboldt, and others to produce a dynamic vision of nature involving population pressure and species competition.[26] On the descriptive side, DeCandolle had clarified the previously indistinct biogeographic terms *station* and *habitation.* The station of a species (synonomous with the less frequently used *habitat*) referred to the specific type of terrain where the species might be found wild, such as a desert, tidal pool, salt marsh, or coniferous forest. Lyell attached an even more explicit meaning to *station,* approaching that of the modern ecological *niche:* "Stations comprehend all the circumstances, whether relating to the animate or inanimate world, which determine whether a given plant or animal can exist in a given locality."[27] *Habitation,* on the other hand, meant simply the geographic location or range of a species—for example, Great Britain, southern Europe, or equatorial South America. The study of plant stations was termed botanical topography; that of plant habitations, plant geography. DeCandolle also divided the globe into twenty botanical provinces, each having a distinct collection of species.[28]

Having summarized DeCandolle's contributions to theory and terminology, Lyell then gave elementary descriptions of the distributions and means of dispersal of each of the major groups of plants and animals. He observed that generalizations about the distribution of plants and the higher animals could be made much more easily than about the invertebrates because the gathering of distributional data for the latter had lagged far behind. This was especially so in the case of the testacea, despite their great importance to the geologist. "We are as yet by no means able to sketch out the submarine provinces of shells, as the botanist has done those of the terrestrial, and even of the subaqueous plants."[29] Even less was known regarding the distribution of echinoderms, crustaceans, zoophytes, and other marine groups which had not enjoyed the attention even of amateur shell collectors.

From his reading of Fleming, Lyell, *et alii*, Forbes undoubtedly recognized that on the Continent ecology and biogeography were nascent sciences; in Britain they were almost nonexistent. He would have noted also that botanists were well ahead of zoologists in describing the distribution of organisms, defining the districts or provinces into which they might be allocated, and outlining some of the relevant environmental conditions which seemed to govern distribution. Zoologists, meanwhile, were beginning to recognize that their understanding of faunal distribution was deficient in comparison with available knowledge of floral distribution and that far less was known about the lower organisms than about the vertebrate groups.[30]

Forbes did not publish extensively during his years as an Edinburgh medical student. Nevertheless, as early as 1834 his short papers on marine invertebrates gave some attention to both the habitats and localities of the species concerned.[31] By this time he was also aware of the generality of the phenomenon he had noted on the Isle of Man, that most benthic (bottom-dwelling) marine species were confined to certain depths; those living in the tidal zone would not be dredged in deep water, and vice versa. These preferences, moreover, were found to vary from one geographic region to another.[32]

During the summer of 1835, Forbes made a tour of France, Germany, and Switzerland. Traveling through the Alps he compiled notes on the characteristic species of Testacea at different elevations. This new curiosity regarding the distribution of terrestrial invertebrates was probably related to his more intimate knowledge of the variation in depth of their marine counterparts. But undoubtedly, he was also aware of the rising study of botanical distribution. In writing up his observations from the Alps, Forbes commented that little attention had been paid to the vertical distribution of animals, although the "influence of elevation on the distribution of *plants* is at present a popular theme with the botanist."[33] The study of elevation in relation to plants had been a prominent theme in Humboldt's *Essai,* but it is likely that Forbes was referring to more recent work. The Swiss botanist Oswald Heer (1809–83), for example, was just then acquiring a reputation for his statistical studies of the distribution, abundance, and association of plant species in the Alps.[34] And the Danish naturalist Joachim Frederik Schouw (1789–1852) had published a general survey of phytogeography during the previous decade.[35] Furthermore, just before his excursion to the Alps, Forbes had joined a botanical field trip led by Adrien de Jussieu (1799–1853) of the Muséum.[36] Although Jussieu did little original phytogeographical research, his works of the 1840s show a complete awareness of the subject, including the zonation of plants with altitude.[37]

Forbes's own countrymen, moreover, were beginning to show an interest in plant geography by the 1830s. Most conspicuous was the new research on the relations of plants and altitude being published by Hewett Cottrell Watson (1804–81). Watson was a Yorkshireman by birth, the son of a magistrate. A sporting injury early in life left him with a permanent limp and redirected his father's intentions for him from a military career to law. In the course of his solicitor apprenticeship, however, Watson became fascinated with the new "science" of phrenology. He then moved to Edinburgh, to study medicine and to meet the prominent phrenologists George and Andrew Combe.

While attending medical classes at the University of Edinburgh (1828–32), Watson became an ardent student of Robert Graham (1786–1845), the professor of botany. Graham was well versed in the principles and systematic relations of his subject, but was not known for innovative teaching, nor did he publish much. He did not employ the microscope in his classes, nor did he encourage the minute examination of plants. His field trips were highly regarded, however, and through them he stimulated in his students an interest in the location and habitats of plants.[38]

The popularity of Graham and botany in Edinburgh at this time is substantiated by the formation of the Botanical Society of Edinburgh in 1836 and his appointment as its first president. Forbes was among the nineteen charter members of the society, and Watson joined later the same year.[39] From the outset, plant geography was a special interest of the society's members.

Watson became the most zealous of Graham's students in the acquisition of phytogeographic information. He received first prize in Graham's essay competition in 1831, the topic for that year being the geographical distribution of plants. His essay never appeared in print,[40] but the following year he did begin to publish the series of works which made him the recognized authority on the distribution of British plants.[41] In the Humboldtian tradition, he was especially interested in ascertaining the relations of climate and altitude to plant distribution. He set himself the task of gathering data on the locales of British species, by personal observation, correspondence with other naturalists, and gleaning of published floras. These data were to be compiled in published tables and recorded on maps, though the best method for accomplishing the latter was a matter of some debate.[42]

In the preface of his *Remarks on the Geographical Distribution of British Plants* (1835), Watson asked that corresponding botanists provide information on the altitude, climate ("temperature and humidity"), dates of first flowering, highest and lowest altitudes of occurrence, and other factors relating to the species and their particular locales.[43] He emphasized that such studies were in their infancy:

> These [local observations], brought together by a comprehensive mind, will at a future day give us an insight into the true philosophy or exact laws of vegetable distribution in Britain; an end which our present materials are quite inadequate to fulfil. In fact, after reading the works of writers on English botany and conversing or corresponding with many others greatly superior to me in botanical skill, I do not hesitate to say (it is hoped without giving offence), that very few indeed appear to have aught beyond the most vague and unconnected notions on the subject.[44]

Referring specifically to data relating plant distribution to elevation, Watson added:

> I have hitherto been compelled to rely almost solely on my own limited and transitory opportunities for observation. This is much to be regretted, so little being published on the subject. . . . And much as my works will show me indebted to botanical friends for their exertion and assistance in other respects, it seems that few of them have felt sufficient interest in that department to which I have attached the most importance.[45]

Watson had established substantial Edinburgh connections prior to settling outside London in 1833. In addition to being Graham's student, he had been elected senior president of the Royal Medical Society of Edinburgh for 1831–32. If he and Forbes were not acquainted at this time, they certainly were in communication by the mid-1830s, because about 1835 Forbes provided Watson with a checklist of species of Manx plants.[46] From that time, their distribution studies progressed along parallel lines. Just as Watson had tried to draw the attention of botanists to plant distribution, Forbes began to emphasize the study of invertebrate distribution. Unfortunately, when their research paths crossed in the 1840s (see Chap. 5), it was under less than amicable circumstances.

After five years of intermittent study, Forbes formally renounced any further intentions of obtaining a medical degree and enrolled as a literary student. His mind was still fixed upon natural history, however, especially the novelties of plants and land snails to be found on the Continent. Hence, in 1837 and 1838, he made tours of France, Algiers, Belgium, Germany, Austria, and Italy.[47] From these travels he began to form some preliminary conceptions of the distribution of the pulmonate, or lung-bearing ("pulmoniferous"), Mollusca throughout Europe. In a sketch of these ideas presented to the British Association in 1838, Forbes stressed that former local catalogues of European land snails had been drawn up according to the political divisions of the continent, which bore little relationship to the natural districts of the Mollusca themselves. He proposed a classification of Europe into six districts, each having a "conchological character of its own; in some certain genera prevail, in others certain species; these divisions may be regarded as climates, and the Flora of each will be found to correspond in its distribution with the Fauna."[48] Although Forbes thought that these districts were to be distinguished primarily by climate, he mentioned several other environmental factors, or "modifying phenomena," which were to be "especially guarded against and marked out by naturalists": "soil and rock," with calcareous rocks (limestone) being regarded as most influential in multiplying the population of a species; proximity of the district to mountains or to the ocean; elevation; and "transportation," a group of influences including man and natural agencies (rivers, winds) which transport species beyond their original domain.[49]

Forbes intended this report as more than just an introduction to the geography of European Mollusca; it was also a prelude to his plea for the cooperation of the zoologists of the British Association in the collection of distributional and environmental data on the land and fresh-water Mollusca of Britain. To facilitate this data collection, he presented a map of the British Isles constructed by William Brand of the Botanical Society of Edinburgh.[50] Brand had divided the map into districts for botanical purposes, and Forbes thought it could be used equally well for recording the British fauna. Forbes exhibited other maps indicating the zones of climate in Britain.

Forbes's report received favorable responses from the Section D president, Sir William Jardine, and secretary, John Richardson.[51] The association subsequently requested that Forbes draw up a report on the "present state of the knowledge of the Geographical Distribution of Pulmoniferous Mollusca in Britain, and the circumstances which influence this distribution."[52]

This was not the first occasion in which the British Association members had exhibited concern with distribution. At the very first meeting in 1831 the subcommittee on zoology and botany recommended that provincial botanists communicate information on their local floras, including data for ascertaining "habitats": soil, temperature, humidity, elevation, and the like. At the 1833 meeting the botanists appointed J. S. Henslow to draw up a report on the state of knowledge on the influence of climate upon vegetation, while the zoologists were asked to consider the conditions that might regulate the distribution of mammals. In 1834, James Wilson was appointed to report on the existing knowledge of insects, especially the Coleoptera (beetles). These requests were part of a larger plan instituted by the association founders, that reports on the state of each science be assembled "in order that scientific students may know where to begin their labours, and in order that those who pursue one branch of science may know how to communicate with the inquirer in another."[53] During the first decade of the association's existence, however, none of these solicited reports on distribution materialized, so that Forbes's 1839 report on the distribution of British land snails was the first biogeographic report to appear.

### Distributional Statistics and the Provincial Societies

During the twelve months prior to submitting his report, Forbes traveled throughout the British Isles gathering data on "pulmoniferous" Mollusca. He visited his old haunts on the Isle of Man and the counties around Edinburgh during the winter. Then in the summer he set out for the extremes of the kingdom: the Shetlands and Orkneys with John Goodsir, then through London to Guernsey alone. He also met with two recognized authorities on the British Mollusca, Joshua Alder of Newcastle and George Johnston of Berwick.[54]

Despite this rigorous itinerary, it must have been clear to Forbes that a truly comprehensive study of the distribution of the terrestrial Mollusca, or any other tribe of animals, could never be completed by one man in one year. With sufficient financial support, the British Association might have sent out a team of naturalists to scour the countryside. But the support of science on such a scale was yet many decades away. The obvious alternative was to solicit the aid of local volunteers who already had some knowledge of the fauna in their home provinces. Great Britain, with her long history of gentlemen-naturalists and natural history societies, was an advantageous place to capitalize on such a program. Moreover, the British Association had greatly facilitated such a program by providing a forum for the meeting of local naturalists and representatives of the natural history societies. The only additional requirement was an enthusiastic and knowledgeable coordinator to join the local observers into a network of reporters. By the late 1830s, Forbes had begun to fill this role. His aspirations in this regard were recorded in a letter to the president of the Natural History Society of Liverpool, circa 1838:

> The British Association has requested me to draw up a report of the Geological and Geographical Distribution of the British Land and Freshwater Mollusca for the meeting next year. As such report cannot be completed satisfactorily without co-operation, I take the liberty of expressing a hope that some member of the Society will be kind enough to furnish a list of the species about Liverpool, with the situation in which they are found. It is to the resources afforded by Local Societies that the naturalists of Britain must especially look for assistance in the great work of the Philosophical Development of the Natural History of our country.[55]

In appealing to the naturalists of provincial scientific societies, Forbes was setting no precedent. The founder and first president of the British Association, William Vernon Harcourt, had suggested the possibilities of this form of data collection, and its coordination by the association, as one of the chief benefits accruing to a national scientific body. In his presidential address to the association in 1831,

Harcourt (who had himself been a leading member of the Yorkshire Philosophical Society) outlined the services which local observers might render to science. Taking geology as an example, Harcourt stated:

I have the pleasure of seeing here the President of the Geological Society of London; and I beg leave to ask him . . . whether in the science of Geology there is not a multitude of facts to be ascertained in every district, on which he would be glad to see a much greater number of observers employed? And if it be so, let me remind him that we have heard today of nine Philosophical Societies in this country alone, which would doubtless find members ready to prosecute any local inquiry that this meeting might, at his suggestion, request them to undertake. It is the same with all parts of Natural History, with Meteorology, and indeed with every science which is founded upon observation, or even upon experiment.[56]

Thus, in marshaling the forces of the provincial natural history societies, Forbes was not creating a new methodology; he was putting into operation one of the functions originally envisioned for the British Association by its founders, albeit a function which had not been extensively used. Yet some credit must go to Forbes for his enthusiastic personality, which inspired the cooperation of naturalists. By comparison, Hewett Watson's more reclusive nature and his commitment to phrenological activities worked against his own efforts at data collection. Partly as a result of this attitude, Watson's major work, the four-volume *Cybele Britannica*,[57] was many years in production, despite the lead which botanical geography enjoyed over animal geography.

When isolated from their historical context, Forbes's and Watson's programs for collecting information on the distribution of animals and plants appear to be an unusual effort to expand in a wholly new direction the disciplinary boundaries of British biology. But it should be remembered that early-nineteenth-century Britain witnessed a reawakening of the Baconian concern for the acquisition of raw data about nature, especially data which varied geographically.[58] In the human sphere especially, there arose a new passion for the collection of statistics on the geography of social phenomena, such as education, labor conditions, poverty, and disease. The British Association added a section for statistics in 1833, and the first statistical societies were instituted shortly thereafter: Manchester in

1833, London in 1834.[59] Not surprisingly, the historian of statistics, Harald Westergaard, has referred to the period 1830 to 1849 as "the era of enthusiasm."[60]

Although "statistics" at that time was usually regarded as a branch of political science, the word also had a broader meaning in which the data of all natural phenomena were included. This broader usage was implied, for example, in an 1838 article in the *Westminster Review* in which *statistics* was defined as "merely a form of knowledge—a mode of arranging and stating facts which belong to various sciences."[61] Thus, distribution data could be regarded as statistics and were in fact occasionally referred to as such.[62]

Much of the impetus toward organizing and formalizing statistical studies in Britain at this time came through the visit of the Belgian mathematician, astronomer, and statistician Adolphe Quetelet (1796–1874). Quetelet attended the 1833 meeting of the British Association and was instrumental in the formation of the statistical section of the association. When the section threatened to be too limited in the scope of its inquiries, Quetelet suggested to London's influential spokesman of science Charles Babbage that a statistical society be established in the metropolis; thus arose the London (later the Royal) Statistical Society.[63]

Interested in statistics of all sorts, Quetelet became involved with British natural history in what was to become one of the most grandiose plans ever envisioned for the collection of natural history data. At the 1841 meeting of the British Association, Quetelet advocated the keeping of registers throughout the kingdom for the collection of information on natural phenomena, including zoological, botanical, and agricultural information. Quetelet was especially interested in accumulating data of a periodical nature, such as the dates of migration of birds, insects and fish, reproduction and mortality of animals, budding of plants and shedding of leaves, and the harvesting of agricultural products. Such data, when compared with social statistics (births, deaths, disease, crime, food consumption, transportation) and physical statistics (weather, tides, earth's temperature and magnetism), were expected to yield useful relationships: "To tabulate these facts, to ascertain the times and circumstances of their maxima and minima, and to show where they coincided with each other, would be highly beneficial to science, and would render statistics the great bond by which all other branches of knowledge would be held together and all applied to the service of man."[64]

Quetelet had already begun the program at a modest level on the Continent and was seeking British participation in a system of simultaneous observations, a nineteenth-century version of the International Geophysical Year.[65] His suggestion was not acted upon immediately, but in 1844 the British Association instituted a Committee for the Registration of Periodical Phenomena of animals and plants. The committee was headed by Richard Owen and included Forbes and seven other naturalists. The following year the committee circulated Quetelet's extended instructions along with lists of British plant and animal species to be observed.[66] And in 1846 considerable interest was expressed in the correlation of meteorological and physical statistics with "scientific agriculture."[67]

The project continued sporadically for some years,[68] but in the end it was inconclusive, due probably to a lack of direction from above, as well as inadequate participation by local naturalists. If the scope of the project was too ambitious for its time, it is nevertheless illustrative of the aspirations of early-nineteenth-century naturalists for the assemblage of raw data. And in this light, Forbes's hopes for the collection of ecological statistics appear less eccentric.

It may have been the absence of a rigorous statistical approach in the early writings of the ecologically minded botanist Richard Brinsley Hinds (1812?–1847?) that led to their neglect by his contemporaries. Hinds had been in on the initial discussions of botanical map design.[69] Then in 1836 he sailed as surgeon-naturalist aboard H.M.S. *Sulphur*. Six years of travel in the Pacific, from the west coast of the Americas to Hong Kong,[70] gave him an even greater appreciation for the influence of climate upon vegetation. Upon his return to Britain in 1842, he published a four-part article, "The Physical Agents of Temperature, Humidity, Light, and Soil, Considered as Developing Climate, and in Connexion with Geographic Botany."[71] The series was a competent summary of the variations in these "physical agents" over the globe, with occasional references to their favorability to different plant genera. The treatment of the subject, however, was broad-brush and somewhat anecdotal, and the statistics provided were largely climatological rather than botanical.

Other British botanists, concerned with such smaller-scale phenomena as the changes in flora with elevation and latitude in the British Isles, did not find Hinds's global perspective relevant or his climatological generalizations innovative. Moreover, in subsequent papers Hinds adopted a thoroughly static, biblical point of view about the original distribution of life on earth, even denying that any plant species had ever become extinct—ideas diametrically opposed to the growing orthodoxy among geologists.[72] His travels may have exposed him to new floras, which in turn suggested new methods of arranging information on present plant distribution,[73] but they also prevented his participating in British Association meetings and other forums where the theoretical basis of plant geography was being discussed. Subsequent realignment with contemporary theory might have placed Hinds at the forefront of phytogeographic research, had he not died a few years later.

### From Terrestrial to Marine Invertebrates

In his report on "pulmoniferous" Mollusca to the British Association in 1839, Forbes was not yet able to draw on the resources of local naturalists as fully as he later would. He acknowledged, nevertheless, the assistance of no fewer than nine naturalists, some of whom later became active in Forbes's dredging program.[74]

The report consisted of three parts: (1) a discussion of the influences affecting the British "pulmoniferous" Mollusca; (2) their distribution; and (3) the relation of this fauna to that of Europe. The opening section, on the influence of environmental factors, was the most original part of the report and from an ecological standpoint unlike anything that had previously been published. Climate and soil he now regarded as the two primary influences. Climate, he felt, was the cause of several phenomena, including the reduced number of species in the northern, colder areas; the reduced numbers of individuals in the northern areas, of species found throughout the kingdom; and the greater "beauty of colouring" shown by species of warmer areas. Other phenomena, such as the increase of species in the central districts over those in some southern districts, were attributed to the mineralogical nature of the soil or rock. Limestone and sand were a positive influence on the propagation of individuals; granite and basalt were negative.

Forbes also enumerated a number of factors which were thought to modify the influence of climate and soil. In addition to those mentioned in his earlier European report (elevation, transportation, proximity to sea and mountains), he cited, for land species, the positive influence of wooded areas (except pines), and for aquatic species, the nature of the body of water (lake, river, canal), its bed (gravel, mud) and the flora found in it. When basing distributional generalizations on observations of dead shells, he warned that errors could easily be introduced by the existence of fossil shells and by shells washed downstream from higher altitudes. These various secondary factors made the study of distribution quite complicated. True principles were only to be obtained by repeated observations of the same species in different areas:

> All these modifying influences being taken into consideration, it behoves us to be very cautious how we judge of the influence of geological and climatal causes on the distribution of a species. The absence of a hill, a wood, a lake, or a ditch, may cause the absence of many species, and lead us to attribute their non-appearance in the district to a climatal cause when the presence of the necessary modifying influence might have called them forth. It is only by a comparison of many districts, and of the face of the country in each, that we can hope to arrive at just conclusions; and it is necessary in every case to ascertain as far as we are able the circumstance under which each species is found in other parts of the world, especially in Europe, ere we can argue fairly on its distribution in our own country.[75]

This first portion of Forbes's report was the most original. His observations did not depend upon accurate measurements of environmental variables, as Humboldt had earlier attempted and as later ecologists perfected. Nevertheless, Forbes's effort to assess the impact of numerous variables made this report one of the most insightful ecological studies of the early nineteenth century.

In the second part of the report Forbes described the distribution of species by dividing the British Isles into ten districts, beginning with the Channel Isles and the southeast of England, and concluding with the north of Scotland and the Shetland Islands. In so doing, he admitted the desirability of using the more refined set of districts

Table 4.1. Forbes's Table of Influences Affecting the British Pulmoniferous Mollusca

| Districts | Primary Influences | | Secondary Influences | |
|---|---|---|---|---|
| | Positive | Negative | Positive | Negative |
| I. Channel Isles | Climate | Structure | Marine | Absence of canals, etc. |
| II. S.E. England | Climate Structure | ......... | Rivers, etc. | ......... |
| III. S.W. England | Climate | Structure | Marine | Want of water in parts |
| IV. N.E. England | Structure | Climate | Woods | ......... |
| V. N.W. England | Structure | Climate | Marine | Elevation |
| VI. N. Ireland | Structure | Climate | Marine | ......... |
| VII. S. Ireland | Climate | Structure | Marine | ......... |
| VIII. S. Scotland | Structure | Climate | Woods | ......... |
| IX. N. Scotland | ......... | Climate Structure | Marine | Elevation Want of wood |
| X. Shetland Isles | ......... | Climate | ........ | Want of wood |

Source: Edward Forbes, "Report on the Distribution of Pulmoniferous Mollusca in the British Isles," *Reports of the British Association for the Advancement of Science,* 1839, pt. 1, p. 132.

enumerated by William Brand in his statistics of British botany (which, in turn, were based on Watson's work); but the available data were not yet adequate for this purpose. A table (Table 4.1) was used to show the primary and secondary influences which predominated in each district: "positive" influences were responsible for increasing the number of species in a district, "negative" influences caused a decrease. Forbes then discussed the ten districts individually, noting in each the principal influences, the number of species, the names of species most abundant in individuals, and relationships to other districts. In the better-known areas he added comments on the characteristic habitats (woods, gardens, hedges, heaths, fens, low ponds, etc.) of some species. The second portion of the report concluded with two tables showing, for each of the seventeen genera, the number of species found in each district, and the number of species found on the various soil and rock types.

Forbes began the final portion of the report by admitting the difficulty of comparing the distribution of British snails with those of Europe. This resulted mainly from the lack of agreement on nomenclature among the naturalists of different countries. "The habit of changing names,—I had almost said,—wantonly,—has been indulged in to an unwarrantable extent among Malacologists." Moreover, there was often disagreement as to whether a new form should be regarded a species or a variety, "some [authors] elevating every little variation to the rank of a species, others attempting definitions more in accordance with the philosophy of natural history."[76] Notwithstanding these problems, Forbes showed in another table the number of species (of nineteen genera) in each of ten European countries. Statistics for the countries other than Britain were derived from the published works of foreign malacologists. The report ended with remarks on the ranges of various genera, and a final table (heavily dependent on the work of Joshua Alder) giving the British districts and general European areas where each of ninety-six British species could be found.

After the 1839 report Forbes did not return to the pulmoniferous Mollusca except to include them in the last volume of the *History of British Mollusca* (1853). His true interests lay with the marine invertebrates—species whose distribution was far less well known. Having demonstrated the fruitfulness of distribution studies in general by his report on the pulmoniferous Mollusca, Forbes was able to convince his fellow zoologists that the association should institute a dredging program to ascertain the distribution of marine invertebrates in British waters. Besides the contributions to zoology and biogeography which would accrue from such a program, much information of great value to geologists would be generated, Forbes argued. The distribution of organisms in space was integrally related to their distribution in time, and this was most obvious for those organisms that were most frequently fossilized, namely the marine invertebrates.

In the discussion following Forbes's 1839 report, Charles Lyell added the weight of his experience to the call for additional ecological and biogeographic studies. He reemphasized the significance of rock type and habitat (land, fresh-water, or marine) to molluscan distribution and the meaning of these relations to the geologist. Without a knowledge of the environments, and especially the depths, in which recent marine species resided, the geologist would be unable to determine the probable environments of fossil species. And without the latter information he would be unable to differentiate a change in species due to the lapse of time from a change due merely to an altered environment (i.e., a facies change). Moreover, an accurate knowledge of recent marine species and their depths was crucial to Lyell's percentage method of determining the ages of Cenozoic strata. Recent strata were assumed to have a high ratio of recent-to-fossil mollusk species; older strata, a lower ratio. Thus incomplete knowledge of existing species would result in lowered ratios and, consequently, the assignment of relative ages that were too great.[77]

Lyell had been well aware of the importance of distribution studies when he wrote the *Principles.* To understand how *fossil* species are distributed spatially and temporally, one must have some understanding of the *present* distribution of plants and animals:

It is only by studying these laws [of geographic distribution] with attention, by observing the positions which groups of species occupy at present, and inquiring how these may be varied in the course of time by migrations, by changes in physical geography, and other causes, that we can hope to learn whether the duration of species be limited, or in what manner the state of the animate world is affected by the endless vicissitudes of the inanimate.[78]

Lyell was not alone in recognizing the need for more data on the habitats of present marine organisms. Henry DelaBeche (1796–1855), later Forbes's superior at the Geological Survey, made this point with specific reference to the Mollusca in his *Researches in Theoretical Geology* (1834):

Conchological works are, in general, exceedingly deficient in information as to the depths at which various shells have been discovered with their animals alive; a circumstance to be much regretted for geologists, as it deprives them, in a great measure, of the assistance they would otherwise derive from organic remains in estimating the probable depth at which a given fossiliferous deposit may have been formed.[79]

DelaBeche's concern with this problem is substantiated by his inclusion, as an appendix to the *Researches,* of a "Table of the situations and depths at which recent Genera of Marine and Estuary shells have been observed."[80] The table, one of the earliest collections of such data to be published, was constructed for DelaBeche by William Broderip, a London magistrate and ardent collector of shells. It listed the depth and typical habitat or substrate for 179 genera of mollusks; general remarks on the habitats of certain annelid and cirriped genera were also included. Thus by the mid-1830s geologists had begun to recognize (though as yet only dimly) the importance of data on the distribution of present organisms for the future advancement of their science. This recognition contributed to the support which Forbes's plans for dredging the British coasts received in 1839. In that year, and intermittently for the next thirty years, the British Association allotted funds specifically "for Researches with the Dredge, with a view to the investigation of the Marine Zoology of Great Britain, the Illustration of the Geographical Distribution of Marine Animals, and the more accurate determination of the Fossils of the Pleiocene Period."[81]

Forbes's own awareness of the connections between marine zoology and geology had grown rapidly during his investigations of 1839.[82] This is reflected especially in the lectures on "Zoo-Geology" which he gave the next year with Samuel Brown (see Chap. 3). He defined "zoo-geology" as "the study of animal conditions, and of the associations of living animal species, as illustrating those of extinct animals, and of the formations containing them."[83] It included the study of animal distribution and the factors (natural and human) which influenced it, the study of marine zonation (the alteration of species assemblages with depth), and the study of the conditions under which fossil species lived. This definition, containing the essences of modern ecology and paleoecology, became the organizing theme of most of Forbes's subsequent research.

Forbes demonstrated how this science of zoo-geology could be put into practice in an important paper of 1840, "On the Associations of Mollusca on the British Coasts, considered with Reference to Pleistocene Geology." This was his first effort to define the zonation of marine organisms, a subject on which he quickly became the British authority. In a manner analogous to his earlier assignment of the Alps Mollusca to zones of elevation, Forbes posited a division of the British coasts into four zones according to depth. Each zone was characterized by a particular assemblage of molluscan species. The four zones were:

(1) the Littoral Zone, lying between high and low water marks;
(2) the Laminarian Zone, from low water to a depth of seven to ten fathoms, dominated by the seaweed *Laminaria;*

(3) the Coralline Zone, from fifteen to thirty fathoms, containing the coralline algae in abundance; and

(4) the Zone of Corals, averaging sixty fathoms in depth, inhabited by the true corals, "a region as yet but imperfectly known."[84]

Submarine zonation seems not to have been noticed by British authors prior to Forbes. It is possible that the data he had obtained by dredging was sufficient to make the zonation obvious, or that he had anticipated it because of the analogous phenomena of alpine zonation in plants. It is also possible that he had observed at least the shallow zones on the Manx coast during his boyhood outings.[85] Moreover, this was not the first time that the general phenomenon of "vertical" or off-shore zonation of marine organisms had been recognized, as Forbes later acknowledged.[86] In scattered publications of the previous thirty years, French and Scandinavian naturalists had noted a variation in the distribution of both algae and invertebrates of the tidal and subtidal zones.[87] Forbes's contribution was to formalize this variation into a series of defined faunal/floral zones and to extend the range of observed zonation beyond the subtidal zone through the use of the dredge.

Two other aspects of Forbes's 1840 paper should be noted. First, it contains one of the earliest comments on man's pollution of the seacoast environment and the resulting alteration to the assemblage of resident species: "When the second zone, or region of laminariae, from the nature of the tides is placed close to a town, the dirt and filth of the town affect it, causing the multiplication of some animals, and diminishing the number of others."[88] Forbes made no ethical judgment on the fact of pollution; it was merely one of several influences modifying faunal zonation.

Second, and more importantly, the entire paper was oriented toward the relationship of present molluscan zonation to the fossil record. Our main route to understanding the changes which have occurred in the "organized creation," Forbes explained, was through the study of fossils:

From the study of them *individually*, we learn the changes which have taken place in genera and species. From the study of them *collectively*, we ascertain the habits of animals during the primeval ages, and much information as to the nature of the localities in which they lived. But to make such study of fossils available in either respect, we must acquaint ourselves with the genera and species of organic beings at present existing, and with their manners, associations, and localities.[89]

The discussion of the four marine zones was thus intended as a step toward elucidating the local faunas, "hoping thereby to assist the geologist in his comparison of the fauna of the later tertiary periods with that of the present day."[90] Such comparisons were bound to be complex, requiring attention to many details. But the result would be a far clearer picture of the earth as it appeared just before the "dawning of the world of man":[91]

By taking into consideration the effect of a change of level on the several zones which I have here pointed out, and by carefully observing the changes of character which take place in those zones under the various modifying influences [tidal exposure, substrate, proximity to a fresh-water source]; by ascertaining correctly the species inhabiting each, and the relative proportions of individuals of those species, and by comparing the associations of living species in the neighbourhood of fossil beds with the associations of species in those beds, we may anticipate a complete elucidation of Pleistocene Geology.[92]

The sciences of ecology, biogeography, and geology were thus interrelated in the thinking of Forbes to a degree quite unusual for naturalists of his era.

Throughout the 1840s Forbes continued to stress his zoo-geology.[93] It figured most prominently in two reports to the British Association and in a lecture at the Royal Institution. The first of the reports (1843) conveyed the results of his eighteen-month dredging sojourn in the Aegean. From this research Forbes was able to define a series of eight zones reaching down to 300 fathoms, each characterized by a distinct assemblage of invertebrates and plants. The environmental factors affecting these marine organisms were set forth in a manner reminiscent of the pulmoniferous Mollusca report (Table 4.2).

Forbes viewed species assemblages not as fixed or static but as fully dynamic. Each zone was the "scene of incessant change," due

Table 4.2. Influences Affecting Distribution of Mollusca and Radiata, According to Forbes

| Pulmoniferous Mollusca (1839) | Marine Mollusca & Radiata (1843) |
|---|---|
| *Primary Influences* | |
| Climate (temperature) | Climate (temperature) |
| Soil (mineralogical character) | Sea composition (salinity, organic matter?) |
| | Depth |
| *Secondary Influences* | |
| Elevation | Fresh-water influx |
| Proximity to mountains | Tides and currents |
| Proximity to sea | Character of sea bottom and geological structure of adjacent coastline |
| Presence of woods, fresh water (for terrestrial species) | |
| Substrate, presence of aquatic plants (for fresh-water species) | |

Sources: Based on Forbes, "Report on the Distribution of Pulmoniferous Mollusca in the British Isles," *Reports of the British Association for the Advancement of Science,* 1839, pt. 1, pp. 127–47; and idem, "Report on the Mollusca and Radiata of the Aegean Sea, and on Their Distribution, Considered as Bearing on Geology," ibid., 1843, pt. 1, pp. 130–93.

to geologic processes and to fluctuations in the populations of the various species.

The death of the individuals of the several species inhabiting them, the continual accession, deposition and sometimes washing away of sediment and coarser deposits, the action of the secondary influences and the changes of elevation which appear to be periodically taking place in the eastern Mediterranean, are ever modifying their character. As each region shallows or deepens, its animal inhabitants must vary in specific associations, for the depression which may cause one species to dwindle away and die will cause another to multiply.[94]

The organisms themselves tend to alter the environment also, sometimes to their detriment, as when calcium-secreting animals convert soft substrates into hard ones:

As the influence of the nature of sea-bottom determines in a great measure the species present on that bottom, the multiplication of individuals dependent on the rapid reproduction of successive generations of Mollusca, &c. will of itself change the ground and render it unfit for the continuation of life in that locality until a new layer of sedimentary matter, uncharged with living organic contents, deposited on the bed formed by the exuviae of the exhausted species, forms a fresh soil for similar or other animals to thrive, attain their maximum, and from the same cause die off.[95]

For Forbes, the species assemblage existed because certain species had common physical requirements. Every species was dependent upon a particular range of temperature and depth, on a particular type of substrate, and so on. If a number of species happened to share these dependencies, they would be found assembled together (providing, of course, that in the history of their creation and dispersion they had been brought into geographic proximity). He placed relatively little emphasis on biological factors, such as feeding relationships or competition for scarce resources.[96] If he ever envisioned the activities of nature as a war or struggle between competing species or individuals, or between predator and prey, he chose not to record such a vision. Unlike Darwin, who in the early 1840s was rethinking the traditional "economy of nature" view in light of DeCandolle and Malthus,[97] Forbes seems never to have abandoned the Linnean conception of harmony in the natural world.

In the final section of the Aegean report, Forbes entered into a discussion of the geological implications of his work. Hypothesizing an elevation of submerged beds into dry land, he set forth the types and states of preservation of organisms that one might expect to find fossilized on Aegean coasts. From the assemblages observed in these hypothetical strata, the attentive zoo-geologist might deduce the probable depth zone in which the assemblage had originally lived. (Forbes demonstrated this method on the strata of an island which had appeared in the Aegean during the previous century.) He might also draw conclusions as to the climate of the former period, from the presence within the assemblages of characteristic northern or southern species. And from close inspection of littoral assemblages and the geologic processes occurring in tidal areas, a clearer understanding would emerge of how alternating fresh-water, marine, and unfossiliferous strata are formed.[98]

Geology was again the focus of a Friday evening lecture given at the Royal Institution in 1844. For this popular forum Forbes chose to concentrate on certain generalizations which had emerged from his British and Aegean dredging experiences: the zonation of seabed invertebrates, noticeable in Tertiary strata as well as in the present oceans; the diminution in numbers of species with increasing depth; the increase in species typical of more northern regions with increasing depth, leading to the conclusion that "parallels in depth [like parallels in elevation] are equivalent to parallels in latitude"; the importance of substrate in determining the resident assemblage of organisms; and the tendency for species with the greatest ranges in depth to have also the largest geographic and/or geological range.[99] This lecture, with its engaging generalizations and well-chosen illustrations, brought Forbes and his zoo-geology to the attention of London society, as the Aegean report had done for his British Association colleagues the previous year.[100]

The third and last of his major zoo-geological contributions was the final report of the dredging committee, given at the 1850 meeting of the association. Extensive tables chronicled ten years of dredging operations, giving the location, depth, substrate, numbers of species of mollusks and radiates and their abundance, for each expedition. A second listing, by species, gave their geographic district, range in depth, and substrate. The seventy-page report concluded with the geographic and geological generalizations of his earlier works, now rendered more certain by a decade of cooperative data collection.[101]

### Marine Biogeography

Dredging and "zoo-geology" diminished in importance in Forbes's thinking after 1850, but his interest in marine biogeography broadened, resulting in publications of regional and global scope. The first of these was a world map of marine life (Fig. 4.1). Forbes divided the globe into nine "homoiozoic belts" symmetrical about the equator, the boundaries of each belt being determined by isotherms. Within these latitudinal belts he defined twenty-five marine provinces, each containing a unique assemblage of species. Insets to the map included a chart showing typical species in each of five

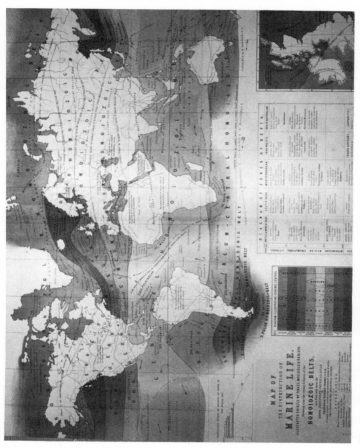

Fig. 4.1. Forbes's map of the distribution of marine life. (From Alexander Keith Johnston, *Physical Atlas of Natural Phenomena*, new and enlarged ed. [Edinburgh, 1856], plate XXXI.)

145

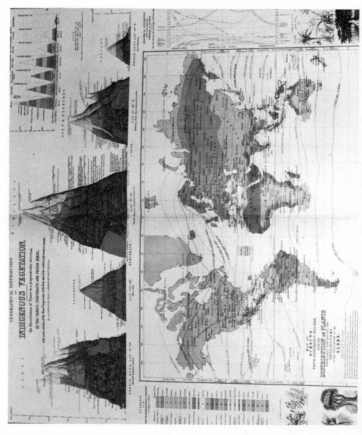

Fig. 4.2. Schouw's map of phytogeographic regions. (From Alexander Keith Johnston, *Physical Atlas of Natural Phenomena*, new and enlarged ed. [Edinburgh, 1856], plate XXV. Originally published in 1823.)

zones of depth for eight of the twenty-five provinces; and a "kite"-diagram illustrating the generic centers and latitudinal ranges of nine genera of mollusks and fishes.[102]

Biogeographic maps were rare but not unheard of in the 1850s. The Germans had pioneered in biogeographic mapmaking in the early nineteenth century, under the stimulus of Humboldt. The earliest were maps of plant distribution, such as Schouw's map of 1823 (Fig. 4.2). Several such maps were included in Berghaus's *Physicalischer Atlas*, which was planned as a supplement to Humboldt's *Kosmos* and was the model used by A. K. Johnston for his *Physical Atlas of Natural Phenomena*, in which Forbes's maps appeared.[103] Forbes's attempt to define the provinces of *marine* life was the first of its kind, so far as I am aware, and his depiction of generic centers was altogether new. The latter idea he may have transferred to biogeography from geology, because he had earlier used kite-diagrams to illustrate the expansion and diminution of fossil genera through geological time.[104]

Forbes's last contribution to biogeography, *The Natural History of the European Seas* (1859), was unfinished when he died and had to be completed by his friend, the geologist Robert A. C. Godwin-Austen (1808–84). This was the first and only book of its kind until Sven Ekman's *Zoogeography of the Sea* of 1953.[105] The dominant organizing principle was the province. The five European provinces outlined in the map of marine life—arctic, Boreal, Celtic, Lusitanian, and Mediterranean—plus two new ones, the Black Sea and the Caspian, were each afforded a chapter's coverage. For each province Forbes gave geographic boundries and subregions, the most prominent physical influences, the characteristic fauna (including diversity and abundance observations) and its zonation, and relations to adjoining provinces.

By far the most interesting are the final chapters, which treat ecological and geological considerations common to all the provinces. Chapter 9, "Distribution of Marine Fauna," is a description of the physical variables that regulate distribution. Temperature is "foremost," with seawater chemistry (including density, salinity, and dissolved oxygen) and coastline and substrate characteristics being secondary. Forbes's concept of marine "outliers" is explained: outliers are populations of species found in isolated patches outside their normal province. Boreal outliers, for example, are organisms of that cold-water province that are located in the deep-water areas of the more southerly, warmer Celtic province. Their presence in the Celtic province was explained historically: during the colder Pleistocene epoch northern species had been able to advance southward; when subsequent warming trends forced their retreat to the north, stragglers were able to remain behind in the deep "oases" of cold water.[106] Here again Forbes had transferred a concept from geology into biogeography; the term *outlier* had been used by Joachim Barrande to denote isolated "colonies" of Upper Palezoic species in Lower Paleozoic strata.[107]

From the introduction to historical outliers in Chapter 9 we pass in Chapter 10 to a larger discussion of "The Early History of the European Seas." Here Forbes and Godwin-Austen ventured into the embryonic sciences of paleogeography, paleoecology, and paleoclimatology, and their results were accordingly tentative and speculative. To understand this discussion, however, we must return again to the early nineteenth century, for we have passed from the purely descriptive aspects of biogeography to its historical side (or as the Victorian naturalist would have expressed it, to the philosophy of the distribution of organisms in space *and time*), and we must therefore consider the earlier developments of the latter line of research.

## Conclusion

We began this chapter by distinguishing, on the one hand, between the study of local distribution (especially zonation) and its ecological parameters, and, on the other, the larger distribution patterns in which historical considerations are most interesting. Although this distinction was implicit in the writings of British naturalists, they seem to have recognized it only vaguely. A noteworthy exception was the botanist Arthur Henfrey (1819–59), author of *The Vegetation of Europe, Its Conditions and Causes* (1852).[108] In successive chapters Henfrey treated what he called the "General" and "Special Influences on the Distribution of Vegetation." Under "General Influences" he discussed ecological factors such as heat, elevation,

wind, exposure, and soil, "the circumtances which *allow* of particular conditions of vegetation in different regions." A separate "class
of phenomena" were the "Special Influences," those "circumstances
which *cause* the peculiar vegetation of particular places."[109] In the
latter case Henfrey referred to the differences in plant species living
under similar climatic conditions in Europe and North America,
often therefore called "representative" species. On this larger scale,
historical considerations become more important: "We must seek
out some view of the original plan upon which the creation of plants
was conducted," giving particular attention to the influence of "external agencies in modifying the conditions with the lapse of
time."[110] For Henfrey, as for Forbes and most of their contemporaries, these larger phenomena were explained in terms of centers of
creation and disperal. These themes will be our concern in the next
chapter.

# 5

# *Whence Came
the Flora and Fauna?*

The descriptive, ecological side of biogeography was only one aspect of the inquiries into distribution which began to occupy British naturalists in the middle decades of the nineteenth century. The other side was temporal, or historical, biogeography, encompassing investigations of how and why the distribution of species might have changed through time. The former, descriptive approach, as we saw in the previous chapter, was pioneered by Humboldt at the beginning of the century and attracted the talents of Fleming, Watson, and Forbes in the 1820s and 1830s. By the 1840s the reservoir of statistics on plant and animal distribution had filled sufficiently that some general biogeographic statements could be advanced. Moreover, the growing interest in the gradualist philosophy of Lyell's *Principles,* coupled with the accumulating data of paleontology, encouraged hypothetical forays into the temporal dimension. For the first time, questions of the origin of present distribution patterns were seen to be resolvable by a combined appeal to theories and data from paleogeography, paleoclimatology, and paleoecology. Edward Forbes's long essay "On the Connexion Between the Distribution of the Existing Flora and Fauna of the British Isles, and the Geological Changes Which Have Affected Their Area," published by the Geological Survey in 1846, became the model for this multifaceted approach to biogeographic problems. The present chapter proposes an interpretation of the origins and fortunes of this innovative and highly controversial essay, in the belief that it was the most significant document in the early development of historical biogeography prior to Darwin's *Origin*.

Since the eighteenth century the central question of biogeography has been simply, Why are organisms *where* they are? When viewed historically or geologically, this question becomes, How did organisms originally come to be where we now find them? The latter question itself involves a number of subordinate issues of which nineteenth-century naturalists were well aware. How was it that a particular species might be distributed in two or more widely separated regions?[1] Or, on the other hand, why did each of the continents have its own species? More specifically, why were the species of isolated but climatically similar regions often closely similar (i.e., belonging to the same genus) but not identical (a generalization which has been dubbed "Buffon's Law")?[2] What had prevented most species from dispersing throughout the entire range of latitutde and climate for which they were apparently adapted?

Prior to the Darwin-Wallace evolutionary interpretation of biogeography there were, in general, five points of view taken toward this complex of natural phenomena: (1) the biblical view; (2) the autochthonous view; (3) the "ignorabimus" view; (4) a preevolutionary view; and (5) the centers-of-creation hypothesis.

The biblical interpretation, an attempt to preserve the Garden of Eden story of Genesis, placed all species originally at a single location in the Middle East. The most famous of such interpretations was that of Linnaeus in his "On the Increase of the Habitable Earth."[3] According to this essay, the Creation had occurred on a single mountainous island which contained all of the habitats and climates necessary to sustain every sort of creature. Subsequent biogeographic history was then merely a matter of dispersal from the island to present locations. But this attractively simple (and religiously orthodox) explanation failed to account satisfactorily for discontinuous distribution or for the dissimilarities in the flora and fauna of the different continents. The other explanations attempted, with varying degrees of success, to obviate these difficulties.

According to the autochthonous viewpoint, species had been created originally in one or many locations, and their present distribution is identical to that original distribution. Aside from geological catastrophes which had periodically caused the extinction of all life forms in various regions, distribution was regarded as static and permanent. The autochthonous position was maintained by many naturalists of the early nineteenth century, including the Danish botanist J. F. Schouw, the German zoologist K. A. Rudolphi, and the French physiologist A. Desmoulins.[4]

In Britain the autochthonous view was closely allied with natural theology. The geographic locations of species were regarded as an integral part of the Creation and therefore established according to divinely inspired laws which were forever incomprehensible to man. In this tradition are the works of Kirby and Spence, William Swainson, and later, Louis Agassiz.[5] Swainson, for example, gave a synopsis of earlier biogeographic theories but concluded that "the limits of every animal have been fixed by an Almighty fiat" and that "the primary causes which have led to different regions of the earth being peopled by different races of animals, and the laws by which their dispersion is regulated, must be forever hid from human research."[6]

Proponents of what has been termed the "ignorabimus" view[7] found the phenomena of biogeography utterly overwhelming. They were resigned to the belief that, if there are laws which have produced the present distribution of organisms, man will probably never be able to discover them. This view derives mainly from Humboldt, who, failing in his attempt to understand the laws of historical biogeography, rejected any further search for such laws and concentrated on the more tractable problem of present distribution and the measurement of limiting physical parameters. This position was also taken by the Scandinavian botanists Gören Wahlenberg and Elias Magnus Fries.[8]

Before Darwin and Wallace, a few naturalists vaguely saw that some biogeographic problems might be solved by an evolutionary hypothesis. In this tradition could be included the German botanist

H. F. Link and the French zoologist Isidore Geoffroy St. Hilaire.[9] Such hypotheses remained undeveloped, however, until the second half of the nineteenth century.

The most commonly accepted notion in early-nineteenth-century historical biogeography was that of centers of creation. According to this view, each species first appeared as one or a pair of individuals at a single location. From that point the species acquired its present distribution by various (often unspecified) means of dispersal. Certain geographic regions, where "creative activity" was thought to have been especially strong, had been unusually prolific of new species and were thus referred to as "foci of creation."[10] In contrast to the previous views, the centers-of-creation/dispersion view seems to have been sufficiently articulated to merit being called a theory. Early forms of the theory appeared in the eighteenth century, in the works of Buffon, Zimmermann, and the Prussian botanist K. L. Willdenow.[11] In the early nineteenth century, centers of creation were discussed by Link, DeCandolle, and Leopold von Buch, among others.[12]

### Lyell and Historical Biogeography

In Britain, Charles Lyell incorporated the theory of centers of creation and dispersion into his uniformitarian interpretation of earth history. He argued that the phenomena of biogeography which we observe today are just those which would appear if, for example, we could completely remove all forms of life from the Western Hemisphere and then introduce, at successive intervals and in the proper climatic regions, a single pair of each species from the Eastern Hemisphere. As the population of each species grew, it would expand until it met with a physical or climatic barrier. The powers of dispersion of the various species being so diverse, some species would easily pass these barriers, while others would remain confined. Thus would arise the particular botanical and zoological provinces we now observe.[13]

Discontinuous populations—that is, the occurrence of a species in two or more isolated provinces, or on a continental area and an adjacent island—were regarded by Lyell to be the product of migration

or the action of fortuitous agencies of transport. Plants were transported by winds, rivers, ocean currents, birds and other animals, and
man; animals were transported by icebergs, floating driftwood, other
animals, and again, man.[14] These modes of dispersal were in progress and could be observed by the attentive naturalist.

There were other, less obvious routes of dispersal which most
naturalists had not contemplated, Lyell thought, because

> they have usually speculated on the phenomena, upon the assumption that
> the physical geography of the globe had undergone no material alteration
> since the introduction of the species now living. So long as this assumption
> was made, the facts relating to the geography of plants and animals appeared
> capricious in the extreme, and by many the subject was pronounced to be so
> full of mystery and anomalies, that the establishment of a satisfactory theory
> was hopeless.[15]

Lyell was referring to major alterations of the earth's surface, specifically the uplifting of mountains like the Alps, which would create
a discontinuous population out of a formerly continuous one. The
movement of land species between islands (and the isolation of
marine species) might also be facilitated by the uplift of the intervening seabed, as was thought to have occurred in the Italian penin-
sular region.

Changes in the earth's geology could thus lead to anomalous biogeographic situations. The same could be said of changes of climate.
While a gradual alteration of climate will be fatal to many species,
those with the capacity to migrate may be able to disperse into formerly uncongenial areas. Equatorial species, for example, might migrate toward the temperate zones during a worldwide warming
trend. Of course the climatic differences between equatorial and
temperate zones involve more than mere temperature; the tropical
climate is characterized by a narrow range of annual temperatures,
whereas the temperate climate experiences wide fluctuations. Hence,
equatorial species would not find totally congenial conditions by
poleward migration. The latter problem would, as Lyell pointed out,
create fewer difficulties for marine species, since ocean temperatures
fluctuate over much narrower ranges than land temperatures. Thus,
"we may easily suppose that most of the testacea, fish, and other

classes, might pass from the equatorial into the temperate regions, if the mean temperature of those regions were transposed."[16]

By the same reasoning, temperature changes over geological time could explain the existence of fossils in regions which their descendents now find uninhabitable. This theory of climatic change was used by Lyell to account for the tropical species of Testacea found fossil in Italian strata, where the climate is now more temperate.[17]

In summation, we find in the *Principles* two modes of theorizing, used to explain two distinct sorts of phenomena. On the one hand, paleogeographical (or geological) hypotheses (i.e., uplift of mountains and seabeds) were invoked to account for present population (spatial) discontinuities. On the other hand, paleoclimatological hypotheses were invoked to account for (temporal) discontinuities in the distribution of fossil and recent representatives of the same species. Lyell discussed the paleoclimatological case at some length, using evidence from paleontology (to argue, for example, that the European climate had been much warmer during the Carboniferous period[18]). The paleogeographical case received relatively little elaboration by comparison.[19] The two theories had also received unequal treatment by earlier authors: while paleoclimatological hypotheses has been used as far back as Robert Hooke,[20] paleogeographical hypotheses had been mentioned only in more recent works, such as those of Willdenow and Milne-Edwards.[21] But both hypotheses were to receive much new evidence through the early nineteenth century from the rapidly advancing discipline of paleontology.

The *Principles* contained one of the earliest discussions of the centers-of-creation/dispersion hypothesis by an English author.[22] Although Lyell did not himself give close study to biogeographic phenomena, his knowledge of the relevant literature made that work an extremely valuable synthesis of the biogeographic observations of others, and thus provided a point of departure for the later biogeographic theorizing of Forbes, Hooker, Darwin, and Wallace. In an 1848 letter to his Geological Survey colleague Andrew Ramsay, Edward Forbes expressed his evaluation of the essentially synthetic nature of the *Principles:* "Respecting Lyell, I do not think that the merit of his Principles lies in originality—but in his working of the *present state* of science into Geology. The leading ideas of both

Hutton & Lyell are older than either & must be culled from many sources. We find one in Strabo, another in Raspe, a third in Henry More, a fourth in Molyneux, a fifth in Leibnitz & so on."[23]

### Forbes and the Centers-of-Creation Doctrine

In the 1830s the hypothesis of centers of creation, and the theories of migration and transport associated with it, constituted one of several alternative solutions to the problems of biogeographic phenomena. In the 1840s the hypothesis grew into a doctrine, with Forbes as one of its leading proponents.[24] The idea probably entered his thinking in the early 1830s,[25] but it was only in the 1840s that he began to speak of the "centre or capital" of a species. By these terms he meant the location most abundant in individuals, or, in the case of a "generic centre," the location of the greatest number of species of a genus.[26]

The devotees of biogeography were beginning to recognize that the primary difficulty confronting the doctrine of single centers of creation for each species lay in accounting for the discontinuous distributions of many modern species. In general there were two methods of surmounting this problem. First, one could assert that the disjoined populations did not in fact belong to the same species, and thereby avoid the question altogether. (Forbes referred to these separated groups as "representative species.") Second, following Lyell one could identify or hypothesize a means of dispersal between the two locations: fortuitous transport across existing barriers by various agents; passage over former land or shallow water "bridges," which have since subsided; or passage at a time when climates were more amenable to the species in question. It was to the latter solutions, those involving paleogeographic and paleoclimatological hypotheses, that Forbes was to make his most innovative, and controversial, contributions.

The expression "representative species" was used to describe species of the same genus which reside in similar environments but in geographically separated regions, for instance the opposite sides of the Atlantic. Forbes's most succinct explanation of the concept appeared in a letter to the geologist Leonard Horner in 1845:

Respecting the doctrine of *representative species* I am very anxious you should understand it, as it is one I lay great stress upon and believe that on its development the fixing of Geology as a science will eventually in part depend.

Example

Take any genus having a wide geographical (or geological) range, dependent on the distribution of many species, each with its own distinct special range (the sum of the *special* ranges making up the great range of the *genus*).

On comparing the species of that genus inhabiting the several hemispheres (North and South—East and West) we shall find that the prevalent species in the Northern hemisphere for instance is *represented* by a *corresponding* species in the Southern—the correspondence or representation depending on such close resemblence [*sic*] between the two forms, that the critical acumen of the naturalist is usually required to define wherein the distinction lies—though the species is certainly distinct.

Sometimes a chain of such representatives is kept up.[27]

Forbes sometimes called this phenomenon "representation *in space,*" to distinguish it from the geological phenomenon of "representation *in time*" (wherein two closely similar fossil species were located in successive strata) and the zonation phenomenon of "representation *in depth*" (two similar species occupying adjacent bathymetric zones). Every species has, thus, "three *maxima* of development."[28]

Critics of the centers-of-creation doctrine, like John Fleming, regarded the concept of representative species as a subterfuge to explain away truly anomalous cases of the discontinuous distribution of a single species. Fleming treated such cases as obvious evidence for the preferable theory of multiple centers of creation.[29] But in general there was little objection to the concept of representative species.

### Prehistoric Lands and Climates

It was through his association with the Scottish geologist James Smith (1782–1867) that Forbes developed an intimate understanding of the use of changes in climate to explain anomalies in the distribution of fossil and recent species. In the course of expeditions along the Scottish coasts aboard his yacht, Smith had acquired an interest in the localities of recent and fossil mollusks. His examination of the strata of raised beaches yielded fossil species which were known to be still living but only in more northerly climates. On this basis, Smith hypothesized that the British climate had been colder during the previous ("Newer Pliocene") epoch and that subsequent warming trends had forced the northward migration of the cold-water mollusks. Forbes accompanied Smith on an expedition in 1839 to examine some of these strata and came away strongly impressed with the power of paleoclimatological theories to account for differences in the distribution of fossil and recent animals.[30] From this point on he invoked both geological and paleoclimatological hypotheses with increasing frequency, whenever there was a relationship between ancient and present distributions to be explained.[31] When used in combination, changes in climate and changes in the relative levels of land and sea could produce ingenious explanations of otherwise anomalous phenomena, as Forbes soon found.

The first hint in Forbes's writings of this union of ideas appeared in a short article read at the Geological Society in 1844. At the time Forbes, as curator of the society, had been required to prepare a report describing a collection of marine fossils from India, presented to the society by two of its traveling members. The Indian fossils turned out to be especially interesting in that they came from strata of two distinct epochs of the Cretaceous period and the two groups of fossils differed greatly in their degree of similarity to European fossils of the same age. Very few of the fossils of the lower (Pondicherry) formation seemed to belong to genera appearing in the comparable European formations (English Lower Greensand and French Neocomien), whereas many fossils of the upper (Verdachellum and Trinconopoly) formation were of species common to Europe (English Upper Greensand). The reason for this increase in similarity of Indian and European faunas through time, Forbes claimed, was not simply a matter of a generally wider distribution of marine species in the later period; rather it was due to a constancy of climate accompanied by "some great change in the distribution of land and sea, and in a greater connection of the Indian and European seas."[32] Since the species of Mollusca and Radiata involved were believed to have had centers of origin in the "Eastern seas"[33] (Indian and western Pacific Oceans), migration was therefore assumed to have been in a westward direction toward Europe. These suggestions were carried no further, however, and apparently elicited little response. A few days after presenting the paper to the Geological Society, Forbes wrote that his conclusions had been "too brief and too deep to be understood by most who were there."[34]

Eighteen months later Forbes set forth the first stage of his most important contribution to biogeographic theory, leaving hardly a trace of the events or thoughts which motivated the work. The contribution was an analysis of the provinces of the British flora, with hypotheses as to their Continental origins. His forum was the Natural History Section of the British Association at Cambridge (1845). As indicated in its title, "On the Distribution of Endemic Plants, more especially those of the British Islands, considered with regard to Geological Changes,"[35] this initial paper concentrated only on the flora of Britain, not its fauna.

The British flora could be divided, Forbes claimed, into five types, or subfloras, based on the distribution patterns of particular species. These five types, in order of increasing numbers of species, were enumerated as follows:

(1) "West Pyrenian," a flora of "very southern character" occupying the mountainous areas of western Ireland and similar to the flora of mountainous northern Spain;

(2) Flora of southwestern England and southern Ireland, a flora similar to that of southwestern France;

(3) Flora of southeastern England, a flora related to that of northern France;

(4) Alpine, occupying the north of England, Scotland, and the mountains of northern Wales;

(5) Germanic, a flora common to most of Britain and Ireland, "mingling with the other floras," and related to that of northern and western Germany.

With these floras defined, the problem was then to ascertain their history. Forbes's thesis was that each of the five floras had been independently introduced into the British Isles at different times and from different directions. The order of the floras given above was also the order of their relative age and period of introduction. The mode of introduction, according to Forbes, was migration from the Continent via various land connections that had intermittently appeared and disappeared, due to geological elevation and subsidence. The migrations had occurred as follows:

(1) The Pyrenean flora crossed over from Spain to Ireland by way of a "great mountain barrier" occupying the present Bay of Biscay. This land bridge had to be mountainous in order to convey plants requiring an alpine environment. The isolation and relatively small extent of the flora indicated that it was quite old.

(2) The southwestern flora had crossed from southwestern France to Devon and Cornwall and then to Ireland via a land bridge traces of which still existed as the Channel Isles (Guernsey and Jersey).

(3) The southeastern flora came across at a time when France and England were joined at the eastern end of the Channel.

(4) The Alpine flora had crossed from Scandinavia during the glacial or Pleistocene epoch.[36] (Nineteenth-century British geologists believed that most of England had been submerged beneath icy seas at that time, the mountains extending above the surface as islands.) Alpine plants had advanced along chains of islands or by icebergs from Norway to Britain, and with the elevation of land and warming of climate at the close of the glacial period, these plants became marooned on mountain summits.

(5) Finally, the Germanic flora crossed from Germany to England and Ireland late in the glacial epoch when the North and Irish seas were thought to have been low-lying plains.

Forbes placed the beginning of this series of migrations in the Miocene epoch because fossil plants of the preceding Eocene epoch were of a tropical character differing greatly from the existing flora. Other fossil evidence suggested relative dates for the second and third floral migrations. Each of these first three floras was then isolated in the British Isles as the land connections disappeared in an eastward-progressing series of land subsidences, commencing in the Bay of Biscay. As evidence that geological changes of this magnitude could have occurred during the Tertiary period, he cited the contemporaneous, 6,000-foot uplift of the Taurus Mountains in Turkey.

The entire train of Forbes's analysis depended on a number of assumptions, some stated and some implicit. First and foremost of his explicit assumptions was that of a unique spatiotemporal center of creation for each species; without this assumption, arguments about discontinuities and dispersion were meaningless. In the discussion that followed Forbes's paper, the botanists John Ball and Charles Babington expressed doubts about the validity of this assumption. Forbes responded that the science of paleontology was utterly dependent upon the assumption; without it there would be "an end to all palaeontology and its value in geological inquiry."[37] In a later paper he defended the idea of centers of creation for both species and genera, arguing that common descent from a single progenitor was implicit in the definition of species as understood by most naturalists.[38]

A second critical assumption, one which became the focus of controversy among biogeographers for years thereafter, was the inadequacy of "natural transport" (dispersion by such fortuitous physical agencies as winds, currents, rivers, and animals) as an explanation for all biogeographic discontinuities.[39] Forbes did not categorically reject natural transport as a means of dispersal[40] but felt that it was "in the majority of cases, insufficient."[41] By presenting the first extensive statement of the theory of land-bridge migration, however, Forbes became the symbol of the subsequent tradition of land-bridge speculation. The repugnance of land-bridge theorizing to Darwin and others would later be a stimulus for their research into the vehicles and efficacy of natural transport.[42]

An unstated assumption in the theory was that the original specific centers of British plants had been located on the European continent, not within Britain itself. Migrations, therefore, had been *from* the Continent *to* Britain, not the reverse. This assumption was grounded in the more general notion that the relatively permanent continents, rather than their oscillating island appendages, were the foci of creations, an assumption which was seldom discussed.

### The "Connexion" Essay

Following the brief 1845 paper which introduced the land-bridge theory for plants, Forbes commenced work on a detailed exposition of his ideas. The theory was presented to a Royal Institution audi-

*Organisms in Space and Time*

ence early in 1846 and was discussed as part of a series of six lectures on biogeography at the London Institution.[43] In the summer of the same year he published the full version of the land-bridge thesis in the first volume of the *Memoirs of the Geological Survey of Great Britain*, under the title "On the Connexion Between the Distribution of the Existing Flora and Fauna of the British Isles, and the Geological Changes Which Have Affected Their Area, Especially During the Epoch of the Northern Drift."[44] I will refer to it hereafter as the "Connexion" essay.

The essay consisted of two parts, one floral and one faunal. The floral section (sixteen pages), primarily an expansion of the earlier British Association paper, included a number of alterations. The central thesis of his research was stated explicitly: "The specific identity, to any extent, of the flora and fauna of one area with those

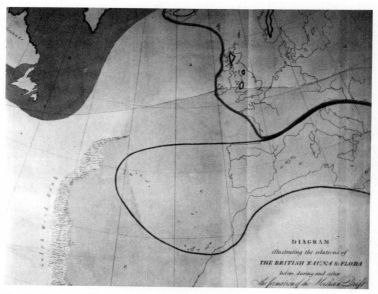

Fig. 5.1. Forbes's "Diagram Illustrating the relations of the British Fauna and Flora Before, During, and After the Formation of the Northern Drift," *Memoirs of the Geological Survey of Great Britain*, vol. 1 (1846), plate 7.

of another, depends on both areas forming, or having formed, part of the same specific centre, or on their having derived their animal and vegetable population by transmission, through migration, over continuous or closely contiguous land, aided, in the case of alpine floras, by transportations on floating masses of ice."[45] The initial assumptions and their supporting evidence were also stated in greater detail.

Lists of plant species were given for each of the five floral provinces. The possibility was raised that the second, third, and fifth floras might have migrated *concurrently* from their respective centers, thus reducing the number of "epochs of migration" from five to three. The explanation previously given for the identity of the fourth (alpine) flora with the subarctic flora of Scandinavia (i.e., transport by icebergs during submersion of most of Great Britain beneath a glacial sea) was now applied broadly to account for the similarity of alpine species throughout middle Europe and central Asia.[46]

The Miocene land mass, which Forbes originally hypothesized as a migration path from northern Spain to Ireland, he now extended westward to include the Azores (Fig. 5.1). The western shore of this land area was declared to be the original, shallow-water home of the *Sargassum* seaweed, whose great floating mass now forms the Sargasso Sea in the mid-Atlantic Ocean: "In all probability, the great semicircular belt of gulf-weed ranging between the 15th and 45th degrees of north latitude, and constant in its place, marks the position of the coastline of that ancient land, and had its parentage on its solid grounds."[47] To support this hypothesis, Forbes cited the conclusions of the Irish algologist William Henry Harvey (1811–66). Harvey believed *Sargassum bacciferum* of the Sargasso Sea to be a floating variety of the attached *Sargassum vulgare,* the former having "migrated from some fixed station."[48]

The faunal section of the "Connexion" essay constituted the bulk of the work. Here Forbes presented new evidence for his epochs of migration from the distribution of marine organisms, especially the Mollusca (both fossil and recent). And it is here that we find clues to the sources of, and motivations for, the work.

He began the faunal section with brief comments on the distinctively northern and southern types of fish and crustacea. He then passed on quickly to the group for which distributional data were far

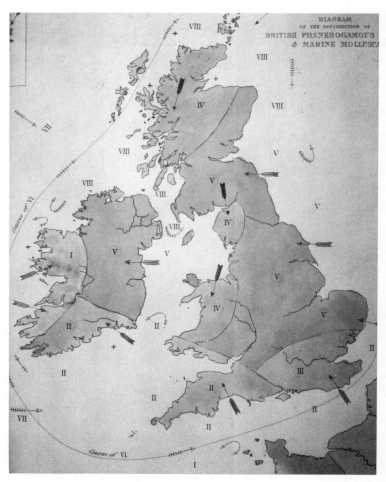

Fig. 5.2. Forbes's "Diagram of the Distribution of British Phanerogamous Plants and Marine Mollusca," *Memoirs of the Geological Survey of Great Britain,* vol. 1 (1846), plate 6.

more abundant (and much better known to himself), the Mollusca. First the distribution of British marine Mollusca was described in terms of nine types, occupying overlapping provinces (see Fig. 5.2):

    I. Southern British Channel and Channel Isles
   II. South British
  III. European (throughout West European shores, Norway to Spain)
  IV. Celtic (exclusively around British Isles)
   V. British (within the Irish Sea)
  VI. Atlantic (southwest England, around west Ireland to the Hebrides, rarely in Irish and North Seas)
 VII. Oceanic (occasional drifters from west and south)
VIII. Boreal (northern British Isles, Scandinavia)
  IX. Arctic (seas north of Britain)

By commencing with the definition of molluscan provinces, Forbes appeared to be following the methodology established in the floral section. But instead of continuing this methodology by relating each of the British molluscan provinces to its Continental counterpart according to present distribution, he turned immediately to the fossil record. By noting the changes that had occurred in the distribution of the marine Mollusca, he garnered new evidence for the changes in British climate and geography. This evidence was then shown to coincide with the changes previously hypothesized to account for terrestrial organisms. This line of argument is shown diagrammatically in Figure 5.3. The reason for this circuitous reasoning was that the fossil record for the Mollusca was sufficiently detailed to permit reaching conclusions directly about past climate and geography, while the record for plants was not. But the conclusions derived from the molluscan evidence could be inserted in place of the lacking plant evidence to support the migration hypothesis.

The enumeration of marine provinces was thus not an end in itself, but rather a key to past geological and climatological conditions, which would, in turn, corroborate Forbes's views on the history of terrestrial migrations. Although each of the marine provinces was given a geographical name, each was based (like the floral provinces) on a particular assemblage of species. And each province could be characterized by its ecology or "climate" (mainly temperature). This

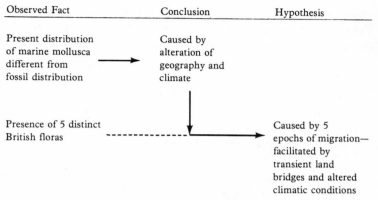

Fig. 5.3. Structure of Forbes's argument in the "Connexion" essay.

mode of classification was then extended to the fossil record by as-
suming that the recent and fossil representatives of each species or
genus had the same ecological requirements. From the appearance of
a particular assemblage of species within a set of strata it could be
argued that the climate during the period of deposition was similar to
the climate in the region where the same assemblage appears today.
Thus, for example, the discovery of an assemblage of fossil mollusks
in southern England whose present counterparts occur only in Arctic
seas indicated that Britain was experiencing a much more frigid
climate when the strata in question were formed. As Forbes pointed
out,[49] he had been preceded in the use of this line of reasoning about
climate, particularly with reference to the glacial or Pleistocene
epoch, by Linnaeus, Lyell, and especially by his friend James Smith.
But none of his predecessors had attacked the subject in the delib-
erate and thorough manner Forbes now employed.

In addition to being an indicator of climate, the Mollusca could
also be used as an indicator of *depth* at the time of deposition. This
was particularly important, since the possibility of migration of littoral or sublittoral organisms depended on the existence of shallow
water as well as a suitable climate. From Forbes's earlier study of
coastal zonation, he knew that particular species assemblages were
characteristic of particular depths. By applying this knowledge to
fossil assemblages, the configuration of land and sea in former
epochs could be made out. Of course, the observing zoo-geologist

must be aware, Forbes warned, that changes in depth correspond to changes in climate in altering the composition of marine species assemblages; hence, in interpreting the fossil data one must be certain not to confuse the two types of changes. The key geological event (actually a series of events) in the history of the British flora and fauna, as Forbes now saw it, was the Pleistocene epoch, "the epoch of glaciers and icebergs, of boulders, and groovings, and scratches."[50] The frigid climate of that epoch had permitted the transmission to Britain of a Scandinavian flora that was subsequently driven into Britain's mountainous areas. The elevation of both land and seabed thereafter had facilitated the migration of the important Germanic flora and fauna to Britain and had altered the distribution of marine invertebrates. Thus, while corroborating his hypotheses of floral migrations, most of the faunal section of the "Connexion" essay was aimed at developing a scenario of geological and climatological events for the Pleistocene.[51] The following summary describes this scenario (see also Table 5.1 ).

At the beginning of the Pleistocene a severe climate gradually engulfed the British Isles. During this time frigid seas covered most of the land with the exception of mountain summits and the southernmost parts of the country; of the terrestrial species acquired during the Miocene and early Pliocene epochs, only those inhabiting these mountainous and southern areas survived.

Arctic marine species migrated south to inhabit British seas, while British (Celtic) species migrated to southern Europe by means of a marine passage between the North and Mediterranean Seas. Alpine plant species reached the exposed portions of the British Isles from Scandinavia either by icebergs or over an Arctic land mass communicating between North America, Greenland, Iceland, and northern Europe.

At the close of the Pleistocene, the climate became less frigid and the glacial seabed was gradually upraised, the North and Irish seas becoming plains. Arctic marine species retired to the north and Celtic species returned from the south; alpine species became marooned on mountain summits.

During the early postglacial epoch Britain acquired most of her present flora (Type V) and fauna by migration from Germany; reindeer and the great Irish elk roamed the largely barren, treeless country. In the later postglacial times, the Irish Sea and then the North

Table 5.1. Forbes's Cenozoic Timetable for the British Isles

| Epoch | Events |
|---|---|
| Historical | Advent of man |
| | Upraised breaches containing modern mollusk fossils |
| Post-Pliocene | Formation of peat deposits |
| (postglacial) | Vast forests covering Britain |
| | Present configuration of Britain completed |
| 2nd Stage | North Sea formed by depression of raised seabed |
| | Irish Sea formed by depression of raised seabed |
| | Formation of fresh-water marls |
| | Flourishing of Irish elk on treeless plains |
| 1st Stage | Migration of Germanic fauna and flora (V)[a] |
| Pleistocene | Glacial seabed upraised gradually |
| (Newer Pliocene, | North Sea and Irish Sea become land |
| Glacial) | Retreat of Arctic forms northward |
| | Isolation of alpine plants |
| | Communication between North and Mediterranean Seas permits passage of Celtic species to Italy |
| | Migration of Scandinavian flora (IV) |
| | Britain covered by glacial seas, except mountains and southernmost England |
| | Severe climate |
| | Formation of Northern Drift |
| | Formation of Mammaliferous Crag |
| Older Pliocene | Migration of flora from N.W. France (III) |
| | Migration of flora from extreme N.W. France and Channel Isles (II) |
| | Formation of Red Crag |
| Miocene | Formation of Coralline Crag |
| | Migration of flora from Spain (I) |
| | Connection of Ireland with Spain |
| | Elevation of seabed throughout Mediterranean |
| Eocene[b] | Extensive changes in land/water configuration exterminate most marine forms |
| | Formation of London Clay |
| | Flora and fauna distinct from present |
| | Warmer climate |

Source: Reconstructed from Forbes, "On the Connexion Between the Distribution of the Existing Flora and Fauna of the British Isles. . . ." *Memoirs of the Geological Survey of Great Britain* 1 (1846):336–432.

[a] Most plant species native to Britain are now regarded as having immigrated from the mainland following the end of the last glacial episode and before the rise in sea

Sea were formed by the break-up or depression of the upraised sea-bed. The land became heavily forested as the climate continued its warming trend toward present levels. The uplift of beaches in Scotland and the appearance of man were the final events in the scenario.

## Origins of the "Connexion"

The "Connexion" essay was a long, complex, and sometimes rambling exposition. This judgment was reflected ten years after its publication in a comment by Darwin, who could then finally say that "I have got it [the essay] up so as to give the heads in a page."[52] It was a major theoretical synthesis, however, in which Forbes brought to bear on a single large problem the many themes which had occupied him over the previous ten years: the distribution of terrestrial species with respect to geography, climate, and elevation; the coastal zonation of marine invertebrates; the comparison of the distribution of Pleistocene fossils with their recent counterparts; and the distribution of Mollusca in the seas of Europe. In merging these various studies, he placed historical biogeography on a solid theoretical foundation by allying it with paleogeography and paleoclimatology. And in the process he was able to produce a much more detailed picture of the historical geology of a particular period and region than had ever been done before.

The essay was also unique because, for the first time, it considered the organisms of a particular place from a thoroughly historical point of view and attempted to explain their distribution as a product of gradual development. In this respect the essay may be viewed as a further instance of the growing tendency to interpret natural phenomena in historical terms. The historicist tendency, which recognized the dimension of time and the evolution of seemingly permanent phenomena, had been invading branch after branch of human

level severed the islands from the Continent, i.e., between about 8000–9000 B.C. and 5500 B.C. See Winifred Pennington, *The History of British Vegetation* (London: English Universities Press, 1969), p. 1. Roman numerals in parentheses designate Forbes's floral types.

[b] The Oligocene epoch, which is now regarded as separating the Eocene and Miocene, was not proposed until 1854. See William B. N. Berry, *Growth of a Prehistoric Time Scale* (San Francisco: W. H. Freeman, 1968), p. 112.

knowledge since the seventeenth century. In geology the historical dimension found its ultimate expositor in Lyell. In the next decade Darwin would apply it successfully to biology. And in the Victorian idea of progress, the historicist tradition showed itself to have permeated man's vision of his own place in the world.[53]

While in retrospect the "Connexion" essay can be seen as a logical event in the widening tradition of treating nature in historical terms, such an explanation leaves many other questions answered. What specific stimuli motivated this new direction to Forbes's thought? Why should he suddenly turn from the basically descriptive marine ecological and paleontological work that had been his forte since the late 1830s to a speculative interpretation of the history of Britain's native species? Why especially did he begin his speculations with the British flora rather than its fauna? Why was he later accused of plagiarism by the plant geographer Hewett Watson? And what led him to advocate land bridges as the solution to biogeographic discontinuities? Was this simply an elaboration of ideas suggested but little developed by Lyell? Was the report of the Cretaceous fossils of southern India the only prior indication of this new trend of thought?

The "Connexion" essay is an enigma in Forbes's thought for which no totally satisfying explanation can be given. It contained ideas from his own experience and from a multitude of sources, not all of which were cited. Nevertheless, the details of his life in the years immediately preceding the essay suggest one possible explanation. Curiously, the essay, which concerned itself principally with the terrestrial flora and the marine invertebrata of Britain, seems to have had its origins not only in Pleistocene geology but in vertebrate paleontology.

The main background against which the "Connexion" episode must be viewed is the primitive but rapidly advancing science of Pleistocene geology of the late 1830s and 1840s. We have seen that Forbes became keenly interested in Pleistocene mollusks while working with James Smith in 1839, and that Pleistocene geology played a notable role in the advent of dredging activities sponsored by the British Association. It was precisely at this time that geologists were first becoming convinced of the unique climatic conditions of the Pleistocene. The cause of a frigid climate and the unusual geological formations of glacial till, known in Britain as the Northern Drift, had not yet been agreed upon. In his 1840 *Etudes sur les glaciers* Louis Agassiz (whom Forbes met in the same year) argued that the existence of vast glaciers throughout Europe, whose remnants could still be seen in the Alps, would account for the Pleistocene phenomena.[54] Most British geologists, including Forbes,[55] preferred the apparently more actualistic (and definitely more diluvialist) interpretation of glacial seas, icebergs, and heavy wave action. Thus there were perplexing phenomena explicable by at least two theories—a situation ripe for debate among geologists and bound to stir interest among all naturalists. In 1844–45 Forbes had participated in Pleistocene fieldwork with the Geological Survey and had undoubtedly entered into discussions with his fellow "hammerers" on the subject of Pleistocene events. As he stated midway through the "Connexion" essay (in reference to the "beds of the glacial epoch"), "My chief purpose in drawing up this essay, is to assist in the elucidation of that most interesting and important formation—one which will engage much of the attention of the geological surveyors—by exhibiting the nature and value of the evidence afforded by organic remains found in those beds, and the bearing of that evidence on the history of animated nature within the area under examination by the Survey."[56]

The "elucidation" of Pleistocene geology was undoubtedly the largest factor governing the final form and emphasis of the "Connexion" essay. But it does not seem to have been the impetus for his preceding British Association report on "Endemic Plants." Moreover, it gives no hint of the stimuli behind the land-bridge methodology. A tentative solution to these problems involves an examination of certain developments in vertebrate paleontology which preceded the "Connexion" essay.

### The Irish Elk

In the 1820s, during Forbes's childhood, the first complete fossil skeleton of the extinct Irish elk, *Megaloceros giganteus,* was unearthed from the peat bogs of the Isle of Man, not far from the estate of Forbes's mother, and transported to Edinburgh for erection in the university museum. Known by various names in the nineteenth century (*Cervus megaceros, Megaceros hibernicus*), *Megaloceros* was an object of wonder because of its huge, broad, mooselike antlers which in the adult have a span of up to twelve feet.[57] It is not known

whether Forbes was a witness in his youth to the excavation of the
elk, but it seems probable that he would have heard about it, for such
an event on his quiet isle would assuredly have created a stir. And he
probably had read the account of the elk in James Parkinson's *Organic Remains of a Former World,* a book he is known to have used as
a boy.[58]

Though he may have studied the Edinburgh museum's skeleton
of *Megaloceros* while a student, no mention of it appears in his
writings until the 1840s. Following his work with James Smith on
the Pleistocene fossils of Scotland and Ireland (1839), Forbes returned to the Isle of Man and spent some time investigating the
Pleistocene strata there. In a subsequent article he compared the
shells in these strata with those obtained by dredging in the adjacent
sea. In passing he mentioned that "the bones of the fossil elk are
found" immediately above the Pleistocene strata.[59] Some months
later he wrote to William Corlett, a Manx resident and amateur geologist who lived near the location where the Edinburgh skeleton had
been excavated, asking for "the particulars of the [elk's] discovery."[60] Since Forbes rarely concerned himself with vertebrates (other
than fish), his inquiry was probably undertaken merely to clarify further the nature and position of the strata in which the elk was found,
especially in relation to the marine beds.

Forbes wrote nothing more on the Irish elk until 1843, when he
composed a four-page manuscript entitled "Note on the age of the
Manx elk."[61] The manuscript was never published. Apparently it
was composed for the use of Richard Owen, who was then preparing
a report for the British Association on British fossil mammalia. In
that report, and in his subsequent book, *British Fossil Mammals and
Birds,* Owen cited information on *Megaloceros* supplied by Forbes.
One of the statements in Owen's work, though not indicated as a
direct quotation, is in fact nearly identical with a passage in Forbes's
manuscript.[62] My point here is that, at Owen's request, Forbes went
to some trouble to compile information for the Manx elk manuscript. And in so doing, it seems very likely that he consulted then (if
he had not done so earlier) the first English account of the elk, published in the *Philosophical Transactions of the Royal Society* in 1697
by the Dublin physician Thomas Molyneux (1661–1733).[63]

Molyneux published only a handful of articles during his lifetime,
but his paper on the Irish elk was apparently well-known, being cited

by both Parkinson and Owen. Now while Owen and the Irish elk probably led Forbes to Molyneux's article, there are two other features of the article which show it to be an important predecessor to the "Connexion" essay. First, Molyneux believed the elk to be most closely related to the North American moose.[64] To explain how the elk had reached Ireland from the New World, Molyneux suggested that between Ireland and North America there had to have been a communication by a land connection, or

> some sort of Intercourse, . . . (though 'tis not easy, I acknowledge, for us at present to explain how) for otherwise I do not see, how we can conceive this Country should be supply'd with this Creature, that for ought I can yet hear, is not to be found in all our Neighbourhood round about us, nay, perhaps in any other Part of *Europe, Asia* or *Africa*. And then 'tis certain as *Ireland* is the last or most Western part of the *Old World;* so 'tis nearest to any Country to the most Eastern Parts of the *New-Canada, New-England, Virginia,* &c. the great Tract of Land, and the only one I yet know, remarkable for plenty of the *Moose-Deer.*[65]

Here was one of the earliest specific instances of a land bridge being hypothesized to explain the discontinuous distribution of a particular species. Of course, by Forbes's time, extinction was a generally accepted fact, and *Megaloceros* fossils had been found in Europe, obviating the need for a transatlantic land bridge. Nevertheless, the former existence of the elk on the Isle of Man, and in the British isles generally, still had to be explained. The solution was at hand at least by 1843 when Forbes recognized that, at the time of the elk's existence, much of the Irish Sea had been "a great plain,"[66] or in other words, a land bridge.

The second unique feature of Molyneux's article appears among what his title refers to as "Remarks on some other things Natural to that Country [Ireland]." Here he called attention to a number of plant species known to be common in the mountainous western parts of Ireland but absent in the rest of Britain. Mentioned specifically were the *Arbutus unedo,* or "Strawbery tree," and the "London Pride," both found in the county of Kerry, the southwesternmost county of Ireland. The former species was known otherwise only in southern France, Italy, and Sicily; the latter, not known elsewhere at all. Molyneux hinted that these plants might be American, like the elk, though he could offer no proof.

Returning to Forbes's 1845 report on "Endemic Plants" which preceded the "Connexion" essay, we recall that the first anomalous distribution pattern which he described was that of the "West Pyrenian" flora—"confined to the west of Ireland, and mostly to the mountains of that district."[67] In the list of species unique to this area Forbes included both *Arbutus unedo* and *Saxifraga umbrosa* ("London Pride"). Since Molyneux's time, these species had been found in northern Spain. Forbes accounted for their existence in these widely separated areas in terms of a former land bridge across the Bay of Biscay, using the same line of reasoning Molyneux had employed for the elk. There is thus a similarity of both observation and explanation in the papers of Molyneux and Forbes.

An 1847 letter from Forbes to Lyell erases any doubts about Forbes's ultimate debt to Molyneux. Lyell had complained that some of Forbes's "Connexion" ideas were extensions of material discussed in the *Principles* which Forbes had failed to cite. In a lengthy response, Forbes insisted that Molyneux, not Lyell, had been the initial source of his ideas:

> Now for Molyneux. For him (one of the most remarkable and enlightened minds Britain ever produced) I claim the clear enunciation of the idea that the present distribution of *animals and plants* has reference to a former distribution of land and water. This I take to be the pith of the hypothesis which preceded such investigations as those alluded to. In his paper on the Irish Elk he was far out as to the facts but wonderfully right in his reasoning (granting his premises). He argued from the Irish fauna and flora the former connection of Ireland with America—one of the boldest speculations in the history of geology, the more so when the age in which he wrote is considered. In the same papers he argued the ancient union of Italy with the neighbouring islands, on similar grounds. These papers are in the Philosophical transactions 100 years ago and were also published separately. I lectured about them in the Royal Instn.[68]

To summarize the events leading to the "Connexion" essay thus far, we began with Forbes's 1839 investigation, with James Smith, of marine fossils indicating an Arctic climate in Britain during the Pleistocene. Earlier research on Scottish coastal geology, along with the marine zoological activities of the British Association dredging committee, showed that in the epochs preceding the present, significant changes in the relative levels of land and sea had occurred, contemporaneous with the changes in climate. The Pleistocene epoch, which had already been the subject of much theorizing regarding the causes of the glacially transported "erratic blocks" and the Northern Drift formation, was acquiring additional interest. Concurrently Richard Owen's work on fossil mammals, presented to the British Association in the early 1840s, emphasized the evidence for the existence of many unusual, now extinct animals in Britain during and after the Pleistocene[69] and their similarity to Continental fossils. Chief among the late Pleistocene mammals was *Megaloceros,* the Irish elk. Because of his acquaintance with the Manx *Megaloceros* Forbes contributed *circa* 1843 to Owen's work. Probably in connection with that research, Forbes was led to the original seventeenth-century account of *Megaloceros* by Molyneux. Along with the description of the elk was Molyneux's hypothesis of a land connection between Ireland and North America and his notice of the unusual flora of southwest Ireland not found elsewhere in the British Isles.

In late 1844 Forbes left the Geological Society curatorship to become paleontologist to the Survey. As a result he became involved immediately in further fieldwork among Pleistocene strata. Probably in early 1845 he settled on the idea of presenting a paper to the British Association in which he would not merely derive the southwest Irish flora from Spain via ancient land connections, but would apply this methodology to explain all of the British floras. From his new knowledge of the Pleistocene, he could argue for the isolation of the alpine flora by the retreat of glacial conditions as well as the migration of the Germanic flora over the plains where *Megaloceros* had roamed.

Forbes's choice of the British flora, rather than its fauna, as the subject of the first (1845) paper may have been due to two factors more immediate than the hint from Molyneux. First, the available data on plant distribution was still far more detailed than that for animals. Forbes had not yet compiled his data on the distribution of marine invertebrata, though he had hopes of doing so in the next year. Second, he may have felt the need to publish a substantial botanical piece, as he had by then been professor of botany at King's College for three years but had not published anything of note on the subject since the late 1830s.[70] Politics may indeed have been partially responsible for the speculative nature of the 1845 paper. Forbes was well aware by that time that in the then poorly supported state of British science, the few naturalists prominent enough to earn a living by their profession did not achieve prominence by common drudgery. Rather, they advocated new and remarkable ideas and displayed a measure of showmanship. This is amply illustrated by his advice on lecturing at the Royal Institution given to an unidentified colleague through a letter (1845) to John Percy:

> His lectures here will, I hope, however, gain him some influential friends. Let his facts and illustrations be as *striking* as possible, that is, as *remarkable to that part of the audience* (more than half) which *consists of those who know nothing at all about the science of the matter, as to those who know and understand.* This is the secret of success in the Royal Institution and in London. It was the secret of Davy and Faraday, and of all who have made a sudden and meteoric reputation in this ugly unphilosophical, lion-hunting centre of the universe.[71]

It seems probable that Forbes hit upon the theme of the 1845 paper not long before presenting it to the British Association, as there are definite signs of his having hurried to produce it in time for the meeting. With more time he might have assembled his statistics on marine invertebrates, but for the moment he confined the paper to plants. The bulk of his botanical data had come, not from personal observation, but from the publications of Hewett Watson. As he later told Lyell, "To get at my results I worked over the localities of above 1600 plants—individually (not very difficult considering how admirably Watson has brought together the data)."[72] Unfortunately he did not cite Watson's work (nor anyone else's). This omission resulted in the one serious charge of professional dishonesty of Forbes's career.

### Conflict with Watson

Watson had determined to devote his life to the collection and co-ordination of the statistics of British plant distribution. He was motivated in part by a belief in Lamarckian transmutation and hoped that his efforts in geographic botany would provide evidence for that theory. After completing the introductory *Remarks on the Geographical Distribution of British Plants* (1835), he began work on his *magnum opus,* the four-volume *Cybele Britannica,* published a volume at a time between 1847 and 1859. Although he was a prime candidate for two chairs of botany (including the King's College professorship, which to his disgust was awarded to Forbes), Watson was never successful in obtaining a university post, mostly for reasons other than scientific competence. He lived a reclusive life in isolation from scientific society and often displayed a hostile attitude toward his colleagues. Thus the personalities of Watson and Forbes were in many ways polar opposites. The two must have met on at least several occasions. They were both involved in a British Association project *circa* 1840 to draw up a map of the British Isles for the use of botanists in recording the localities of plant species. Even then there seems to have been some minor disagreement, between Watson on the one hand, and Forbes and William Brand on the other, over the degree of geographic detail to be included on the map.[73] Their antipathies may, in fact, have originated during student years in Edinburgh: in 1834 the ever-jesting Forbes published a short piece satirizing phrenology, an attitude that Watson, the future editor of the *Phrenological Journal,* could hardly have appreciated.[74]

Watson did not attend the 1845 meeting of the British Association, but he heard of Forbes's "Endemic Plants" paper soon thereafter and immediately began to collect evidence to support a charge of plagiarism.[75] The charge was published in 1847 as an appendix to the first volume of the *Cybele Britannica.* In it Watson compared the floral groupings in Forbes's essays of 1845 and 1846 with those he himself had published in 1835.[76] The comparison, summarized in tabular form, is as follows:

| *Forbes's Floras* | *Watson's Types* |
|---|---|
| 1. S.W. Ireland | |
| 2. S.W. England | I. S.W. England |
| 3. S.E. England | II. S.E. England |
| 4. Alpine Plants | VI. Mountain plants of England and Scotland |
| 5. Generally distributed | IV. Plants more generally distributed |
| | III. Plants of S. England decreasing northwards |
| | V. Plants of Scotland and N. England decreasing southwards |

Thus, Forbes's floras 2, 3, 4, and 5 correspond to Watson's types I, II, VI, and IV, respectively; Watson did not recognize Forbes's flora 1, and he felt that Forbes had "suppressed" his types III and V.

Watson concluded that, with the exception of the southwest Irish flora, the two systems were so similar that the one had to have been derived from the other. And Watson felt that Forbes, in not citing this derivation, was implying that the system of floras was entirely original with him. Already other authors were beginning to cite the floral provinces as Forbes's innovation.[77] So Watson felt compelled to set the record straight by publicly announcing that Forbes's "alleged 'floras' were little else than a garbled reproduction of the 'types of distribution'—taken from a ten-year-old volume without acknowledgement." Forbes could not, in fact, have contributed significantly to the statistics of geographic botany, Watson insisted, because "whatever may be his scientific merits in other respects, that gentleman's repute, as a botanist, is more academical than personal."[78] In direct support of his claim, Watson noted that Forbes had borrowed a copy of Watson's *Remarks* from the Linnean Society Library on 16 June 1845, only four days before presenting his "Endemic Plants" report to the British Association. "With that work before him, slight and sketchy as it is allowed to be, an 'ingenious' copyist might have written the paper in less than three hours."[79]

Forbes never answered, nor even explicitly acknowledged Watson's charge in print. In expanding the "Endemic Plants" paper into the "Connexion" essay, however, he cited Watson's work no fewer than six times. And in noting that the completeness of British floral works was essential to the type of analysis he was attempting, Forbes added that "the essays of Mr. H. C. Watson may be cited as among the most remarkable, and to them I must refer geologists who would wish to learn more respecting our indigenous flora, than it is here necessary to state."[80] Forbes's only other published comment on Watson appeared in an 1852 review of botanical works. Alluding to the latter's attack upon himself, he described Watson as "indefatigable and deservedly illustrious in statistics, but grown misanthropic by working overmuch when in ill humour, [taking] a melancholy pleasure in attributing evil motives to his fellow-labourers."[81]

Although there may have been no direct exchange between Forbes and Watson over the issue, there was considerable communication with intermediaries and some effort made to prevent Watson's complaint from reaching print.[82] A few months after Forbes's reading of the "Endemic Plants" paper, Joseph Hooker wrote to Darwin:

I have not seen Forbes since studying his paper and really do not know what to say when I do, for he will be sure to ask me about it, and most unfortunately he does not seem to know the Geographic Distrib. of the English Plants. I must confess to have taken his modification of Watson's types of vegetation as correct; and this for granted, but I had occasion to look closely at this the other day and find his S.E. Flora, numbered III., to be altogether a fallacy: all or about all the 20 species on whose supposed presence he founded it, being as common or more in the W. or N. as in the E. or S. and some of them not existing in the S.E. at all! or if so as introduced species. I now see the cause for Watson's being so peculiarly savage and offering me proof that all that is correct is mere plagiarism. I still however quite acquit Forbes of any intentional piracy. He has long and early appreciated Watson's views and has fancied that he has grounds for modifying them. I do all I can to appease W[atson], but in vain, he threatens to denounce F[orbes] publicly and if he does I fear that it will read awkwardly for our friend. I need not ask you to say nothing of this, except you can offer some way or means of keeping these, almost the only 2 philosophical Brit. Botanists, out of a broil, at which all the dirty species-mongers will chuckle.[83]

Hooker continued his analysis of Forbes's and Watson's floral systems. Six months later he wrote again to Darwin, announcing "the distressing result, that I fear I must haul out of all participating with [Forbes]."[84]

Hooker's confirmation of Watson's claims meant that the conflict was not merely a product of Watson's misanthropic personality. It also makes the unanswered questions in this episode between "almost the only 2 philosophical Brit. Botanists" all the more curious. Why did Forbes fail to cite his debt to Watson? And why did he not acknowledge this failure? In most cases he seems to have been quite conscientious in citing the work of others; it was for this reason that Darwin was surprised at Forbes's treatment of Lyell's contributions, as he noted in an 1846 letter to Hooker: "I think Forbes ought to allude a little to Lyell's work on nearly the same subject as his speculations; not that I mean that Forbes wishes to take the smallest credit from him or any man alive; no man, as far as I see, likes so much to give credit to others, or more soars above the petty craving for self-celebrity."[85]

Forbes recognized the importance of Hooker's opinions in the case and was anxious that his side be clearly understood. Two of his letters to Hooker, previously unpublished, provide answers to most of the questions remaining. Not long after the "Connexion" essay had appeared, he wrote Hooker that

Nobody is more ready than I am to proclaim Watson's merits and indefatigable work. I grant the excellence of his [floral] types and their truth—but when they did not concern the question surely I did more than enough in quoting them. The types I required were *those of migration* (according to my view—of *foreign relations* at any rate) and were not classified by him. Yet I did not put them forth as mine—since they were simple statements of facts known to every British botanist. What I claimed and claim was the attempt to explain the causes of these things and through what series of events they were brought to pass (as essential a chapter in Botanical Geography and therefore in Botany as any other in the Flower-books). This Watson's want of a sufficient variety of natural history and geological knowledge prevented his doing or being likely to do. I fancied—here vainness—that he would have been pleased at my coming into the field with the collateral sciences of Zoology and Geology to aid Botany. And no doubt he would have been pleased had I buttered him *more geologico* to begin with. I think that at heart he must grant my *essay* does him justice but he can't forgive the omission of his name in the abstracts. If I quoted authorities in the abstracts I could not have found room for the conclusions—*which are all that an abstract should consist of.* He had no excuse for putting attacks in print when he knew the full paper was out, whilst he made no attempt to get hold of it. (I have an impression that even in the original abstract drawn up by myself and printed in the Gardener's Chronicle Watson's name is mentioned. If you have that paper bound will you refer for me to the report of the Cambridge meeting and see). I have trust further in Watson's calmer judgment and in my own theory that I feel sure he will adopt it in the end.

I must have a discussion with Darwin about these things.[86]

Six months later, after the first volume of Watson's *Cybele* had appeared, Forbes corresponded at length again with Hooker reiterating his position and agonizing over the proper mode of response.

All you say about Watson and the *Cybele* is so far from offending me that it delights me to find you speak out on the state of the case, as, conscious of not having voluntarily done injury to Watson, I am more anxious to know *exactly* how the case appears to others in order that I may avoid a wrong course in replying or noticing [?] Watson's attack. You have written me as I would write myself to any friend. Any sneers of Watson at my views I don't care about for if they be true they will not last and if not, the sooner they go to the devil the better: I believe them true—or would not have put them forward. But I am bound to offer some reply to his accusations of motives and to his misstatements (inexcusable as he knows how matters really were) respecting my doings. Our Survey volume is not a very accessible book—otherwise there would be no need for this—but there are many who will see his attack (especially since maliciously reprinted by Newman) and be completely misled as to the nature of the pretensions I put forward in my essay.

If it had occurred to me that Watson's love for personal glorification had so far exceeded his love of the search after truth, as he has shown it to be, I would with pleasure have trumpeted him to his heart's content—and not too much either for you know how highly I appreciate his labours, much more highly indeed than I can get all my botanical friends to admit. But such a notion never entered into my head and I (simply) thought that by showing how through the combination of Geology with Botany we got new clues, Watson would have been pleased. I did not call "the five floras," modifications of his—because I did not and cannot regard them as such: they being *types of external relations, his* types of *internal relations.* I never meant to substitute them for his, because both I looked upon as equally true—but as meaning different things. Moreover I do not put them forward as any new things, but as expressions of facts well known to all British Botanists. What I claimed for myself was the explanation of the causes of them—which explanation Watson—thoughtlessly, as he will find by and by—sneers at. If I have the luck at any time to get leisure and working room in Edinburgh I mean to treat the whole natural history question in similar outline though fuller form with respect to Europe generally and the borders of the ancient glacial sea. (I believe such outlines give a stimulus and direction to research) —and Watson will then find that, fiercely tho he has attacked me I can, when space and the proper place are at hand do him full honour for his special researches. But in limited essays, I do hold that space spent in butter, *more geologico,* is space mis-spent and when I wrote of his "invaluable" researches I wrote what I meant—though for that one word he wants a thousand.[87]

These letters now make the battle lines distinct. There is no question that Forbes had relied more heavily upon Watson's *Researches* for his phytogeographic data than upon any other source, and that he should have made some reference to that debt in the initial ("Endemic Plants") paper. His argument to Hooker that such papers were only "abstracts" and that there was no space in abstracts for references is not especially convincing; certainly one or two key references could have been included without adding significantly to the length of the abstract. And certainly it was not unusual for references to be included in papers presented to the British Association.

More substantive, however, was the disagreement between Forbes and Watson as to what it was in Forbes's paper (and the later essay) that was truly significant. Watson felt that the only important point was the division of the British flora into geographical groupings. This being so, Forbes had erred twice: by failing to note that Watson had accomplished the same division process ten years earlier, and by producing a set of groups demonstrably inferior to Watson's (though based largely on Watson's data). By comparison Forbes's geological hypotheses were to Watson fanciful, disprovable, and based on a misinterpretation of botanical evidence.

To Forbes, however, the priority was just the reverse. The primary thrust of his research program was geological: to establish how and when the various components of the British flora (and later, fauna) had arrived in Britain. Determining what those components were was an essential but subsidiary exercise. Moreover, the components could not be taken directly from Watson; they had to be reworked because of a change in assumptions. Where Watson's floral types were based solely on the present distribution and association of species within Britain, Forbes regarded each of his floras as being part of a temporally dependent, European grouping. The two systems would thus necessarily disagree, and any attempt to compare them directly was misguided.

In truth, Watson was probably not competent to judge of the geological aspects of Forbes's theory. And on the zoological evidence presented in the "Connexion" essay Watson had nothing to say except that it consisted of " 'facts' . . . found under water by a man not remarkably conscientious, and to whom it had become a sort of necessity to find them."[88] His perception of the issues was undoubtedly influenced by his proprietary concern for the six floral types he had labored long to determine. This labor had been little noticed or appreciated by his "unphilosophical" countrymen, who as yet attached little significance to distribution studies. Even those who had argued for more distribution research were not uniformly impressed with Watson's efforts. John Fleming, for example, reviewed the early volumes of the *Cybele* in 1854 and asserted:

> We do consider the merit of Mr. Watson, in having either in his "Remarks" or in his Cybele, distributed British plants into *types*, as of small

amount. Whoever has examined, with any degree of care, the *loca natalia* of the "Philosophica Botanica" of Linnaeus, or Adanson's preface to his "Familles des Plantes" must have been prepared for the groups exhibited in the "Cybele," especially if he followed up his researches by a study of the generalizations of Wallenberg, Wildenow [*sic*], and Humboldt. By the aid, however, of even the earlier works, our author's labours in constructing either his "Remarks" or his "Cybele," required industry rather than originality; while, under the guidance of Schow, and aided by Turner's "Botanist's Guide," the composition of his useful work became scarcely more than a mechanical operation, conducted, however, by one to whom the subject was familiar in all its bearings. We may add, that Professor E. Forbes's references to Mr. Watson's labours are decided and complimentary.[89]

For Watson then to discover that a fast-rising younger *zoologist* was suddenly gaining attention by writing on Watson's chosen subject and using his data without the least recognition would have been upsetting to men far more temperate than Watson. In addition, his discouragement may have been exacerbated by Forbes's success in constructing an historical hypothesis to account for the British flora, while his own efforts to demonstrate the evolutionary hypothesis of Lamarck had been unfruitful.

Forbes probably hoped to satisfy Watson's complaints about "Endemic Plants" with generous references to him in the "Connexion" essay. But Watson would not be placated except by a total capitulation to his interpretation of the events, so the denunciatory appendix of the *Cybele Britannica* went to press. In the final (1859) volume of the *Cybele,* published after Forbes's death, Watson made further acrimonious allusions to Forbes.[90] But in an open reference to the "Connexion" essay, with partially laudatory comments on Forbes's idea of the isolation of alpine plants, Watson's tone showed signs of softening:

Neither ought the treatise by Edward Forbes, on the supposed origin and dates of the present flora of Britain, to be wholly condemned by those who are better acquainted with the special facts of vegetable distribution in Britain and Europe, than were the geologists and general botanists, who universally committed themselves to wholesale eulogy of an essay so deceptive and inaccurate. Although blundering and false in its botanical illustrations, and perhaps not less untrue in some of its zoological assertions, that treatise by Edward Forbes may still be allowed to have evinced remarkably suggestive conceptions of science, larger and more comprehensive than those which have characterised the writings of English botanists, present or past, with extremely few exceptions.[91]

This unfortunate controversy, the first to strike the infant science of biogeography, might never have occurred but for faulty communications. Through correspondence and meetings Forbes was in touch regularly with a great many British naturalists, professional and amateur, of the 1840s, but Watson was never among them. The boisterous "Red Lions" dining sessions, which Forbes helped organize at the 1839 and subsequent British Association meetings, brought together the naturalists of the nation in a convivial atmosphere where light-hearted satire of scientific events was a featured item of the menu. Had Watson attended the 1845 meeting, an exchange of comments after Forbes's paper or during a dinner might have been the end of the affair. But Watson rarely attended association meetings, and rarely if ever the Red Lions gatherings. He was very much a peripheral member of the community of naturalists, not because of his competence or contributions but because of a preference for seclusion.

### Reception of the "Connexion" Essay

In the course of composing the "Connexion" essay, Forbes wrote that it would be "a coup d'oeil of the history of the British flora and fauna of a very novel kind."[92] The essay did indeed receive much acclaim in the late 1840s. Phrases such as "highly philosophical" and "ingenious and skillful" were used to describe it.[93] Even those who did not accept all its points regarded it as strikingly original. In his presidential address to the 1846 meeting of the British Association, Roderick Murchison gave a brief review of the essay, asserting that it would "introduce a new class of inquiries into natural history, which will link it on more closely than ever to geology and geography. In short, this paper may be viewed as the first attempt to explain the *causes* of the zoological and botanical features of any region anciently in connexion."[94] Murchison emphasized two points in the essay as being of particular value. First, the isolation theory for alpine plants explained phenomena which had long puzzled botanical geographers, a point which "even Humboldt himself" would admit. Second, Forbes's interpretation of the Pleistocene confirmed by independent evidence that the "Alpine glacialists [i.e., Agassiz and his followers] had erroneously applied their views" and that the opposing theory of glacial seas, long advocated by Murchison and other English geologists, was the correct one.[95]

Lyell was also enthusiastic about the essay, thinking it "one of the most original treatises, and so far as I have yet studied it (for I mean to read it again), one of the soundest as well as boldest that I have ever had the pleasure of pursuing."[96] He was less than pleased, however, that his own ideas on the effects of geological and climatological changes on plant and animal migration had received no citation in the essay. In a long letter to Forbes he cited a number of instances, beginning with the first edition of the *Principles,* in which his ideas had preceded Forbes's essay, in order "that you may take an opportunity on some future occasion, if you think fit, to acknowledge my labours."[97] Although Lyell was clearly disturbed about the omission of references to his work, he was almost apologetic in raising the issue: "I am perfectly aware that there is no one who is in the habit of doing more justice to any claim I may have in our science than yourself, and therefore I attribute to mere accident any omission you may have made in citing me, especially as I have no doubt you think the publicity of a work which has gone through six editions is enough to satisfy any man, and supersede tedious historical details."[98]

In his reply to Lyell, Forbes affirmed that his omissions were inadvertent. He had written the "Connexion" essay under the pressure of a deadline set for publication of the Geological Survey's first *Memoir,* and in the process had lost two crucial months to illness. At the same time he had been preparing two sets of lectures and overseeing the two-volume *Travels in Lycia* through the press:

Under such circumstances many references I should have liked to quote were lost sight of and omitted. . . . The plan of my essay was purely *inductive,* and consequently did not admit of more citation than was absolutely necessary for my purpose. . . . It was my wish to have appended notes and extracts in an appendix, and to have given a bibliography of the scientific literature bearing upon the subjects treated of. In this way I could have done the fullest justice to everyone who had touched upon them; but illness and the printers prevented the fulfillment of the intention."[99]

Forbes added that he wished he had recalled Lyell's discussion of the climate and geology in relation to the Sicilian Mollusca, as it would have substantiated his own argument. But in general, references to the *Principles* ought not to be necessary, he thought, for the very reason that the work was so widely known and regarded.

> There cannot be a warmer admirer or more grateful pupil of your 'Principles' than myself. I have read every edition, and most often over; and much that I have done has grown up from the seed sown by you. My not quoting them oftener, however, is not an accident, but because I did not consider allusions to them necessary. I wrote for naturalists and geologists—who are, or ought to be, as familiar with them as myself.[100]

The following year (1847) Leonard Horner reviewed the essay at length in his presidential address to the Geological Society. Horner drew attention to Forbes's debt to Lyell on the subject, but nevertheless praised the essay as an "admirable example of the light to be derived from other branches of natural history in the prosecution of geological inquiries . . . so interesting and attractive throughout, so suggestive of great views."[101] In general, geologists were the most appreciative of the "Connexion" essay. The immediate reactions of biologists are less well recorded, perhaps because so few of them had until this time been concerned with biogeography. Only the responses of Hooker and Darwin are well documented. Hooker became an advocate of land-bridge theorizing during the 1850s, employing it to explain the discontinuous distribution of plants in the southern oceans. In volume 2 (*Flora Novae-Zelandiae*) of *The Botany of the Antarctic Voyage of H.M. Discovery Ships "Erebus" and "Terror,"* Hooker described the "Connexion" essay as "the most original and able essay that has ever appeared on this subject [plant distribution and migration], and though I cannot subscribe to all its botanical details, I consider that the mode of reasoning adopted is sound, and of universal application."[102]

Darwin, however, was adamant in his objections to land-bridge theories from the beginning. In general his criticisms were two. First, his knowledge of, and fascination with, natural means of transport immediately provoked him to question Forbes's initial assumption of their inadequacy. He realized that Forbes's geological hypotheses might stimulate geologists, but they could also hinder biological research. In 1860 he wrote to Lyell: "I quite agree in admiration of Forbes' Essay, yet, on my life, I think it has done, in some respects, as much mischief as good. Those who believe in vast continental extensions will never investigate means of distribution."[103] Secondly, Darwin did not see sufficient geological evidence to support the fluctuations in the relative levels of land and sea of the degree and rapidity required by Forbes. He did not deny the possibility of continental elevation and subsidence, of course, but he insisted that the available geological evidence did not independently confirm the existence of the continental extensions Forbes had hypothesized as paths of migration.[104]

Correspondence between Forbes and Darwin during the period when Forbes was composing the "Connexion" essay indicates that Forbes attempted to answer all of Darwin's objections.[105] Darwin remained unconvinced, but he admitted to Hooker that "I the more regret Forbes cannot more satisfactorily prove his views, as I heartily wish they were established, and to a limited extent I fully believe they are true; but his boldness is astounding."[106] Darwin realized that if the existence of land bridges could be proved, many biogeographic questions would be settled and the doctrine of *multiple* centers of creation for each species (which both he and Forbes opposed) could be finally discredited.[107] But he could not give in to land-bridge theorizing on those grounds alone.

## Migrationists and Extensionists

By 1850 the "Connexion" essay was well known at home and abroad. Despite a variety of criticisms of it, Forbes remained confident: "I intend to reply to D'Archiac in full, sooner or later," he wrote Lyell, "but am waiting till a sufficient number of objectors to my views have come forward. Watson (who is curiously enough cited as the originator of views against which he has violently and malignantly protested, being crazy), Grisebach, C. Martens [*sic*], D'Archiac and Agassiz have all now written against them and it will be much less trouble to answer all in a batch than to fight them singly. Their arguments are easily enough upset."[108] He continued to advocate land-bridge views for the remaining four years of his life, though he published no further extensive works on the subject. He did pursue additional biogeographic evidence to support his ideas about the northward and southward movements of marine invertebrates as a consequence of changes in geography and climate.[109] In this regard Robert M'Andrew provided him with dredging data on a remnant ("outlier") deep-water fauna off the coast of Spain which included many British species. Forbes regarded this data as an extremely significant confirmation of his theory of an ancient Irish-Spanish connection.[110]

The vogue of land-bridge hypotheses reached a peak in the late 1850s and early sixties, and is thus beyond the period of the present study. But as it is one of the most fascinating episodes in the history of biogeography and has never been adequately recounted, an outline of the principal developments will make a fitting contrast to the lethargic state of distribution studies at the beginning of the century, whence we began this discussion.

In his much acclaimed treatise *Geographie Botanique Raisonnée* (1855), Alphonse De Candolle adopted Forbes's hypothesis of a Miocene extension of the European continent to the Azores and Canaries.[111] The following year Oswald Heer extended the Tertiary peninsula all the way to America. Many plant species of the Azores, Madeira, and the Canaries, he insisted, were "American types,"[112] as were some land snails and insects. He noted further that in Matthew Maury's recent bathymetric map of the Atlantic[113] there was a "vast maritime plateau" on either side of a valley crossing the ocean between twenty and forty degrees north latitude. This submarine plateau connected "the Atlantic islands, as well as the whole space between the European continent, Newfoundland and Acadia." Judging from the facts of biogeography, Heer claimed, "we must admit that during the miocene period the maritime plateau . . . was solid ground"—an "ancient Atlantis," he called it.[114]

In America Asa Gray countered Heer's explanation with the suggestion that the migration route of plants from America to Europe had been across Asia, not over an Atlantic land bridge.[115] But "Atlantis" continued to spread. In 1860 "the sunken island of Atlantis" was the topic of a lecture by the prominent professor of botany at the University of Vienna, Franz Unger. To Unger the similarities between the Tertiary flora of Europe and the present flora of North America and the Atlantic islands demonstrated unmistakably "some connection or other" in the past. Agents of transport like winds, waves, and migratory animals were just not a satisfactory explanation for the similarities:

> The number of species diffused in this way is a very limited one, and can never reach a sufficiently high figure to influence the character of the vegetation of a foreign country. The plants imported by wind and waves always remain more or less strangers, or rather curiosities, which never mix properly with the natives of the soil, and show by their very look that they are intruders. . . .
>
> All these considerations force us to the conclusion that there must have been a continental connection. *In the Tertiary period, or at the time when lignite was formed, Europe must have been connected with North America, and the Atlantic Ocean must have been divided at one place or another by a continent.*[116]

Unger imagined this continent to extend from Iceland in the north to the Azores and Canaries in the south. But when it came to defining specific coastlines, he demurred.

> At present it is impossible to speak more precisely on this subject. Perhaps a more accurate definition of the extent and connection of this central continent might be given by availing ourselves of the well-known soundings taken in the Atlantic Ocean; but it would always be a difficult and dangerous undertaking, and we might be thrown by the waves of this treacherous ocean of speculation from one hidden rock upon the other.[117]

Although cautious about geographic details, Under did not hesitate to associate this new Atlantis with the legendary Atlantis civilization of Plato's *Timaeus*. How could that ancient tradition be "entirely imaginary," he asked rhetorically, "since we have shown that its most important substratum is sound, and that at one time a continent did exist in the Atlantic Ocean."[118] He admitted that there was a discrepancy of timing, for the Tertiary age of geologists was presumed to have long preceded the advent of man. But he predicted that "the united efforts of philologists and naturalists" would resolve this difficulty.

Unger's lecture may have been the most speculative offshoot of the "Connexion" essay, but it was hardly the last. Meanwhile, in

1856 Darwin, who was then laboring over the biogeographic portions of the *Origin*, became embroiled in discussions with Lyell and Hooker over the reality and efficacy of land bridges. Darwin insisted upon remaining a "migrationist," or advocate of natural transport, and referred to Lyell and Hooker as "continentalists" or "extensionists" for their continued support of theories involving continental extension. When new works of the extensionist ilk appeared, such as those by S. P. Woodward and T. V. Wollaston, Darwin's agitation increased.[119] As he wrote to Lyell,

My blood gets hot with passion and turns cold alternately at the geological strides, which many of your disciples are taking.

Here, poor Forbes made a continent to North America and another (or the same) to the Gulf weed; Hooker makes one from New Zealand to South America and round the World to Kerguelen Land. Here is Wollaston speaking of Madeira and P. Santo "as the sure and certain witnesses of a former continent." Here is Woodward writes [*sic*] to me, if you grant a continent over 200 or 300 miles of ocean depths (as if that was nothing), why not extend a continent to every island in the Pacific and Atlantic Oceans? And all this within the existence of recent species! If you do not stop this, if there be a lower region for the punishment of geologists, I believe, my great master, you will go there. Why, your disciples in a slow and creeping manner beat all the old Catastrophists who ever lived. You will live to be the great chief of the Catastrophists.[120]

Darwin detailed his objections to extensionism in letters to Lyell and Hooker but won no immediate converts.

In the mid-1860s the extensionists were still growing in numbers. Hooker wrote to Darwin in 1866 that the camp of Forbes's followers included Heer and Unger, George Hartung, Wollaston, R. T. Lowe, Andrew Murray, and possibly Alfred Russell Wallace.[121] By this time, however, Hooker had begun to doubt his own extensionist position. In preparing a review of the arguments for a talk before the British Association at Nottingham, he felt uncomfortable about taking either side, but finally leaned toward Darwin and migrationism.[122] Fifteen years later, in another address to the association, he felt more confident in taking Darwin's position. Summing up the history of the study of geographical distribution, Hooker reflected: "As Humboldt was its founder, and Forbes its reformer, so we must regard Darwin as its latest and greatest lawgiver."[123]

## Conclusion

Hooker's loss of faith in extensionist arguments was due in great measure to the oceanic soundings made during the *Challenger* expedition.[124] Unlimited continental extensions could not be supported once the basic topography of the ocean bottom was established. But the formulation of land-bridge hypotheses did not cease altogether. More cautious use of Forbes's method of theorizing, in support of more modest claims, continued into the twentieth century.[125] And given the recent developments in continental drift and plate tectonics research, it appears that the victory of Darwin and the migrationists may have been, indeed, only partial.[126] Current tectonic theory indicates, for example, that the African and South American continents were joined and, therefore, that biogeographic continuity existed probably as late as the Jurassic period (ca. 150 million years ago), and that land migration between the temperate climes of Europe and North America was possible even later. This timing, of course, is considerably earlier than Forbes and the extensionists had envisioned. But it substantiates the principle, championed by Forbes in the "Connexion" essay, that our understanding of the movements of plants and animals in past eras need not be dictated absolutely by the present configuration of the oceans and continents.

When the nineteenth century began, the "distribution of organized beings in space and time" was an unknown phrase, and the subject matter it designated drew only occasional speculations. By the 1840s Forbes and Watson had become the acknowledged leaders of the British assault on the subject, and the subject itself had become synonymous with philosophical natural history. Their syntheses incorporated the zoological, botanical, and paleontological findings of a batallion of less philosophical but nevertheless essential collectors. In the latter half of the century the biogeographic preeminence of Forbes and Watson was eclipsed by that of Wallace and Hooker. With the tool of Darwinism, solutions to the puzzles of historical biogeography came much more easily. The wonder is, perhaps, that in the pre-*Origin* years Forbes and Watson saw the puzzles, if not the solutions, as clearly as they did.

# 6

# *A Darwinian Epilogue*

This inquiry into the early-nineteenth-century vogue of idealism and distribution studies has demonstrated (if indeed any demonstration was necessary) the richness and complexity of British contributions to natural history in the pre-*Origin* era. British efforts to acquire and promulgate the thought of earlier Continental naturalists were manifold. And by the 1840s outright modifications of imported ideas and the creation of entirely original concepts and lines of research became frequent. After a century of collecting, naming, and arranging —and little else—British naturalists were returning to the theoretical frame of mind of their late-seventeenth-century forebears.

The age of philosophical natural history began in the 1820s, first with the Pythagorean efforts of William MacLeay and the quinarians to create a circular system of taxonomy, and then with Robert Knox's aspiration of reforming British comparative anatomy by teaching the transcendental precepts of Geoffroy and the Naturphilosophen. The quinarian quest had become moribund by the end of the 1830s; transcendentalism, however, was then just beginning to win devotees. Richard Owen and Edward Forbes soon became the leaders of the transcendental movement, but numerous other naturalists, many with connections to Knox and/or Edinburgh, were drawn into the seemingly profound possibilities of science based on a priori patterns. The original stimulus for this movement can be found in the philosophy of transcendental idealism developed by Immanuel Kant in late-eighteenth-century Germany. It seems, however, that most British naturalists cared little or understood little of the complexities of Kant's true teachings. Their idealism was more Platonic—justified by a belief that their God had created nature in accordance with simple, unifying concepts of geometry and logic, not by the argument that their minds invoked such concepts involuntarily in the act of perceiving nature. Thus, while the Romantic revival of idealism in general must be attributed to Kant, the idealism that British naturalists subsequently came to appreciate was from more familiar sources: Plato and Henry More.

It was in the 1830s, too, that the British biogeographic tradition arose. Buoyed by the enthusiasm of the British Association and the Humboldtian urge to anatomize statistically the earth's surface, naturalists began to concern themselves with the spatial and then the temporal placement of God's creatures. Here, too, patterns were perceived. But only rarely, as in Forbes's suggestion of fossil polarity, were these patterns regarded as manifestations of Divine or a priori ideas. They came to be explained, first, in terms of ecological parameters and, later, as the result of the geographic or climatological accidents of the geological past. Forbes and Hewett Watson, acting under the inspiration of John Fleming and Charles Lyell, organized research programs which were models for their generation.

The subsequent fortunes of the transcendental and biogeographic movements could hardly have been more diverse. After the appearance of M'Cosh's and Dickie's *Typical Forms and Special Ends* in 1856, idealism was all but forgotten. By then Forbes, Swainson, Brown, and Barry were dead, while Owen and Carpenter had been drawn to other research problems. When in 1857 Knox penned his essay "Zoology: Its Present Phasis and Future Prospects,"[1] he prophesied a coming "renaissance" in which transcendentalism would reign over natural history. But this was his last contribution to the transcendental tradition. The following year a renaissance did indeed begin, but it was the renaissance initiated by the reading of the papers of Darwin and Wallace at the Linnean Society. Acceptance of the evolutionary theory spelled the demise of transcendental natural history, at least for the nineteenth century. The most fundamental of the transcendentalists' doctrines, the unity of type, was no longer a principle of Divine design or a category of the mind. "Unity of type," as Darwin pointed out in the *Origin*, "is explained by unity of descent."[2] Similarly, the concept of homologous structures among different species, arising from the unity of type according to the transcendentalist, was redefined by the Darwinist to be the result of common ancestry.[3]

Knox saw nothing new in Darwin's theory and opposed it adamantly. A few naturalists who had subscribed to transcendental doctrines in their younger days, like Huxley and Carpenter and even M'Cosh, became supporters of Darwinism. But most remained opposed to evolutionary theories. Owen's opposition is well known. Goodsir, though less vocal, was equally negative. He brought the subject before his anatomy students in 1862:

> No one would be inclined to deny that the general aspects of the human body, and the body of a higher ape, resemble one another more than do the aspects of the frames of the highest and the lowest ape. But I have, I trust, satisfied you that the human body presents a whole series of perfected arrangements of structure, bearing immediately on the higher conscious or rational principle of man—arrangements which are deficient in all apes alike, and which thus collectively, by their absence, distinguish all the apes from man corporeally as precisely as their instinctive form of consciousness separates them from man psychically.[4]

As was so often the case, the relationship of mankind to the rest of animated nature was, in Goodsir's eyes, the great stumbling block for theories of descent. Transcendental theory, on the other hand, encountered no such difficulties.

Darwin, for his part, was at all times antagonistic toward idealistic explanations. Of Forbes's fossil "polarity" he wrote Hooker that it "makes me sick—it is like 'magnetism' turning a table."[5] But as much as Darwin devalued transcendentalist explanations for the order in nature, it must be recognized that he, like the transcendentalists, was searching for an alternative to teleological explanations for nature's order. Moreover, his disgust with "polarities" and other such abstractions made him all the more eager to work out and defend his case for natural selection.

In contrast to the fate of transcendentalism, distribution studies contributed directly to Darwin's program. The anomalous distribution of finches and tortoises in the Galapagos had, after all, been a key stimulus to his first questioning of the doctrine of special creation in the 1830s. The subject was again at the forefront of his thought in 1856 while he composed his "big book,"[6] and it occupied two substantial chapters in the 1859 "abstract." The *Origin*, in turn, gave new meaning and fresh energy to biogeographic research.

The history of biogeography (both descriptive and historical) in the later nineteenth century is yet to be written.[7] The continuing interest in the subject shown by Darwin and Lyell and the major advances fashioned by Wallace, Hooker, and Sclater (to cite only the most prominent British workers) demonstrate, however, that the efforts of Forbes and Watson inaugurated a research tradition of lasting significance.

But the age of "philosophical natural history" had ended. Shorn of transcendentalism and reclothed in the theory of descent with modification, philosophical natural history was transformed into Darwinian biology. The "philosophical naturalist"—the term and the man—concluded thirty years of highest respectability by quickly becoming an anachronism.

So, while biogeography became well integrated into the fabric of post-*Origin* biology, the predilections of naturalists which led John Theodore Merz to describe the early nineteenth century as the "morphological period"[8] were, by 1860, all but snuffed out. But the passing of idealism was not a death, only an eclipse. Advocates of morphology, in both pure and hybrid forms, have reemerged in the twentieth century with D'Arcy Thompson leading the way.[9] In view of the repeated appearances which idealism has made throughout the history of scientific thought, one might well ask if they are related to shifts in the attitude or world view of the broader culture. The positivistic and scientistic sentiments which bloomed in the Victorian era and survived into our own century seem generally to have been antagonistic toward idealism in science. Conversely, the disillusion and hostility toward science and technology which have surfaced in the latter half of the twentieth century may spawn a new form of idealism in science,[10] just as Kant's idealism was a response to dissatisfactions with the established Newtonian, analytic science of the late eighteenth century. The parallel is not altogether absurd. Our increasingly incomprehensible space-age technologies, accompanied by political disorder and environmental transfiguration, all had late-eighteenth-century analogues. Perhaps the next episode of scientific idealism will have its roots in, for example, modern developments in Eastern philosophy, with additional nutrients being supplied by relativity theory, ecology, psychology, or parapsychology. The twenty-first century may see a new Naturphilosophie.

*Notes*
*Bibliography*
*Index*

# Notes

## Abbreviations

A few of the more frequently cited sources have been abbreviated in the notes and bibliography as follows:

| | |
|---|---|
| *Ann. Mag. Nat. Hist.* | *Annals and Magazine of Natural History* |
| *DNB* | *Dictionary of National Biography* |
| *DSB* | *Dictionary of Scientific Biography* |
| *Edinb. New Phil. J.* | *Edinburgh New Philosophical Journal* |
| *Hist. Sci.* | *History of Science* |
| *J. Hist. Biol.* | *Journal of the History of Biology* |
| *Mem. Geol. Surv.* | *Memoirs of the Geological Survey of Great Britain* |
| *Phil. Trans.* | *Philosophical Transactions of the Royal Society of London* |
| *Proc. Roy. Inst.* | *Proceedings of the Royal Institution of Great Britain* |
| *Proc. Roy. Soc. Edinb.* | *Proceedings of the Royal Society of Edinburgh* |
| *Proc. Roy. Soc. Lond.* | *Proceedings of the Royal Society of London* |
| *Q.J. Geol. Soc.* | *Quarterly Journal of the Geological Society of London* |

199

| | |
|---|---|
| *Rpt. Brit. Assn.* | *Reports of the British Association for the Advancement of Science* |
| *Trans. Bot. Soc. Edinb.* | *Transactions of the Botanical Society of Edinburgh* |
| *Trans. Roy. Soc. Edinb.* | *Transactions of the Royal Society of Edinburgh* |

## Introduction

1  Charles Darwin, *Journal of Researches into the Geology and Natural History of the various countries visited by H.M.S. "Beagle"* . . . (London: Henry Colburn, 1839; facsimile reprint, New York: Hafner Publishing Co., 1952), p. 210. Italics mine. In later editions, this section was revised and the phrase "philosophical naturalist" was omitted.

2  Robert Knox, ed. and trans., "The Comparative Osteography of the Skeleton and Dentar System, in the Five Classes of Vertebral Animals, Recent and Fossil," by Henri Marie DeBlainville, *Lancet,* October 1839, p. 138. Italics mine.

3  Charles Darwin and Alfred Russel Wallace, *Evolution by Natural Selection* (Cambridge: Cambridge University Press, 1958), p. 36; Gertrude Himmelfarb, *Darwin and the Darwinian Revolution* (Gloucester, Mass.: Peter Smith, 1967), p. 196.

4  Ralph Waldo Emerson to Samuel Brown, 23 July 1848, Edinburgh University Library MS Dc.2.76/22.

5  *Life and Letters of Thomas Henry Huxley,* ed. Leonard Huxley, 2 vols. (London: Macmillan, 1900), 1:94.

6  For a fascinating survey of the entire British natural history tradition, see David Elliston Allen, *The Naturalist in Britain: A Social History* (London: Allen Lane, 1976).

7  Charles Babbage, *Reflections on the Decline of Science in England and on Some of its Causes* (London: B. Fellows, 1830).

8  *Life and Letters of Sir Joseph Dalton Hooker,* ed. Leonard Huxley, 2 vols. (New York: D. Appleton & Co., 1918), 2:298.

9  See John C. Greene, "Reflections on the Progress of Darwin Studies," *J. Hist. Biol.* 8 (1975): 243–273; Bert J. Loewenberg, "Darwin and Darwin Studies, 1959–1963," *Hist. Sci.* 4 (1965):15–54.

10  James Grierson, "General Observations on Geology and Geognosy, and the Nature of These Respective Studies," *Memoirs of the Wernerian Society* 5 (1823–25):408–9.

11  Robert Knox, "Contributions to the Philosophy of Zoology," *Zoologist* 13 (1855):4837.
12  William B. Carpenter, *Principles of Comparative Physiology*, 4th ed. (Philadelphia: Blanchard and Lea, 1854), p. 33. Italics are Carpenter's.
13  The Bridgewater Treatises were a series of eight books published between 1833 and 1836, commissioned by the eighth earl of Bridgewater, to illustrate the "power, wisdom, and goodness of God" with the latest evidence from science.
14  Two recent articles have inaugurated the study of this idealist version of the argument from design: Peter J. Bowler, "Darwinism and the Argument from Design: Suggestions for a Re-evaluation," *J. Hist. Biol.* 10 (1977):29–43; and Dov Ospovat, "Perfect Adaptation and Teleological Explanation: Approaches to the Problem of the History of Life in the Mid-Nineteenth Century," *Studies in History of Biology* 2 (1978):33–56.
15  Joseph Hooker to Charles Darwin, 28 September 1845, Cambridge University Library, Darwin Papers, vol. 100, fols. 71–72. Italics mine.
16  The absence of any such society in the nineteenth century may well be a major reason for the neglect of ecology and biogeography by twenty-century historians of British science, in comparison to the great attention paid to the geological side of distribution studies. For the latter, see esp. Martin J. S. Rudwick, *The Meaning of Fossils: Episodes in the History of Palaeontology*, 2nd ed. (New York: Neale Watson Academic Publications, 1976); Peter J. Bowler, *Fossils and Progress: Paleontology and the Idea of Progressive Evolution in the Nineteenth Century* (New York: Neale Watson Academic Publications, 1976); and Roy Porter, *The Making of Geology: Earth Science in Britain, 1660–1815* (Cambridge: Cambridge University Press, 1977). Similar assessments of biogeography and ecology have not reached print as of this writing, but two are expected: Janet Browne, "C. R. Darwin and J. D. Hooker: Episodes in the History of Plant Geography, 1840–1860" (Ph.D. diss., University of London, 1978); and Frank N. Egerton, *Hewett C. Watson, a Victorian Scientist* (in preparation).
17  Historians of the physical sciences have been more attentive to the influence of idealism in early Victorian science than have their biological counterparts. See esp. L. Pearce Williams, *Michael Faraday* (New York: Simon & Schuster, 1971), and *The Origins of Field Theory* (New York: Random House, 1966); Joseph Agassi, *Faraday as a Natural Philosopher* (Chicago: University of Chicago Press, 1971); Robert C. Stauffer, "Speculation and Experiment in the Background of

Oersted's Discovery of Electromagnetism," *Isis* 48 (1957):33–50; D. M. Knight, "The Physical Sciences and the Romantic Movement," *Hist. Sci.* 9 (1970):54–75; and Walter F. Cannon, "History in Depth: The Early Victorian Period," *Hist. Sci.* 3 (1965):20–38.

## Chapter 1: The Continental Background

1   See Paul Farber, "The Type-Concept in Zoology during the First Half of the Nineteenth Century," *J. Hist. Biol.* 9 (1976):93–119.

2   The classic treatment of the philosophical conflicts of this period is E. A. Burtt, *The Metaphysical Foundations of Modern Science* (New York: Harcourt, Brace & Co., 1925; rev. ed., 1932).

3   Extensive discussions of Kant's scientific outlook may be found in Gerd Buchdahl, *Metaphysics and the Philosophy of Science, The Classical Origins: Descartes to Kant* (Oxford: Basil Blackwell, 1969); and Gordon G. Brittan, Jr., *Kant's Theory of Science* (Princeton: Princeton University Press, 1978).

4   See Donald Worster, *Nature's Economy: The Roots of Ecology* (San Francisco: Sierra Club Books, 1977), chap. 4.

5   For discussions of the ethos of Naturphilosophie, see Alexander Gode-von Aesch, *Natural Science in German Romanticism* (New York: Columbia University Press, 1941); L. Pearce Williams, "Kant, *Naturphilosophie*, and Scientific Method," in Ronald N. Giere and Richard S. Westfall, eds., *Foundations of Scientific Method: The Nineteenth Century* (Bloomington: Indiana University Press, 1973), pp. 3–22; Barry Gower, "Speculation in Physics: The History and Practice of *Naturphilosophie,*" *Studies in History and Philosophy of Science*, 3 (1973):301–56; Walter D. Wetzels, "Aspects of Natural Science in German Romanticism," *Studies in Romanticism*, 10 (1971):44–59; and Timothy Lenoir, "Generational Factors in the Origin of *Romantische Naturphilosophie,*" *J. Hist. Biol.* 11 (1978):57–100.

6   See above, Introduction, n. 17.

7   The idea of nature as a single, hierarchical series of species, rising from rocks and minerals up through plants and animals to man, was a popular belief from Plato through the Neoplatonists and Leibniz to the eighteenth century, as A. O. Lovejoy demonstrated in his classic essay *The Great Chain of Being* (Cambridge: Cambridge University Press, 1936). H. B. Nisbet, (*Goethe and the Scientific Tradition,* Publications of the Institute of Germanic Studies, vol. 14 [London: University of London, 1972], pp. 6–12) argues that Goethe's belief in

the great chain of being was influenced mainly by his reading of Charles Bonnet's *Contemplation de la nature* (1764).

8    J. W. von Goethe, *Versuch, die Metamorphose der Pflanzen zu erklaren* (Gothe, 1790), trans. Agnes Arber as "Goethe's Botany," *Chronica Botanica* 10 (1946):63–126. See also Arber's distinguished study of plant morphology, *The Natural Philosophy of Plant Form* (Cambridge: Cambridge University Press, 1950), pp. 40–46, 59; and C. S. Sherrington, *Goethe on Nature and on Science*, 2nd ed. (Cambridge: Cambridge University Press, 1949), pp. 19–23; J. H. F. Kohlbrugge "Historisch-Kristische Studien über Goethe als Naturforscher," *Zoologische Annalen* 5 (1913):82–228; Frank J. Lipp, "Goethe the Botanist," *Garden Journal* 25, no. 1 (1975):2–9. For a review of more recent contributions and reactions to idealistic plant morphology in the Goethean tradition, see Richard H. Eyde, "The Foliar Theory of the Flower," *American Scientist* 63 (1975):430–37. An especially useful discussion of the ideal type, or *Urtyp*, concept is in Lenoir's "Generational Factors" (n. 5, above).

9    The term *morphologie* was in fact coined by Goethe and appeared in his diaries as early as 1796; see George A. Wells, "Goethe and Evolution," *Journal of the History of Ideas* 28 (1967):537–50.

10    F. J. Cole, *A History of Comparative Anatomy from Aristotle to the Eighteenth Century* (London: Macmillan, 1944), pp. 467–68.

11    E. S. Russell, *Form and Function: A Contribution to the History of Animal Morphology* (London: John Murray, 1916), p. 206. I have depended heavily on this classic study, an invaluable guide to understanding the development of comparative anatomy and morphology in this period, and on the historical sections of Richard Owen's *On the Archetype and Homologies of the Vertebrate Skeleton* (London: John Van Voorst, 1848), pp. 72–80. Also, R. O[wen], "Oken, Lorenz," *Encyclopaedia Brittannica*, 9th ed. (1884).

12    William Coleman, *Georges Cuvier, Zoologist: A Study in the History of Evolution Theory* (Cambridge: Harvard University Press, 1964), p. 7.

13    Étienne Geoffroy Saint-Hilaire, *Philosophie anatomique*, 2 vols. (Paris: Mequignon-Marvis, 1818; privately printed by the author, 1822).

14    See Owsei Temkin, "The Idea of Descent in Post-Romantic German Biology: 1848–1858," in Bentley Glass et al., eds., *Forerunners of Darwin, 1745–1859* (Baltimore: Johns Hopkins Press, 1959), pp. 323–55; two essays by Arthur O. Lovejoy, "Kant and Evolution" and "Herder: Progressionism without Transformation," ibid., pp. 173–221; and Arber, *Natural Philosophy of Plant Form*, p. 59.

15    Russell, *Form and Function*, pp. 66–69. J. F. Meckel was also appar-

ently a limited transmutationist, though his belief in transforming forces within the organism would seem to place him closer to Lamarck than Geoffroy; see ibid., pp. 92–93, 228.

16   The divergence of Cuvier's and Geoffroy's views was no mere matter of details but a conflict of philosophies. As Russell emphasized (*Form and Function,* p. 78), "The contrast between the teleological attitude, with its insistence on the priority of function to structure, and the morphological attitude, with its conviction of the priority of structure to function, is one of the most fundamental in biology."

17   See Toby A. Appel, "The Cuvier-Geoffroy Debate and the Structure of Nineteenth-Century French Zoology" (Ph.D. diss., Princeton University, 1975); Michel Guédes, "Goethe et Geoffroy Saint-Hilaire," *Histoire et Nature* 3 (1973):27–45.

18   William H. Austin, "More, Henry," *DSB;* P. M. Rattansi, "Cudworth, Ralph," *DSB;* Burtt, *Metaphysical Foundations,* chap. 5; William B. Hunter, Jr., "The Seventeenth-Century Doctrine of Plastic Nature," *Harvard Theological Review* 43 (1950):197–213.

19   See Timothy Lenoir, "The Göttingen School and the Development of Transcendental Naturphilosophie in the Romantic Era," *Studies in History of Biology* 5 (1981):111–205; and E. S. Shaffer, "Coleridge and Natural Philosophy: A Review of Recent Literary and Historical Research," *Hist. Sci.* 12 (1974):284–98.

20   See Susan F. Cannon, *Science in Culture: The Early Victorian Period* (New York: Science History Publications, 1978), chap. 2; H. Aarsleff, "Locke's Reputation in Nineteenth-Century England," *Monist* 55 (1971):392–422; J. B. Schneewind, "Sidgwick and the Cambridge Moralists," *Monist* 58 (1974):371–404. For a general survey of Romanticism in England, see F. Copleston, *A History of Philosophy* (Garden City, N.Y.: Image Books, 1967), vol. 8, pt. 1, chap. 6.

21   William Whewell, *Philosophy of the Inductive Sciences,* 2 vols. (London: John W. Parker, 1840). See Robert E. Butts, ed., *William Whewell's Theory of Scientific Method* (Pittsburgh: University of Pittsburgh Press, 1968), pp. 5–6. Richard Yeo has argued that Whewell's idealist philosophy of science arose from theological motivations, especially the desire to reconcile the Christian belief in the spiritual nature of the mind with the materialist search for scientific knowledge; see his article "William Whewell, Natural Theology, and the Philosophy of Science in Mid-Nineteenth-Century Britain," *Annals of Science* 36 (1979):493–516. The influence of Kant in Whewell's philosophy is discussed in Robert Blanché, *Le Rationalisme de Whewell* (Paris:

Librairie Félix Alcan, 1935); and G. C. Seward, *Die Theoretische Philosophie William Whewells und der Kantische Einfluss* (Tübingen: Christian Gulde, 1938).

22  See, for example, E. W. Strong, "William Whewell and John Stuart Mill: Their Controversy about Scientific Knowledge," *Journal of the History of Ideas* 16 (1955):209–31.

23  George Simonds Boulger, "MacLeay, William Sharp," *DNB;* [George Busk], obituary for W. S. MacLeay, *Proceedings of the Linnean Society of London,* 1864–65, pp. c–ciii.

24  W. S. MacLeay, *Horae Entomolgicae; or, Essays on the Annulose Animals,* 1 vol. in 2 pts. (London: S. Bagster, 1819–21). Mary P. Winsor has treated the complexities of quinarianism at greater length in her authoritative *Starfish, Jellyfish, and the Order of Life: Issues in Nineteenth-Century Science* (New Haven: Yale University Press, 1976), pp. 81–97.

25  W. S. MacLeay, "Remarks on the Comparative Anatomy of certain Birds of Cuba, with a view to their respective Places in the System of Nature or to their Relations with other Animals," *Transactions of the Linnean Society* 16 (1833):9. This paper was read before the society in 1826–27.

26  See Leonard Jenyns, "Report on the Recent Progress and Present State of Zoology," *Rpt. Brit. Assn.,* 1834, pp. 152–57.

27  See John Lindley, "Some Account of the Spherical and Numerical System of Nature of M. Elias Fries," *Philosophical Magazine* 68 (1826):81–91, a translated abstract from E. M. Fries, *Systema Orbis Vegetabilis* (Lund: Typographia Academica, 1825); W. S. MacLeay, "Remarks on the Identity of Certain General Laws Which Have Been Lately Observed to Regulate the Natural Distribution of Insects and Fungi," *Transactions of the Linnean Society of London* 14 (1822):46–68.

28  William Swainson, *A Treatise on the Geography and Classification of Animals* (London: Longman, Rees, Orme, Brown, Green & Longman, 1835), pp. 201–99. See also Swainson's "On the Series of Nature, and on the Relations of Animals: Remarks Occasioned by a Review of the Preliminary Discourse on Natural History," *Entomological Magazine* 3 (1835):1–12, in which he cites over a dozen prominent adherents to the circular theory.

29  Edward Newman, *Sphinx Vespiformis: An Essay* (London: F. Westley and A. H. Davis, 1832); idem, "Further Observations on the Septenary System," *Entomological Magazine* 4 (1837):234–51.

30  Winsor, *Starfish, Jellyfish,* p. 87; Huxley, *Life and Letters of Hooker,*

1:84. For a contemporary critique of the quinary system, see Peter Rylands, "On the Quinary, or Natural, System of M'Leay, Swainson, Vigors, &c.," *Magazine of Natural History* 9 (1836):130–38, 175–82.

## Chapter 2: Robert Knox

1   On scientific and social aspects of the Scottish Enlightenment period, see the following: J. B. Morrell, "Reflections on the History of Scottish Science," *Hist. Sci.* 12 (1974):81–94, and "The University of Edinburgh in the Late Eighteenth Century: Its Scientific Eminence and Academic Structure," *Isis* 62 (1971):158–71; Steven Shapin, "Property, Patronage, and the Politics of Science: The Founding of the Royal Society of Edinburgh," *British Journal for the History of Science* 7 (1974):1–41, and "The Audience for Science in Eighteenth Century Edinburgh," *Hist. Sci.* 12 (1974):95–121; J. R. R. Christie, "The Rise and Fall of Scottish Science," in M. Crosland, ed., *The Emergence of Science in Western Europe* (London: Macmillan, 1976), pp. 111–26, and "The Origins and Development of the Scottish Scientific Community, 1680–1760," *Hist. Sci.* 12 (1974):122–41; John Clive, "The Social Background of the Scottish Renaissance," in N. T. Phillipson and Rosalind Mitchison, eds., *Scotland in the Age of Improvement: Essays in Scottish History in the Eighteenth Century* (Edinburgh: University Press, 1970), pp. 225–44; N. T. Phillipson, "Culture and Society in the Eighteenth-Century Province: The Case of Edinburgh and the Scottish Enlightenment," in Lawrence Stone, ed., *The University in Society* (Princeton: Princeton University Press, 1974), 2:407–48; Douglas Young, *Edinburgh in the Age of Sir Walter Scott* (Norman: University of Oklahoma Press, 1965); Michael Joyce, *Edinburgh: The Golden Age, 1769–1832* (London: Longmans, Green and Co., 1951); John Anderson, *A History of Edinburgh* (Edinburgh: A. Fullerton and Co., 1856).

2   René Wellek, *Immanuel Kant in England, 1793–1838* (Princeton: Princeton University Press, 1931), pp. 3–11, 32, 40–44, 51, 62, 255. See also William Ralph Inge, *The Platonic Tradition in English Religious Thought* (New York: Longmans, Green and Co., 1926).

3   See Morrell, "The University of Edinburgh"; John D. Comrie, *History of Scottish Medicine*, 2nd ed., 2 vols. (London: Wellcome Historical Medical Museum, 1932); Vern Bullough and Bonnie Bullough, "The Causes of the Scottish Medical Renaissance of the Eighteenth Century," *Bulletin of the History of Medicine* 45 (1971):13–28.

4   Alexander Monro *primus, Essay on Comparative Anatomy* (London: J.

Nourse, 1744). These lectures were published anonymously by a student apparently without Monro's consent; see F. J. Cole, *A History of Comparative Anatomy from Aristotle to the Eighteenth Century* (London: Macmillan, 1949), p. 20. Monro's *Essay* is also discussed by John Barclay in his *Introductory Lectures,* p. 145 (see below, n. 6).

5  Alexander Monro *secundus, The Structure and Physiology of Fishes Explained, and Compared with Those of Man and Other Animals* (Edinburgh: C. Elliot, 1785). See Comrie, *History of Scottish Medicine,* 1: 321, 323.

6  This account of Barclay is based on John Barclay, *Introductory Lectures to a Course of Anatomy . . . with a Memoir of the Life of the Author, by George Ballingall, M.D.* (Edinburgh: Maclachlan and Stewart, 1827); John Struthers, *Historical Sketch of the Edinburgh Anatomical School* (Edinburgh: Maclachlan and Stewart, 1867); and Comrie, *History of Scottish Medicine,* 2:493–96. Barclay's many published writings include *The Muscular Motions of the Human Body* (Edinburgh: Laing and Constable, 1808); *Description of the Arteries of the Human Body* (Edinburgh: Bryce, 1812); and *An Inquiry into the Opinions, Ancient and Modern, Concerning Life and Organization* (Edinburgh: Bell & Bradfute, 1822).

7  Comrie, *History of Scottish Medicine,* 2:495; Richard Owen, *On the Archetype and Homologies of the Vertebrate Skeleton* (London: John Van Voorst, 1848), pp. 166–67.

8  There is no modern, full-length scientific biography of Knox. His life was admirably chronicled in the nineteenth century by his student and partner, Henry Lonsdale: *A Sketch of the Life and Writings of Robert Knox the Anatomist* (London: Macmillan, 1870). His personal difficulties and public image are discussed in some detail in Isobel Rae, *Knox, the Anatomist* (Springfield, Ill.: Charles C Thomas Publishers, 1964). Useful articles include Andrew S. Currie, "Robert Knox (1791–1862): Anatomist, Scientist, and Martyr," *Proceedings of the Royal Society of Medicine* 26 (1932):39–46; Lloyd G. Stevenson, "E. D. Worthington on Student Life in Edinburgh, with a Character Sketch of Robert Knox," *Journal of the History of Medicine and Allied Sciences* 19 (1964):71–73; Vern L. Bullough, "Knox, Robert," *DSB.*

9  Rae, *Knox,* pp. 8–9. See also John L. Thornton, *John Abernethy: A Biography* (London: printed for the author, 1953).

10  The Hunterian Museum of Comparative Anatomy, subsequently operated by the Royal College of Surgeons of England, was the first museum of its kind. Little appreciated by Hunter's own generation, it achieved prominence in the nineteenth century under the conservator-

ships of William Clift and Richard Owen. See Cole, *History of Comparative Anatomy,* pp. 460–63; and John Abernethy, *Physiological Lectures, Exhibiting a General View of Mr. Hunter's Physiology, and of His Researches in Comparative Anatomy* (London: Longman, Hurst, Rees, Orme, and Brown, 1817), pp. 9–12. Hunter's writings on comparative anatomy and natural history were later assembled by Owen in vol. 4 of James F. Palmer, ed., *The Works of John Hunter F.R.S. with Notes,* 4 vols. (London: Longman, Rees, Orme, Brown, Green and Longman, 1835–37); and in John Hunter, *Essays and Observations on Natural History, Anatomy, Physiology, Psychology, and Geology,* 2 vols. (London: John Van Voorst, 1861). See also Stephen J. Cross, "John Hunter, the Animal Oeconomy, and Late Eighteenth-Century Physiological Discourse," *Studies in History of Biology* 5 (1981):1–110.

11  Never modest about his "French connections," Knox was still dropping their names thirty-five years later: "The distinguished zoologists, . . . Geoffroy and DeBlainville, colleagues of M. Cuvier, . . . whose friendship I had the pleasure of enjoying uninterruptedly from 1821 to the period of their decease" (Knox, "On Organic Harmonies: Anatomical Co-relations, and Methods of Zoology and Paleontology," *Lancet,* August 1856, p. 246).

12  Robert Knox, *Great Artists and Great Anatomists: A Biographical and Philosophical Study* (London: John Van Voorst, 1852; reprinted, New York: AMS Press, 1977), pp. 2–4.

13  Ibid., p. 4.

14  Ibid., pp. 11–12.

15  Robert Knox, "Introduction to Inquiries into the Philosophy of Zoology," *Lancet,* June 1855, p. 625.

16  Knox claimed to be "intimately acquainted" with the works of German comparative anatomists as early as 1823; see his "Account of the *Foramen centrale* of the Retina, Generally Called the *Foramen of Soemmering,* as Seen in the Eyes of Certain Reptiles," *Memoirs of the Wernerian Society* 5 (1823–25):1–7.

Curiously, there was an earlier flow of ideas from Edinburgh *to* the German transcendentalists when, in the 1790s, Schelling and Novalis (Friedrich von Hardenberg) were inspired by the a priori principle of "excitability" in the medical system of Dr. John Brown; see John Neubauer, "Dr. John Brown (1735–88) and Early German Romanticism," *Journal of the History of Ideas* 28 (1967):367–82.

17  Knox, "Introduction to Inquiries into the Philosophy of Zoology," p. 625. See also his *Great Artists,* pp. 92, 114.

18  Knox, *Great Artists,* pp. 20, 66, 205–6.

19  Knox, "On Organic Harmonies," pp. 270, 299.
20  See Knox's preface to Henri Milne-Edwards, *A Manual of Zoology,* trans. R. Knox, ed. C. Carter Blake, 2nd ed. (London: Henry Renshaw, 1863), pp. vii–viii; also Knox, *Great Artists,* p. 92.
21  Knox, "On Organic Harmonies," p. 247. See also Knox, *Great Artists,* p. 206; Knox, *The Races of Men: A Fragment* (Philadelphia: Lea & Blanchard, 1850), pp. 20, 291.
22  Lonsdale, *Sketch of Knox,* pp. 22–23.
23  Robert Knox, "Observations on the Comparative Anatomy of the Eye," *Trans. Roy. Soc. Edinb.* 10 (1826):43–78. A partial listing of Knox's publications appears in the *Royal Society Catalogue of Scientific Papers;* not included are numerous articles published in medical journals.
24  Lonsdale, *Sketch of Knox,* p. 36. See also Knox, "On the Wombat of Flinders," *Edinb. New Phil. J.* 1 (1826):104–12.
25  The vote was not unanimous, however, as an opposing faction attempted to have the physician-naturalist Robert E. Grant installed. See Rae, *Knox,* p. 36.
26  Comrie, *History of Scottish Medicine,* 2:500; Rae, *Knox,* pp. 44–45.
27  Why Knox ceased these lectures after three years is not known. Most likely the demands made on his time by his main anatomy course and by work at the museum forced him to forego them. Lack of student interest seems an unlikely cause, given Knox's prowess at lecturing and the spreading interest in zoology in Britain at this time. Political pressure from competitors also seems improbable.
28  Lonsdale, *Sketch of Knox,* p. 43.
29  Ibid., p. 144.
30  Comrie, *History of Scottish Medicine,* 2:500.
31  Lonsdale, *Sketch of Knox,* pp. 280–81; "The Late Dr. Robert Knox," *Lancet,* January 1863, pp. 19–20. See below, Chap. 3.
32  Lonsdale, *Sketch of Knox,* pp. 132–33.
33  Knox, *Great Artists,* pp. 211–12; see also pp. 73, 112. Johann Herrmann Ferdinand von Autenrieth (1772–1835) was professor of medicine at the University of Tübingen.
34  Lonsdale, *Sketch of Knox,* pp. 246–47.
35  Ibid., p. 244. This was also the opinion of an anonymous reviewer of Knox's *Great Artists and Great Anatomists;* see *Athenaeum,* 1852, p. 935.
36  Robert Knox, ed. and trans., *A System of Human Anatomy: Translated from the Fourth Edition of the French of H. Cloquet, M.D. With Notes and a Corrected Nomenclature* (Edinburgh: Maclachlan and Stewart,

1828); idem, *The Anatomy of the Bones of the Human Body; Represented in a Series of Engravings, Copied From the Elegant Tables of Sue & Albinus. By Edward Mitchell, Engraver. With Explanatory References by the late John Barclay, M.D., F.R.S.E.,* A new edition (Edinburgh: Edward Mitchell, 1829); Pierre Auguste Béclard, *Elements of General Anatomy,* translated from the last edition of the French, . . . with notes and corrections (Edinburgh: Maclachlan and Stewart, 1830). See Knox's comments on his 1821 encounter with Béclard in "Xavier Bichat, His Life and Labours: A Biographical and Philosophical Study," *Lancet,* November 1854, p. 395.

37  Announcement of DeBlainville's lectures on the comparative anatomy of the skeleton, edited by Robert Knox, *Lancet,* September 1839, p. 5.

38  Henri Marie DeBlainville, "The Comparative Osteography of the Skeleton and Dentar System, in the Five Classes of Vertebral Animals, Recent and Fossil," edited (from the French) and additionally illustrated with numerous notes, observations and drawings, by Robert Knox, *Lancet,* September–November 1839, pp. 137–45, 185–92, 217–22, 297–307.

39  Robert Knox, "Recollections of Researches into the Natural and Economic History of Certain Species of the Clupeadae, Coregoni, and Salmonidae," *Rpt. Brit. Assn.,* 1846, pt. 2, pp. 79–80; idem, "On the Application of the Method, Discovered by the Late Dr. Thibert, of Modeling and Colouring After Nature All Kinds of Fishes," ibid., p. 80.

40  On the Burke and Hare episode see Rae, *Knox,* chaps. 5–10; William Roughead, ed., *Notable British Trials: Burke and Hare* (London: William Hodge, 1921); and James Moores Ball, *The Sack-'em-up Men: An Account of the Rise and Fall of the Modern Resurrectionists* (Edinburgh: Oliver and Boyd, 1928). Dylan Thomas's filmscript *The Doctor and the Devils* (New York: James Laughlin, 1953) is also based on these events.

41  James A. Ross and Hugh W. Y. Taylor, "Robert Knox's Catalogue," *Journal of the History of Medicine* 10 (1955):269–76; Rae, *Knox,* p. 103.

42  Lonsdale, *Sketch of Knox,* p. 196.

43  Cecil Howard Turner, *The Inhumanists* (London: Alexander Ouseley, 1932), p. 286.

44  Rae, *Knox,* p. 131.

45  Lonsdale, *Sketch of Knox,* p. 163.

46  Rae, *Knox,* chap. 14.

47  See Bibliography.

48  Robert Knox, "Contributions to the Philosophy of Zoology," *Zoologist* 13 (1855):4840.

49  Ibid., p. 4841. Knox did not cite the specific works of Vicq d'Azyr which inspired him. It may have been the *Système anatomique: Quadrupèdes* (Paris, 1792) or the undated *Discours sur l'anatomie comparée.*

50  Robert Knox, "Observations on the Structure of the Stomach of the Peruvian Lama; to Which are Prefixed Remarks on the Analogical Reasoning of Anatomists, in the Determination *a priori* of Unknown Species and Unknown Structures," *Trans. Roy. Soc. Edinb.* 11 (1831): 479–98. See also Knox, "On Organic Harmonies."

51  Knox, "Observations on the Structure of the Stomach of the Peruvian Lama," p. 486.

52  Ibid.

53  DeBlainville, "Comparative Osteography," p. 217.

54  Ibid., annotation by Knox, p. 222.

55  Knox, "Observations on the Structure of the Stomach of the Peruvian Lama," pp. 486–87. Teleological reasoning came under attack by a number of other British biologists in the 1830s. See below, Chap. 3; and Dov Ospovat, "Perfect Adaptation and Teleological Explanation: Approaches to the Problem of the History of Life in the Mid-Nineteenth Century," *Studies in History of Biology* 2 (1978):33–56.

56  Robert Knox, "Contributions to Anatomy and Physiology: On some Varieties in Human Structure, with Remarks on the Doctrine of 'Unity of Organization,'" *London Medical Gazette*, n.s. 2 (1843):589. Italics are Knox's.

57  DeBlainville, "Comparative Osteography," annotation by Knox, p. 138. See also the annotations to pp. 141, 145, and 191 of these lectures. Knox reiterated the need for caution against "the too hasty adoption of extreme transcendental views" in "Contributions to the Philosophy of Zoology," p. 4841.

58  Knox, "Contributions to Anatomy and Physiology," p. 500.

59  Knox, *Great Artists*, p. 63. For other expressions of Knox's allegiance to the unity-of-organization doctrine, see Knox, "Contributions to Anatomy and Physiology," pp. 499–502, 529–32, 554–56, 586–91, 637–40.

60  Knox, "Introduction to Inquiries into the Philosophy of Zoology," p. 625.

61  Ibid.

62  Knox, *Great Artists*, pp. 13, 17, 72.

63  Cuvier had undermined the *scala naturae* by dividing the animal kingdom taxonomically into four separate, unconnected groups or *em-*

*branchements.* Unable to accept the taxonomy of Cuvier, DeBlainville retreated to the single series concept. In the lectures which Knox translated in 1839, DeBlainville stated at the outset that he had undertaken the lectures as "the only means of convincing the incredulous in science, and proving, by demonstration, the distinctions which exist in animal species, and their arrangement in a series" (DeBlainville, "Comparative Osterography," p. 137). See also Toby A. Appel, "Henri de Blainville and the Animal Series: A Nineteenth-Century Chain of Being," *J. Hist. Biol.* 13 (1980):291–319.

64 Robert Knox, "Inquiries into the Philosophy of Zoology," *Zoologist* 13 (1855):4790. See also Knox, "Introduction to Inquiries into the Philosophy of Zoology," p. 627.

65 DeBlainville, "Comparative Osteography," annotation by Knox, p. 137. See also Knox, "Introduction to Inquiries into the Philosophy of Zoology," p. 627.

66 Knox, "Inquiries into the Philosophy of Zoology," p. 4790.

67 Knox, "Introduction to Inquiries into the Philosophy of Zoology," p. 627. See also Knox, "Contributions to the Philosophy of Zoology," p. 4838.

68 Robert Knox, "Zoology: Its Present Phasis and Future Prospects," *Zoologist* 15 (1857):5482.

69 Knox studied the Salmonidae intermittently over a period of twenty-five years. See for example: "Observations on the Natural History of the Salmon," *Rpt. Brit. Assn.,* 1831–32, pp. 587–89; "The Present Position of the Salmon Question, Considered Physiologically," *Zoologist* 14 (1856):4985–92; and *Fish and Fishing in the Lone Glens of Scotland* (London: G. Routledge & Co., 1854).

70 Robert Knox, "Some Observations on the *Salmo estuarius,* or Estuary Trout," *Zoologist* 13 (1855):4666.

71 Knox, "Inquiries into the Philosophy of Zoology," p. 4790.

72 Ibid.

73 Knox, "Some Observations on the *Salmo estuarius,*" pp. 4667–68.

74 Knox, "Zoology: Its Present Phasis and Future Prospects," p. 5491.

75 Arthur Lovejoy implied that Knox entertained transmutationist or "evolutionistic" ideas, based on the embryonic recapitulation of earlier forms or present lower forms. I do not think that the bulk of Knox's writings will support this claim, however, unless we confine "transmutation" to the production of various species from genetically isolated genera. See Lovejoy, "The Argument of Organic Evolution before the *Origin of Species,* 1830–1858," in Bentley Glass et al., eds.

*Forerunners of Darwin, 1745–1859* (Baltimore: Johns Hopkins Press, 1959), pp. 409–10.

76 Knox, *Great Artists*, p. 43.

77 Knox, "Introduction to Inquiries into the Philosophy of Zoology," p. 627.

78 Knox, "On Organic Harmonies," p. 300; "Some Observations on the *Salmo estuarius*," pp. 4665, 4667; "Zoology: Its Present Phasis and Future Prospects," p. 5494.

79 Knox seems to have agreed with Buffon on the artificiality of species. "Species are only real in so far as regards man's observing powers: they seem to form no part of Natures [*sic*] scheme or plan, which obviously fills up all gaps, leaving no link deficient in the great chain. A serial unity connects all, the past, the present, and the future. Those who fancy that gaps exist mistake merely a deficiency in their own knowledge for a part of Nature's scheme" (Knox, "Inquiries into the Philosophy of Zoology," p. 4791). Knox did claim that genera, or "natural families," are real, though if the "great chain" is indeed without gaps, it is not clear how genera are to be distinguished by the naturalist (a point which seems not to have bothered Knox).

80 Knox, "Introduction to Inquiries into the Philosophy of Zoology," p. 627. Italics are Knox's.

81 See Barry Gower, "Speculation in Physics: The History and Practice of *Naturphilosophie*," *Studies in the History and Philosophy of Science* 3 (1973):301–56.

82 Knox, "Contributions to Anatomy and Physiology," p. 555; see also pp. 500 and 588; and "Zoology: Its Present Phasis and Future Prospects," p. 5492. Knox's "law of species" was, he declared, only an extension of Buffon's concept of the *moule interieur*, the permanent form or mould which Nature causes each species to attain ("Zoology: Its Present Phasis and Future Prospects," pp. 5498–99).

83 Knox, "Contributions to Anatomy and Physiology," p. 640. Italics are Knox's.

84 Lorenz Oken, *Elements of Physiophilosophy* (1809), trans. Alfred Tulk (London: Ray Society, 1847), pp. 21, 182.

85 Owen, *On the Archetype and Homologies of the Vertebrate Skeleton*, pp. 171–72; Richard Owen, "Darwin *on the Origin of Species*," *Edinburgh Review* 111 (1860):506; J. B. Stallo, *General Principles of the Philosophy of Nature* (Boston: Wm. Crosby and H. P. Nichols, 1848), p. 273. See also E. S. Russell, *Form and Function: A Contribution to the History of Animal Morphology* (London: John Murray, 1916), pp. 111–

12; and Roy M. MacLeod, "Evolutionism and Richard Owen, 1830–1868: An Episode in Darwin's Century," *Isis* 56 (1965):269–70.

86    On essentialism, see David L. Hull, "The Effect of Essentialism on Taxonomy: Two Thousand Years of Stasis," *British Journal for the Philosophy of Science* 15 (1964–65):314–32; idem, *Darwin and His Critics: The Reception of Darwin's Theory of Evolution by the Scientific Community* (Cambridge: Harvard University Press, 1973), chap. 5. Essentialism has also been referred to as "typological thinking"; see Ernest Mayr, "Darwin and the Evolutionary Theory in Biology," in *Evolution and Anthropology: A Centennial Appraisal* (Washington, D.C.: Anthropological Society of America, 1959), pp. 1–10.

87    See, for example, Knox, *Great Artists*, pp. 21–22, 81, and "Contributions to Anatomy and Physiology," p. 531.

88    Knox, *The Races of Men*, p. 230. For an elaboration of Knox's racial theories, see M. D. Biddiss, "The Politics of Anatomy: Dr. Robert Knox and Victorian Racism," *Proceedings of the Royal Society of Medicine* 69 (1976):245–50. Biddiss argues briefly that Knox's racial theory was an extrapolation from his transcendental anatomy.

89    Review of *Great Artists and Great Anatomists* and *A Manual of Artistic Anatomy* by Robert Knox, *Athenaeum*, 1852, p. 937.

90    Lonsdale, *Sketch of Knox*, p. 32.

91    Ball, *The Sack-'em-up Men*, p. 96.

## Chapter 3: The Specific and the Transcendental

1    C. Carter Blake, "The Life of Dr. Knox," *Journal of Anthropology*, 1870–71, p. 334.

2    *DNB;* D. L. Emblen, *Peter Mark Roget: The Word and the Man* (New York: Crowell, 1970).

3    Peter Mark Roget, *Animal and Vegetable Physiology Considered with Reference to Natural Theology*, 2 vols. (London: William Pickering, 1834), 1:47–48. Italics in original.

4    Ibid., pp. 48–49. Italics in original.

5    Ibid., 2:635–36.

6    Ibid., p. 637. Roget singled out Serres and Lamarck as particularly guilty of speculative excesses.

7    "The enlarged views to which we are conducted by the study of comparative physiology afford us a glimpse of some of the plans or models of structure which appear to have been followed in the formation of the animal world. The analogies of form discernible in corresponding organs, throughout a very extensive series of tribes, have been lately

traced and developed with extraordinary care by the modern naturalists of the French and German schools, and especially by Cuvier, Blainville, Savigny, Geoffroi St. Hilaire, Oken, Carus, and Milne Edwards. The conclusions they have drawn from their labours, though sometimes over-strained, are always ingenious, and in general satisfactory; and they strongly tend to prove, that several distinct types, or standards of figure, have been adhered to in all the multiplicity of forms with which it has pleased the Author of nature to diversify the animal creation" (Roget, "Physiology," *Encyclopaedia Britannica*, 7th ed. [1838]; printed separately as *Outlines of Physiology: with an Appendix on Phrenology*, 1st American ed. [Philadelphia: Lea and Blanchard, 1839], p. 45).

8   In the preface to *Animal and Vegetable Physiology*, Roget acknowledged his dependence on the works of Cuvier, Blumenbach, Carus, Home, Meckel, DeBlainville, Latreille, and Geoffroy, among others.

9   See Jane Oppenheimer, "An Embryological Enigma in the *Origin of Species*," in Bentley Glass et al., eds., *Forerunners of Darwin: 1745–1859* (Baltimore: Johns Hopkins Press, 1959), pp. 310–15. Biographical details on Barry are from *DNB;* J.B., "Memoir of the Late Martin Barry, M.D., F.R.SS. L and E.," *Edinburgh Medical Journal* 1 (1855): 81–91; and *Proc. Roy. Soc. Lond.* 7 (1854–55):577–82.

10  Martin Barry, "On the Unity of Structure in the Animal Kingdom," *Edinb. New Phil. J.* 22 (1836–37):141.

11  Ibid., p. 118. For an extensive discussion of the prevalence of Von Baer's law in British thinking, see Dov Ospovat, "The Influence of Karl Ernst von Baer's Embryology, 1828–1859: A Reappraisal in Light of Richard Owen's and William B. Carpenter's 'Palaeontological Application of "Von Baer's Law,"' " *J. Hist. Biol.* 9 (1976):1–28.

12  Barry, "Unity of Structure," p. 127.

13  Ibid., pp. 126–27.

14  Barry elaborated upon these concepts in a sequel essay, "Further Observations on the Unity of Structure in the Animal Kingdom, and on Congenital Anomalies, including 'Hermaphrodites'; with some Remarks on Embryology, as facilitating Animal Nomenclature, Classification, and the study of Comparative Anatomy," *Edinb. New Phil. J.* 22 (1836–37):345–64.

15  Ibid., pp. 348, 350.

16  Martin Barry, "Researches in Embryology," *Phil. Trans.* 128 (1838): 301–41, and 129 (1839):307–80; idem, "A Contribution to the Physiology of Cells," ibid. 130 (1840):529–93.

17  K. Bryn Thomas, "Carpenter, William Benjamin," *DSB;* Andrew

Taylor, "Obituary Notice of William Benjamin Carpenter, C.B., M.D., LL.D., F.R.S.," *Trans. Bot. Soc. Edinb.* 16 (1886):303–8; Robert M. Young, *Mind, Brain, and Adaptation in the Nineteenth Century* (Oxford: Clarendon Press, 1970), pp. 210–20; Harold L. Burstyn, "Pioneering in Large-Scale Scientific Organization: The *Challenger* Expedition and Its Report. I. Launching the Expediton," *Proc. Roy. Soc. Edinb.* (B), 72 (1972):47–61.

18  J. Estlin Carpenter, "Introductory Memoir" to William B. Carpenter, *Nature and Man: Essays Scientific and Philosophical* (New York: D. Appleton and Co., 1889), p. 10.

19  Ibid., pp. 11, 17. Carpenter's biographer relates that Carpenter "at this time preferred to dwell on large and general conceptions, to discover analogies, to follow out principles, rather than to come into close contact with actual facts" (ibid., p. 15).

20  Ibid., pp. 16, 22.

21  William B. Carpenter, "On the Structure and Functions of the Organs of Respiration, in the Animal and Vegetable Kingdoms," *West of England Journal of Science and Literature*, no. 4 (1835), p. 221.

22  Ibid., p. 223.

23  Ibid., *West of England Journal of Science and Literature*, no. 5 (1836), p. 286. Carpenter's quotation is from Roget, *Animal and Vegetable Physiology*, 2:625.

24  William B. Carpenter, "On Unity of Function in Organized Beings," *Edinb. New Phil. J.* 23 (1837):92–114. This paper was read to the Royal Medical Society of Edinburgh in April 1837. Like Barry, Carpenter had just spent a term as president of Royal Physical Society; see Carpenter, *Nature and Man*, p. 19. Apparently neither Carpenter nor Barry attended the classes of Knox, though they must have been acquainted with his ideas through other students.

25  Carpenter, "Unity of Function," p. 100.

26  Ibid., pp. 107–8.

27  Ibid., p. 108.

28  Ibid.

29  William Whewell, *History of the Inductive Sciences, from the Earliest to the Present Times*, 3 vols. (London: John W. Parker, 1837), 3:470–71. Compare Baden Powell's treatment of formal and final causes in *The Connexion of Natural and Divine Truth; or, The Study of the Inductive Philosophy Considered as Subservient to Theology* (London: John W. Parker, 1838), pp. 37–41, 128–36.

30  William B. Carpenter, "Physiology an Inductive Science," *British and Foreign Medical Review* 5 (1838):338. In an "addition" to the third

edition of the *History* (1857) Whewell took a more moderate position on the teleology-morphology issue, citing Richard Owen's work and admitting that "a new view as to Unity of Plan will almost necessarily displace or modify some of the old views respecting Final Causes" (3rd ed., 3:559). Carpenter maintained his opposition to final causes in biology as late as the 1880s; see Carpenter, "The Argument from Design in the Organic World," in *Nature and Man*, p. 413. For a more detailed account of the Whewell-Carpenter disagreement, see Dov Ospovat, "Perfect Adaptation and Teleological Explanation: Approaches to the Problem of the History of Life in the Mid-Nineteenth Century," *Studies in History of Biology* 2 (1978):37–39.

31  William B. Carpenter, *Principles of General and Comparative Physiology, Intended as an Introduction to the Study of Human Physiology, and as a Guide to the Philosophical Pursuit of Natural History* (London: J. Churchill, 1839; 2nd ed., 1841; 3rd ed., 1851; 4th ed., 1854). For contemporary assessments of the value of this text, see Carpenter, *Nature and Man*, pp. 64–69.

32  Carpenter, *Principles,* 2nd ed., chaps. 3 and 17.

33  See my article "Edward Forbes (1815–1854): An Annotated List of Published and Unpublished Writings," *Journal of the Society for the Bibliography of Natural History* 9 (1979):171–218. Forbes's life was chronicled in George Wilson and Archibald Geikie, *Memoir of Edward Forbes, F.R.S.* (Cambridge: Macmillan, 1861). A more recent analysis is contained in my unpublished doctoral dissertation, "Organisms in Space and Time: Edward Forbes (1815–1854) and New Dimensions for Early Victorian Natural History" (Johns Hopkins University, 1975). I have discussed Forbes's role in British oceanography in "The Early Dredgers: 'Naturalizing' in British Seas, 1830–1850," *J. Hist. Biol.* 12 (1979):293–368.

34  The Reverend Richard Owen, *The Life of Richard Owen,* 2 vols. (London: John Murray, 1894), 1:408.

35  Wilson and Geikie, *Memoir,* p. 266.

36  Samuel M. Brown and Edward Forbes, *Popular Lectures on the Philosophy of the Sciences* (Edinburgh: n.p., [1840]), p. 1.

37  Ibid., pp. 7–8.

38  There is no explicit evidence of a Forbes-Whewell connection in 1840, although certainly in the next few years Forbes would come to know both Whewell and his philosophy well. Forbes's closest associate in Cambridge during this period was probably the botanist C. C. Babington, a student of Henslow. Babington was only moderately interested in transcendentalism; it is interesting to note, however, that his post-

humously published *Memorials Journal and Botanical Correspondence* (Cambridge: Macmillan and Bowes, 1897) contains contributions by the Germanophile Connop Thirlwall.

39  Edward Forbes, *An Inaugural Lecture on Botany, Considered as a Science, and as a Branch of Medical Education* (London: John Van Voorst, 1843), p. 21.

40  Edward Forbes, "On the Morphology of the Reproductive System of Sertularian Zoophytes, and its Analogy with that of the Flowering Plants," *Rpt. Brit. Assn.*, 1844, pt. 2, pp. 68–69.

41  Ibid.; italics are Forbes's.

42  Ibid., p. 69.

43  Ibid.

44  *Athenaeum*, 1844, p. 978. This quotation is a reporter's paraphrase of Owen's reactons; hence the use of the simple past tense.

45  R. Q. Couch, "On the Morphology of the Different Organs of Zoophytes," *Ann. Mag. Nat. Hist.* 15 (1845):161–66.

46  Wilson and Geikie, *Memoir*, pp. 344, 370.

47  Edward Forbes, "On Some Important Analogies Between the Animal and Vegetable Kingdoms," *Athenaeum*, 1845, p. 199.

48  Fries discussed polarity in his *Systema Orbis Vegetabilis: Primas Lineas Novae Constructionis* (Lund: Typographia Academica, 1825); see John Lindley's abstract of the introduction to Fries's work, *Philosophical Magazine* 68 (1826):81–91; Forbes, "On the Manifestation of Polarity in the Distribution of Organized Beings in Time," *Proc. Roy. Inst.* 1 (1851–54):428–33. Fries, interestingly, was immediately made an honorary foreign member of the Botanical Society of Edinburgh upon its founding in 1836, while Forbes was a charter member of the society and its foreign secretary until 1840.

49  John Lindley, *Introduction to Botany*, 4th ed., 2 vols. (London: Longman, Brown, Green and Longmans, 1848), 1:165; William Whewell, *Philosophy of the Inductive Sciences*, 1st ed., 2 vols. (London: John W. Parker, 1840), vol. 1, Book 5. See especially William Whewell, "On the Idea of Polarity," *Athenaeum*, 1849, pp. 119–20.

50  Forbes, "On Some Important Analogies."

51  Edward Forbes, "On the Supposed Analogy Between the Life of an Individual and the Duration of a Species," *Edinb. New Phil. J.* 53 (1852):130–35.

52  This theme had been discussed by the Italian geologist G. B. Brocchi, and by Charles Lyell in the *Principles of Geology*, 3 vols. (London: John Murray, 1830–33), 2:128–30. See Frank N. Egerton, "Studies of Animal Populations from Lamarck to Darwin," *J. Hist. Biol.* 1 (1968): 235.

53  Forbes, "On the Supposed Analogy," pp. 133–34.
54  Ibid., p. 134. In J. H. Balfour, "Sketch of the Life of the Late Professor Edward Forbes," *Ann. Mag. Nat. Hist.*, 2nd ser. 15 (1855):45–46, are illustrations used by Forbes in this lecture which were not published elsewhere. See also Edward Forbes, "On the Distribution of Freshwater Animals and Plants," *Athenaeum*, 1850, p. 290.
55  Forbes, "Distribution of Freshwater Animals and Plants."
56  Wilson and Geikie, *Memoir*, p. 429 (italics are Forbes's). On Forbes's Platonism see ibid., pp. 546–47; and Walter F. Cannon, "The Bases of Darwin's Achievement: A Revaluation," *Victorian Studies* 5 (1961–62):112–15. Compare Edward Forbes, "Inaugural Lecture," *Monthly Journal of Medical Science* 18 (1854):565.
57  Wilson and Geikie, *Memoir*, p. 429; Edward Forbes, "The Future of Geology," *Westminster Review*, n.s. 2 (1852):76; [T. H. Huxley], "Professor Edward Forbes, F.R.S.," *Literary Gazette*, 1854, pp. 1016–18.
58  Owen, *The Life of Richard Owen*, 1:27. See also Wesley C. Williams, "Owen, Richard," *DSB*.
59  Henry Lonsdale, *A Sketch of the Life and Writings of Robert Knox the Anatomist* (London: Macmillan, 1870), pp. 280–81. Though Lonsdale seems emphatic about the Knox-Owen relationship, Owen's biographer mentions Barclay, not Knox, as Owen's mentor. Officially Barclay was still lecturing during the period when Owen attended medical classes in Edinburgh (October 1824–April 1825). Knox did not formally assume Barclay's lectures until the following autumn, though he may have assisted Barclay with the lectures during the year of Owen's attendance. See George Ballingall, "Life of Dr. Barclay," in John Barclay, *Introductory Lectures to a Course of Anatomy* (Edinburgh: Maclachlan and Stewart, 1827), p. xviii.
60  See Owen's account of this period in his *On the Anatomy of Vertebrates* (London, 1866–68; reprint, New York: AMS Press, 1973), pp. 786–89. Also E. S. Russell, *Form and Function: A Contribution to the History of Animal Morphology* (London: John Murray, 1916), chap. 8; Roy M. MacLeod, "Evolutionism and Richard Owen, 1830–1868: An Episode in Darwin's Century," *Isis* 56 (1965):259–80, esp. 265–70.
61  Ospovat, "Perfect Adaptation and Teleological Explanation," p. 37.
62  Richard Owen, "A Description of a Specimen of the *Plesiosaurus Macrocephalus*, Conybeare, in the Collection of Viscount Cole, M.P., D.C.L., F.G.S., &c.," *Transactions of the Geological Society of London* (1838):517–18.
63  The year before, Whewell had written (speaking of Geoffroy's ideas in general) that "we may venture to say that they are hardly yet generally

understood with sufficient distinctness to justify the mere historian of science in attempting such an explanation" (*History of the Inductive Sciences*, 3rd ed., 3:380). And referring specifically to Geoffroy's statement of the vertebral theory of the skull, Whewell cautioned, "How far the application of the principle, as here proposed, is just, I must leave philosophical physiologists to decide" (ibid., p. 371). A little earlier Leonard Jenyns had mentioned Geoffroy's "peculiar views respecting the *unity of composition* in animals," and implied that they were well enough known not to require elaboration; but he did not suggest that they were accepted in Britain ("Report on the Recent Progress and Present State of Zoology," *Rpt. Brit. Assn.*, 1834, pt. 1, pp. 150–51.

64   Richard Owen, *Lectures on the Comparative Anatomy and Physiology of the Invertebrate Animals* (London: Longman, Brown, Green, and Longmans, 1843), pp. 366–71.

65   Ibid., p. 368.

66   Ibid., pp. 374, 379.

67   Owen had also begun the first drafts of his subsequent "Archetype and Homologies" report about this time, and had solicited Darwin's comments thereon; see Owen, *Life*, 1:208–9. Knox and Owen rarely referred in print to each other's work, nor am I aware of any correspondence between the two. Owen did describe Knox as "this able comparative anatomist" in "On the Anatomy of the Dugong," *Proceedings of the Zoological Society of London*, 27 March 1838, p. 43.

68   Robert Knox, "Contributions to Anatomy and Physiology," *London Medical Gazette*, n.s. 2 (1843):530–31.

69   Ibid., p. 501.

70   Owen to Whewell, 31 October 1837, Trinity College Library, Cambridge, Add. ms. a.210, no. 54.

71   Ibid.

72   See especially Richard Owen, *On the Nature of Limbs* (London: John Van Voorst, 1849), pp. 85–86. Whewell's philosophy became increasingly Platonic in later years as well.

73   I. Todhunter, *William Whewell, D.D.: An Account of His Writings with Selections from His Literary and Scientific Correspondence*, 2 vols. (London: Macmillan and Co., 1876), 1:137.

74   For example, Whewell's *Indications of the Creator: Extracts, Bearing upon Theology, from the History and the Philosophy of the Inductive Sciences*, 2nd ed. (London: Parker, 1846), p. 13, and his *History of the Inductive Sciences*, 3rd ed., 3 vols. (London: John W. Parker and Son, 1857), 3:553–58. See also Michael Ruse, "The Scientific Methodology

of William Whewell," *Centaurus* 20 (1976):227–57; and John H. Brooke, "Richard Owen, William Whewell, and the *Vestiges,*" *British Journal for the History of Science* 10 (1977):132–45. For another, more detailed account of the Owen-Whewell relationship, see the recent, fascinating book by Ruse, *The Darwinian Revolution* (Chicago: University of Chicago Press, 1979), pp. 116–27.

75  Richard Owen, *Lectures on the Comparative Anatomy and Physiology of the Vertebrate Animals, Delivered at the Royal College of Surgeons of England, in 1844 and 1846* (London: Longman, Brown, Green and Longmans, 1846), p. 48.

76  See especially Owen, *On the Anatomy of Vertebrates,* p. vii.

77  [William B. Carpenter], "Professor Owen *on the Comparative Anatomy and Physiology of the Vertebrate Animals,*" *British and Foreign Medico-Chirurgical Review* 23 (1847):472.

78  Ibid., pp. 489–90.

79  Richard Owen, "Report on the Archetype and Homologies of the Vertebrate Skeleton," *Rpt. Brit. Assn.,* 1846, pt. 1, pp. 169–340. Widespread interest in this treatise led to its separate publication in 1848 as *On the Archetype and Homologies of the Vertebrate Skeleton* (London: John Van Voorst). See also Owen's "On the Vertebrate Structure of the Skull," *Athenaeum,* 1846, pp. 1004–5, and "On the Homologies of the Bones collectively called 'Temporal' in Human Anatomy," ibid., pp. 968–69, with subsequent comments by Louis Agassiz.

80  Owen, *Archetype and Homologies,* p. 79.

81  Ibid., pp. 171–72.

82  Ibid., pp. 168–69.

83  Owen, *On the Nature of Limbs* (London: John Van Voorst, 1849), pp. 1–3.

84  Carpenter, *Principles,* 4th ed., p. 132.

85  Ibid., p. 39.

86  Ibid., p. 46.

87  Ibid., p. 41.

88  Ibid., p. 123.

89  Ibid., p. 124.

90  J. Estlin Carpenter, in Carpenter, *Nature and Man,* p. 117.

91  William B. Carpenter, "Man the Interpreter of Nature" (Presidential Address to the British Association, Brighton, 1872), in *Nature and Man,* pp. 185–210. See also "The Phasis of Force" (1857), ibid., pp. 173–84. These and other aspects of Carpenter's thought are discussed in Roger Smith, "The Human Significance of Biology: Carpenter,

Darwin, and the *vera causa*," in U. C. Knoepflmacher and G. B. Tennyson, eds., *Nature and the Victorian Imagination* (Berkeley and Los Angeles: University of California Press, 1977), pp. 216–30.

Carpenter may have taken the title of his presidential address from the first aphorism of Whewell's *Philosophy of the Inductive Sciences* (p. xvii): "Man is the Interpreter of Nature, Science the Right Interpretation."

92 Richard Owen, Presidential Address, *Rpt. Brit. Assn.*, 1858, p. lxviii.

93 Huxley was for a time positively disposed toward the unity-of-plan doctrine, as well as the circular taxonomic system of MacLeay and Swainson. See Leonard Huxley, ed., *Life and Letters of Thomas Henry Huxley*, 2 vols. (London: Macmillan, 1900), 1:92–93; Mary P. Winsor, *Starfish, Jellyfish, and the Order of Life* (New Haven: Yale University Press, 1976), pp. 87–97, 118–19, 140–41, 170.

94 T. H. Huxley, "Owen's Position in the History of Anatomical Science," in Owen, *Life of Richard Owen*, 2:315.

95 Ibid., p. 312.

96 Ibid., pp. 320–21.

97 Ibid., p. 316.

98 Ibid., p. 319.

99 Biographical material on Brown is scarce. See [John Brown], "Dr. Samuel Brown," *North British Review* 26 (1857):376–406. Samuel wrote of his father's work in *Some Account of Itinerating Libraries and Their Founder* (Edinburgh: William Blackwood and Sons, 1856).

100 F. Szabadváng, "Mitscherlich, Eilhard," *DSB*. Mitscherlich's statement of the law of isomorphism was that "an equal number of atoms, combined in the same way, produce the same crystal forms and the crystal form does not depend on the nature of the atoms, but only on their number and mode of combination." See also Evan Melhado, "Mitscherlich's Discovery of Isomorphism," *Historical Studies in the Physical Sciences* 11 (1980):87–123; I thank Dr. Harold Burstyn for calling my attention to this article.

101 Samuel M. Brown, *Lectures on the Atomic Theory, and Essays Scientific and Literary*, 2 vols. (Edinburgh: T. Constable and Co., 1858), preface by J[ohn] B[rown], p. vii, and 1:78. David M. Knight has discussed the unity-of-matter theme in his recent book, *The Transcendental Part of Chemistry* (Folkestone: Dawson, 1978).

102 J[ohn] B[rown], Preface to Samuel Brown, *Lectures*, 1:vii.

103 Brown, *Lectures*, p. 78.

104 Gordon Goodwin, "MacVicar, John Gibson," *DNB;* John M'Murtrie, "Rev. John Gibson Macvicar, LL.D., D.D., Minister of Moffat," *Trans. Bot. Soc. Edinb.* 16 (1886):95–98; Henry Lonsdale, "Biograph-

ical Memoir of John Goodsir," in *The Anatomical Memoirs of John Goodsir,* ed. William Turner, 2 vols. (Edinburgh: Adam and Charles Black, 1868), 1:14. Little has been written about the philosophical MacVicar. The *Royal Society Catalogue* lists nineteen articles under his name; not included, however, are his contributions to the *Quarterly Journal of Agriculture* (which he edited for a time), and to medical journals, especially the *Edinburgh Medical Journal.*

105  John Gibson MacVicar, *Elements of the Economy of Nature; or, The Principles of Physics, Chemistry, and Physiology: Founded on the Recently Discovered Phenomena of Light, Electro-Magnetism, and Atomic Chemistry* (Edinburgh: Adam Black, 1830), esp. p. 528 and plate I. A considerably revised second edition was published in 1856. The final form of MacVicar's chemical philosophy appears in volumes 2 and 3 of his *Sketch of a Philosophy.* 4 vols. (London: William & Norgate, 1868–74).

106  MacVicar, *Elements of the Economy of Nature,* p. xi.

107  M'Murtrie, "Rev. John Gibson MacVicar," p. 97.

108  MacVicar, *Elements of the Economy of Nature,* p. 4. See Humphrey Davy, *Elements of Chemical Philosophy* (London: J. Johnson and Co., 1812), pp. 182, 488–89.

109  MacVicar, *Elements of the Economy of Nature,* p. 4.

110  [Samuel M. Brown], "Sir Humphrey Davy," *North British Review* 2 (1844):53–86, reprinted in Brown's *Lectures on the Atomic Theory,* 1: 246–98.

111  [John Brown], "Dr. Samuel Brown," p. 384.

112  Jessie Aitkin Wilson, *Memoir of George Wilson* (Edinburgh: Edmonston and Douglas, 1860), p. 209.

113  Whewell, *Philosophy of the Inductive Sciences,* 1st ed., 1:xxxvii.

114  Brown and Forbes, *Popular Lectures on the Philosophy of the Sciences,* p. 4; italics are Brown's.

115  Brown published a series of essays on the history of chemistry (collected in the *Lectures on the Atomic Theory*), and also the drama *The Tragedy of Galileo Galilei* (Edinburgh: James Hogg, 1850).

116  Lonsdale, "Biographical Memoir of John Goodsir," pp. 68–69.

117  Samuel M. Brown, "Experimental Researches on the Production of Silicon from Paracyanogen," *Proc. Roy. Soc. Edinb.* 1 (1841):341–43; idem, *Two Processes for Silicon* (Edinburgh: A. and D. Black, 1843). Brown's experiments are described in more detail in Knight, *The Transcendental Part of Chemistry,* pp. 194–201.

118  Wilson and Geikie, *Memoir,* p. 361. See also ibid., pp. 340–42; [Edward Forbes], "Carbon and Silicon," *Literary Gazette,* 1844, pp. 39–40.

119   George Wilson, *A Letter from George Wilson, M.D. Lecturer on Chemistry, to the Right Honourable Sir James Forrest, Bart.* . . . (Edinburgh: Neill and Co., 1843); *Testimonials in Favour of Dr. Samuel Brown, now a Candidate for the Chair of Chemistry in the University of Edinburgh* (Edinburgh: Neill and Co., 1843). See also Wilson, *Memoir of George Wilson,* pp. 310–11, 314.

120   Brown, *Lectures on the Atomic Theory,* vol. 1.

121   [John Brown], "Dr. Samuel Brown," pp. 387, 390; [Forbes], "Carbon and Silicon," p. 39; Brown, *Lectures on the Atomic Theory,* 1:2.

122   George Wilson and John Crombie Brown, "Account of a Repetition of Several of Dr. Samuel Brown's Processes for the Conversion of Carbon into Silicon," *Trans. Roy. Soc. Edinb.* 15 (1844):547–59, and *Proc. Roy. Soc. Edinb.* 1 (1844):468–70. Justus Liebig quickly denounced Brown's experiments, judging him to be "totally unacquainted with the principles of chemical analysis" (*Familiar Letters on Chemistry, and its Relation to Commerce, Physiology, and Agriculture* [Philadelphia: James M. Campbell & Co., 1843], p. 21). Forbes objected to Liebig's attack as unnecessarily abusive ("Carbon and Silicon," p. 39).

123   The major biographical source on Goodsir is the memoir by Henry Lonsdale (Knox's biographer) in Turner, ed., *The Anatomical Memoirs of John Goodsir,* 1:1–203 (hereafter Goodsir, *Anatomical Memoirs*). Also useful are two obituaries: J. H. Balfour, *Trans. Bot. Soc. Edinb.* 9 (1867):118–27; and *Proc. Roy. Soc. Lond.* 16 (1868):xiv–xvi.

124   Lonsdale, "Biographical Memoir of John Goodsir," p. 14.

125   See, for example, Edward Forbes and John Goodsir, "Notice of Zoological Researches in Orkney and Shetland During the Month of June 1839," *Rpt. Brit. Assn.,* 1839, pt. 2, pp. 79–83; idem, "On Some Remarkable Marine Invertebrata New to the British Seas," *Trans. Roy. Soc. Edinb.* 20 (1853):307–16. Harry Goodsir had commenced a promising career in the study of the Crustacea, but perished with Sir John Franklin's Arctic expedition in 1847.

126   Lonsdale, "Biographical Memoir of John Goodsir," pp. 23–28. Forbes's biographers claim that Forbes and Goodsir first met in Knox's dissecting room in 1831.

127   John Goodsir, "On the Origin and Development of the Pulps and Sacs of the Human Teeth," *Edinburgh Medical and Surgical Journal* 51 (1839):1–38; Lonsdale, "Biographical Memoir of John Goodsir," pp. 35–44.

128   Lonsdale, "Biographical Memoir of John Goodsir," p. 56.

129   Rudolph Virchow, *Die Cellularpathologie in ihrer Begrundung auf Physiologische und Pathologische Gewebelehre* (Berlin: A. Hirschwald, 1858). See also Richard H. Follis, Jr., "A Note on the Centenary of

John Goodsir's 'Anatomical and Pathological Observations,'" *Bulletin of the History of Medicine* 18 (1945):438–44.

130 Most of these papers appear in Goodsir's *Anatomical Memoirs*. Some also appeared earlier in John Goodsir and Harry D. S. Goodsir, *Anatomical and Pathological Observations* (Edinburgh: Myles Macphail, 1845).

131 John Goodsir, "On the Employment of Mathematical Modes of Investigation in the Determination of Organic Forms," *Anatomical Memoirs*, 2:206.

132 Ibid., p. 209.

133 Ibid., p. 213.

134 John Goodsir, "On Life and Organization," *Anatomical Memoirs*, 1:289–90.

135 See John Goodsir, "A Brief Review of the Present State of Organic Electricity," *Anatomical Memoirs*, 2:306–44. On DuBois-Reymond and others of the German school of biophysics, see P. C. Cranefield, "The Organic Physics of 1847 and the Biophysics of Today," *Journal of the History of Medicine* 12 (1957):407–23.

136 Goodsir, "On the Employment of Mathematical Modes," pp. 209–19. Goodsir's citations were to Henry Moseley, "On the Geometrical Forms of Turbinated and Discoid Shells," *Phil. Trans.* 128 (1838):351–70; and D. R. Hay, *The Geometric Beauty of the Human Figure Defined, To Which Is Prefixed a System of Aesthetic Proportion Appliable to Architecture and the Other Formative Arts* (Edinburgh and London: William Blackwood and Sons, 1851), p. xiv. Goodsir knew Hay through the Edinburgh Aesthetic Club and was in fact responsible for portions of the latter's work. See Lonsdale, "Biographical Memoir of John Goodsir," pp. 142–43.

137 Lonsdale, "Biographical Memoir of John Goodsir," chap. 6.

138 William Hamilton, *Discussions on Philosophy and Literature, Education and University Reform* (London: Longman, Brown, Green and Longmans, 1852).

139 Goodsir, "On Life and Organization," p. 304.

140 Ibid., p. 305.

141 Lonsdale states ("Biographical Memoir of John Goodsir," p. 156) that Goodsir "all along seems to have had a desire to emulate Richard Owen, whom he esteemed more highly than any other British authority as a teleologist and comparative anatomist."

142 John Goodsir, "On the Morphological Relations of the Nervous System in the Annulose and Vertebrate Types of Organization," *Anatomical Memoirs*, 2:84.

143 John Goodsir, "On the Morphological Constitution of the Skeleton of

the Vertebrate Head," *Anatomical Memoirs*, 2:88–197, and "On the Morphological Constitution of the Limbs," ibid., pp. 198–203.

144 Lonsdale, "Biographical Memoir of John Goodsir," p. 177.

145 See ibid., pp. 59–61; Wilson, *Memoir of George Wilson*, pp. 225–31; Philip F. Rehbock, "The Early Dredgers: 'Naturalizing' in British Seas, 1830–1850," *J. Hist. Biol.* 12 (1979):293–368, with Forbes's figure of the dredge on p. 305.

146 Lonsdale, "Biographical Memoir of John Goodsir, " p. 180.

147 Lorenz Oken, *The Elements of Physiophilosophy*, trans. Alfred Tulk (London: Ray Society, 1847); K. E. Von Baer, "Fragments Relating to Philosophical Zoology," trans. T. H. Huxley, in Arthur Henfrey and Thomas Henry Huxley, eds., *Scientific Memoirs* . . . (London: Taylor and Francis, 1853; reprint, New York and London: Johnson Reprint Corp., 1966), pp. 176–238.

148 See, for example, John Gibson MacVicar, "Vegetable Morphology: Its General Principles," *Trans. Bot. Soc. Edinb.* 6 (1860):401–18; idem, "The First Lines of Morphology and Organic Development, Geometrically Considered," *Edinb. New Phil. J.*, n.s. 14 (1861):1–15; W. MacDonald, "On the Homologies of the Vertebrate Skeleton and its Analogies amongst the Invertebrata," *Athenaeum*, 1856, p. 1095; W. Mitchell, "Analogy between the Serial Arrangements of the Leaves of Plants and Crystalline Forms," *Trans. Bot. Soc. Edinb.*, 5 (1857):207–10; idem, "On the Correspondence Between the Serial Internodes of Plants and Serial Crystalline Forms," ibid., 6 (1858):31–35.

149 James McMullen Rigg, "McCosh, James," *DNB;* William M. Sloane, *The Life of James M'Cosh: A Record Chiefly Autobiographical* (New York: Charles Scribner's Sons, 1896).

150 James M'Cosh, "Morphological Analogy Between the Disposition of the Branches of Exogenous Plants and the Venation of Their Leaves," *Literary Gazette*, 1852, p. 716; idem, "Some Further Observations on the Correspondence Between the Leaf-venation and Ramification of the Plant," *Rpt. Brit. Assn.*, 1854, pt. 2, p. 100; also idem, "Some Remarks on the Plant, Morphologically Considered," *Botanical Gazette* 3 (1851):118–23.

151 [James M'Cosh], "Typical Forms: Goethe, Professor Owen, Mr. Fairbairn," *North British Review* 15 (1851):389–418. I have not discussed John Hutton Balfour (1808–84) here; his textbook, *A Manual of Botany, being an Introduction to the Study of the Structure, Physiology, and Classification of Plants* (London: Griffin, 1849), included some discussion of ideal plant morphology. Balfour was professor of botany

at Edinburgh from 1845, and a prominent founding member of the Botanical Society of Edinburgh. Judging from the contents of its *Transactions,* the society was one of the most active locations in Britain for discussions of ideal plant morphology in the 1850s.

On Schleiden, see his *Principles of Scientific Botany; or, Botany as an Inductive Science,* trans. Edwin Lankester (London: Longman, Brown, Green, and Longmans, 1849; New York: Kraus Reprint Co., 1969), esp. pp. 124–26, 310–14.

152 [M'Cosh], "Typical Forms," pp. 395, 397.
153 Ibid., p. 402.
154 Ibid.
155 Ibid., p. 410.
156 Ibid., p. 411.
157 James M'Cosh and George Dickie, *Typical Forms and Special Ends in Creation* (Edinburgh: Thomas Constable and Co., 1856), p. 1.
158 Ibid., p. 428.
159 Ibid., p. 430.
160 Ibid., p. 6.
161 Ibid., p. 26.
162 For biographical details on Swainson, see Iris M. Winchester, "William Swainson, F.R.S., 1789–1853 and Henry Gabriel Swainson, 1830–1892," *Turnbull Library Record,* n.s. 1 (1967):6–19; and *DSB.* On MacLeay, see above, Chap. 1.
163 William Swainson, *A Treatise on the Geography and Classification of Animals* (London: Longman, Rees, Orme, Brown, Green and Longman, 1835), pp. 1–2.
164 Ibid., p. 3.
165 For another discussion of Swainson's ideas, see M. P. Kinch, "Geographical Distribution and the Origin of Life: The Development of Early-Nineteenth-Century British Explanations," *J. Hist. Biol.* 13 (1980):107–9.
166 See Peter J. Bowler, *Fossils and Progress: Paleontology and the Idea of Progressive Evolution in the Nineteenth Century* (New York: Neale Watson Academic Publications, 1976), pp. 47–62.
167 Lyell, *Principles of Geology,* vol. 1, bk. 1, chap. 9; [Edward Forbes], "The Future of Geology," *Westminster Review,* n.s. 2 (1852):84–86.
168 Edward Forbes, "On the Cystideae of the Silurian Rocks of the British Islands," *Mem. Geol. Surv.* 2 (1848):526. See also Forbes, "On the Cystidea Found in British Rocks, and on Recent Additions to our Knowledge of the Fossil Echinodermata," *Athenaeum,* 1847, p. 744.
169 Forbes, "On the Cystideae of the Silurian Rocks," p. 532.

170  Ibid., pp. 483, 527–28. See Leopold von Buch, "On the Cystidea (a New Family of Radiated Animals), Introduced by an Account of the *Caryocrinus ornatus,* Say," *Q. J. Geol. Soc.* 2, pt. 2 (1845–46):20–42. Forbes's high opinion of von Buch is evidenced in an obituary on the Prussian geologist in the *Literary Gazette,* 1853, p. 253.

171  Forbes, "On the Cystideae of the Silurian Rocks," p. 533.

172  Ibid., p. 534.

173  Notations on Darwin's reprint of Forbes's "On the Cystideae of the Silurian Rocks," Cambridge University Library, pp. 526, 532, 534.

174  Edward Forbes, "Anniversary Address of the President," *Q.J. Geol. Soc.* 10 (1854):lxxvii–lxxxi; idem, "On the Manifestation of Polarity in the Distribution of Organized Beings in Time," *Proc. Royal Inst.* 1 (1851–54):428–33; Wilson and Geikie, *Memoir,* p. 543.

175  Forbes's own term. "Neozoic" appears occasionally in later nine-teenth-century texts, such as A. J. Jukes-Brown, *The Student's Hand-book of Historical Geology* (London: George Bell, 1886), pp. 4, 257. It apparently did not survive into the twentieth century.

176  Forbes, "On the Manifestation of Polarity," p. 432.

177  Ibid., pp. 430–31.

178  See for example, James M. Valentine, "How Many Marine Inverte-brate Fossil Species? A New Approximation," *Journal of Paleontology* 44 (1970):412.

179  Forbes, "On the Manifestation of Polarity," p. 432.

180  Ibid.

181  Immanuel Kant, *Critique of Pure Reason,* trans. Norman Kemp Smith (New York: St. Martin's Press, 1929), pp. 74–78; Whewell, *Philosophy of the Inductive Sciences,* 1:125–28.

182  Forbes, "On the Manifestation of Polarity," p. 428.

183  [Forbes], "The Future of Geology," p. 91.

184  Forbes, "Anniversary Address of the President," p. lxiii.

185  Ibid., p. lxxxi.

186  Whewell, *Philosophy of the Inductive Sciences,* 1:374. Interestingly, Whewell had lectured on the general concept of polarity at the Royal Institution in 1849 ("On the Idea of Polarity," *Athenaeum,* 1849, pp. 119–20).

187  Forbes, "On the Manifestation of Polarity," p. 429.

188  Edward Forbes, "On the Supposed Analogy Between the Life of an Individual and the Duration of a Species," *Edinb. New Phil. J.* 53 (1852):134.

189  Edward Forbes to Andrew Ramsay, 1 August 1854, Imperial College Archives, Ramsay Papers; Andrew C. Ramsay, "On the Former Prob-

able Existence of Palaeozoic Glaciers," *Rpt. Brit. Assn.,* 1854, pt. 2, pp. 93–94; idem, "On the Occurrence of Angular, Subangular, Polished and Striated Fragments and Boulders in the Permian Breccia of Shropshire, Worcestershire, etc.; and on the Probable Existence of Glaciers and Icebergs in the Permian Epoch," *Q.J. Geol. Soc.* 11 (1855):187–205.

190 Ramsay, "On the Occurrence of Angular Fragments," p. 205. For Forbes's support of Ramsay's discovery, see letter, Forbes to Charles Lyell, 17 September 1854, American Philosophical Society, Lyell Papers, no. 189.

191 [Forbes], "The Future of Geology," p. 86.

192 *Sir Charles Lyell's Scientific Journals on the Species Question,* ed. Leonard G. Wilson (New Haven: Yale University Press, 1979), p. 146.

193 Roderick Murchison, *Siluria: The History of the Oldest Known Rocks containing Organic Remains,* 2nd ed. (London: John Murray, 1854), p. 469.

194 [Edward Forbes], "Siluria," *Quarterly Review* 95 (1854):372.

195 S. P. Woodward, *A Manual of the Mollusca* (London: Virtue Brothers, 1866), p. 128. M'Cosh and Dickie described Forbes's "polarity" noncommittally in their *Typical Forms and Special Ends in Creation,* pp. 322–24.

196 C.F.A. Pantin, "Alfred Russel Wallace: His Pre-Darwinian Essay of 1855," *Proceedings of the Linnean Society* 171 (1958–59):139–53. See also Pantin, "Alfred Russel Wallace, F.R.S., and His Essays of 1858 and 1855," *Notes and Records of the Royal Society* 14 (1959):67–84.

197 Alfred R. Wallace, "On the Law Which Has Regulated the Introduction of New Species," *Ann. Mag. Nat. Hist.,* 2nd ser. 16 (1855):192, 195. See also H. Lewis McKinney, *Wallace and Natural Selection* (New Haven: Yale University Press, 1972), pp. 44–46, 97.

198 Wallace, "On the Law Which Has Regulated the Introduction of New Species," p. 192.

199 Alfred R. Wallace, *Contributions to the Theory of Natural Selection* (London: Macmillan, 1875), p. 45.

200 Forbes, "On the Manifestation of Polarity," p. 433.

*Chapter 4: Zonation, Provinces, and Biogeographic Statistics*

1 See the Hippocratic treatise "On Airs, Waters, and Places," in the *Genuine Works of Hippocrates,* trans. Francis Adams (New York: William Wood, 1928), pp. 156–83; G. Miller, "Airs, Waters, and

Places in History," *Journal of the History of Medicine and Allied Sciences* 17 (1962):129–40; Frank N. Egerton, "Ancient Sources for Animal Demography," *Isis* 59 (1968):175–89. The term *ecology* was coined by Ernst Haeckel in his *Generelle Morphologie der Organismen*, 2 vols. in 1 (Berlin: Georg Reimer, 1866), 2:286–89. As an active scientific discipline, ecology clearly is a twentieth-century phenomenon, but for an account of ecological doctrines since the eighteenth century, see Donald Worster's most interesting *Nature's Economy: The Roots of Ecology* (San Francisco: Sierra Club Books, 1977).

2   C. Linnaeus, "The Oeconomy of Nature," in *Miscellaneous Tracts relating to Natural History, Husbandry, and Physick* by B. Stillingfleet (London: J. Dodsby, 1791), pp. 31–108; idem, "On the Police of Nature," in *Select Dissertations from the Amoenitates Academicae, A Supplement to Mr. Stillingfleet's Tracts Relating to Natural History,* trans. F. J. Brand, 2 vols. (London: G. Robinson, 1781), 1:129–66. See also Carl von Linne, *L'Equilibre de la nature* translated by Bernard Jasmin with introduction and notes by Camille Limoges (Paris: J. Vrin, 1972).

3   Valuable in this regard is R. C. Stauffer, "Ecology in the Long Manuscript Version of Darwin's *Origin of Species* and Linnaeus's *Oeconomy of Nature,*" *Proceedings of the American Philosophical Society* 104 (1960):235–41.

4   Alexander von Humboldt and Aimé Bonpland, *Essai sur la géographie des plantes* (Paris: Fr. Schoell, 1807). Humboldt's research on heat patterns and biogeography appeared in "On Isothermal Lines, and the Distribution of Heat over the Globe," *Edinburgh Philosophical Journal* 3 (1820):1–20, 256–74; 4 (1820–21):23–37, 262–81; 5 (1821):28–39. See also William T. Stearn, "Humboldt's *Essai sur la Géographie des Plantes,*" *Journal of the Society for the Bibliography of Natural History* 3 (1960):351–57.

Although Humboldt's work was the first to popularize the study of plant distribution, it was not the first to deal with the subject. Perhaps the first was Giambattista della Porta, *Phytognomonica* (Naples: H. Saluianum, 1588). Appearing in the eighteenth century were Joseph Pitton de Tournefort, *Relation d'un Voyage du Levant*, 2 vols. (Paris: L'Imprimerie Royale, 1717), which documented the changes in vegetation accompanying increases in elevation; and C. Linnaeus, *Stationes Plantarum* (Uppsala: L. M. Hojer, 1754); see G. Einar Du Rietz, "Linnaeus as a Phytogeographer," *Vegetatio acta Geobotanica* 7 (1956–57):161–68.

5   Alexander von Humboldt, "New Inquiries into the Laws Which are Observed in the Distribution of Vegetable Forms," *Edinb. Phil. J.* 6

(1822):282. Italics are Humboldt's. On the development of botanical arithmetic, see Janet Browne's innovative paper, "Darwin's Botanical Arithmetic and the 'Principle of Divergence,' 1854-1858," *J. Hist. Biol.* 13 (1980):53-89.

6  E. A. W. Zimmermann, *Specimen Zoologiae Geographicae Quadrupedum domicilia et migrationes sistens* (Leiden, 1777); see also F. S. Bodenheimer, "Zimmermann's *Specimen Zoologiae Geographicae Quadrupedum*, a Remarkable Zoogeographical Publication at the End of the Eighteenth Century," *Archives Internationales d'Histoire des Sciences* 8 (1955): 351-57; J. C. Fabricius, *Philosophia Entomologica* (Hamburg: C. E. Bohnii, 1778); Gottfried Reinhold Treviranus, *Biologie; oder, Philosophie der Lebenden Natur für Naturforscher und Aerzte*, 6 vols. in 3 (Göttingen: J. F. Röwer, 1802-22); Humboldt, "New Inquiries into the Laws Which are Observed in the Distribution of Vegetable Forms," *Edinb. Phil. J.* 6 (1822):273-87. The onset of biogeographic thinking among German naturalists in the late eighteenth and early nineteenth centuries is a subject ripe for research at the present time.

7  Dawson Turner and Lewis Weston Dillwyn, *The Botanist's Guide through England and Wales*, 2 vols. (London: Phillips and Fardon, 1805).

8  If one examines, for example, the conchological works published prior to this time, the rarity of careful and systematic observations relating to habitats and distribution (either local or regional) is immediately apparent. See Emanuel Mendes da Costa, *Elements of Conchology* (London: Benjamin White, 1776); E[dward] Donovan, *The Natural History of British Shells*, 5 vols. in 3 (London: printed for Donovan and for F. and C. Rivington, 1799-1803). Somewhat more thorough in their inclusion of data on the localities of species were Thomas Brown, *The Elements of Conchology* (London: Lackington, Allen and Company, 1816), and W[illiam] Turton, *A Manual of the Land and Fresh-water Shells of the British Islands* (London: Longman, Rees, Orme, Brown and Green, 1831).

9  Robert Brown, "On the Proteaceae of Jussieu," *Transactions of the Linnean Society of London* 10 (1810-11):20-24; idem, "General Remarks, Geographical and Systematical, on the Botany of Terra Australis," and appendix to Matthew Flinders, *A Voyage to Terra Australis*, vol. 2 (London: G. & W. Nicol, 1814), pp. 61-70.

10  William Kirby and William Spence, *An Introduction to Entomology; or, Elements of the Natural History of Insects*, 4 vols. (London: Longman, Hurst, Rees, Orme and Brown, 1815-26), 4:484.

11    The primary biographical source on Fleming is the memoir by John Duns in John Fleming, *The Lithology of Edinburgh* (Edinburgh: William P. Kennedy, 1859).

12    John Fleming, *The Philosophy of Zoology*, 2 vols. (Edinburgh: Archibald Constable, 1822), 1:vii.

13    John Fleming, *History of British Animals* (London: Duncan and Malcolm, 1828; 2nd ed., 1842), p. xii.

14    Fleming, *Philosophy of Zoology*, 1:49–53. This was a total reversal of the Linnean view which held that plants were dependent on animals to keep their numbers from growing too large and thereby upsetting nature's balance. The polity of nature was also a principal theme in Fleming's lectures at New College. See John Fleming, *The Institutes of Natural Science* (Edinburgh: privately printed, [1846]).

15    Fleming, *Philosophy of Zoology*, 1:53.

16    Ibid., 1:xi–xii. This argument was often used in subsequent works, especially to defend the study of invertebrates. Edward Forbes, for example, wrote that "in the grand system of nature, size is of small account, and elephants and mites, however different in bigness, reckon of equal value as links in the chain of organization. God's works are never left unfinished. None is too minute for the display of infinite perfection" (Edward Forbes and Sylvanus Hanley, *A History of British Mollusca and their Shells*, 4 vols. [London: John Van Voorst, 1848–53], 1:xiv).

17    Fleming, *Philosophy of Zoology*, vol. 2, part 2. A knowledge of these factors was essential, Fleming claimed, not only to a full appreciation of nature, but to any attempts to naturalize exotic species (ibid., 2:105–6).

18    Ibid., p. 87.

19    Ibid., p. 106.

20    John Fleming, *Molluscous Animals* (Edinburgh: Adam and Charles Black, 1837), pp. 20–21. This work formed the article "Mollusca" in the seventh edition of the *Encyclopaedia Britannica*. The "helminthologist," now one who studies worms, especially parasitic types, was originally responsible for the large and nebulous Linnean class Vermes, which included the Mollusca.

21    Fleming, *Philosophy of Zoology*, 2:106–9.

22    Ibid., 1:xv.

23    Duns, "Memoir," chap. 1.

24    George Wilson and Archibald Geikie, *Memoir of Edward Forbes, F.R.S.* (Cambridge: Macmillan, 1861), pp. 83, 154; Augustin-Pyramus DeCandolle and K. Sprengel, *Elements of the Philosophy of Plants* (Edinburgh: W. Blackwood, 1821).

25   Charles Lyell, *Principles of Geology*, 3 vols. (London: John Murray, 1830–33; reprint, New York: Johnson Reprint Corp., 1969). All references to the *Principles* appearing in this and subsequent chapters refer to the reprint of the original edition, unless otherwise noted.

26   Augustin-Pyramus DeCandolle, "Géographie botanique," in *Dictionnaire des Sciences Naturelles*, 18 (1820):359–422; Lyell, *Principles*, 2: 131–40; see Frank N. Eggerton, "Studies of Animal Populations from Lamarck to Darwin," *J. Hist. Biol.* 1 (1968):231–32.

27   Lyell, *Principles*, 2:130.

28   Ibid., 2:69, 71.

29   Ibid., 2:107.

30   See, for example, William Kirby, "Introductory Address, Explanatory of the Views of the Zoological Club, Delivered at its Foundation, November 29, 1823," *Zoological Journal* 2 (1826):1–8; Leonard Jenyns, "On the Recent Progress and Present State of Zoology," *Rpt. Brit. Assn.*, 1834, pp. 143–251.

31   See for example, Edward Forbes, "On the British Species of the Genus Patella," [Edinburgh] *University Journal*, January 1834, p. 6.

32   Edward Forbes, "Notice of Sixteen Species of Testacea new to Scotland," *Athenaeum*, 1836, p. 634.

33   Edward Forbes, "On the Comparative Elevation of Testacea in the Alps," *Magazine of Zoology and Botany* 1 (1837):257–59; see also Wilson and Geikie, *Memoir*, pp. 222–23. Forbes's first observations of plant localities occurred during his visit to Norway in the summer of 1833; see "Journal in Norge," Edinburgh University Library MS., pp. 8–8*a*; J. H. Balfour, "Sketch of the Life of the late Professor Edward Forbes," *Ann. Mag. Nat. Hist.* 2nd ser. 15 (1855):36.

34   Heer's dissertation, *Beiträge zur Pflanzengeographie* (Zurich, 1835) was the first treatise on the geography of plants of the Swiss Alps (Heine Tobien, "Heer, Oswald," *DSB*). See also Alphonse DeCandolle, "Mémoires sur la Géographie Botanique de la Suisse, par M. Oswald Heer," *Bibliotheque Universelle des Sciences, Belle-lettres et Arts: Sciences* 7 (1837):198–201.

35   Joachim Frederik Schouw, *Grundzüge einer allgemeinen Pflanzengeographie* (Berlin: Reimer, 1823).

36   Wilson and Geikie, *Memoir*, p. 219.

37   See Adrien de Jussieu, *Botanique: Cours élémentaire d'histoire naturelle* (Paris: Victor Masson, 1848; 1st ed., 1842), Dixième Leçon; idem, *Géographie botanique* (Paris: [1845]), reprinted from Charles D'Orbigney's *Dictionnaire universel d'histoire naturelle* (1842–61).

38   Graham coauthored a short phytogeographic report to the British Association with James Townsend MacKay, curator of the botanical

garden at Trinity College, Dublin: "Comparative View of the More Remarkable Plants Which Characterize the Neighbourhood of Dublin, the Neighbourhood of Edinburgh, and the Southwest of Scotland," *Rpt. Brit. Assn.*, 1836, pt. 1, pp. 253–57. Graham worked many years on a comprehensive flora of Britain but failed to complete it before his death (J. H. B[alfour], obituary on Robert Graham, *Ann. Mag. Nat. Hist.* 16 [1845]:283–86).

39  *First Annual Report and Proceedings of the Botanical Society of Edinburgh,* 1836. On the early history and aims of the society, see David Elliston Allen, *The Naturalist in Britain: A Social History* (London: Allen Lane, 1976), pp. 109–10, 114; and idem, "H. C. Watson and the Origin of Exchange Clubs," *Proceedings of the Botanical Society of the British Isles* 6 (1965):110–12.

40  A summary of the contents of this first essay and other details of Watson's career are given in Frank N. Egerton's essay "Hewett Watson, Great Britain's First Phytogeographer," *Huntia* 3 (1979):87–102.

41  Hewett C. Watson, "Observations Made During the Summer of 1832, on the Temperature and Vegetation of the Scottish Highland Mountains, in Connection With Their Height Above the Sea," *Edinb. New Phil. J.* 14 (1833):317–24; idem, *Outlines of the Geographical Distribution of British Plants* (Edinburgh: privately printed, 1832), the second edition published as *Remarks on the Geographical Distribution of British Plants; Chiefly in Connection with Latitude, Elevation and Climate* (London: Longman, Rees, Orme, Brown, Green, and Longman, 1835). Watson's *Outlines* received high praise in a review appearing in the *Magazine of Natural History* 6 (1833):265–67.

42  Hewett C. Watson, "Observations on the Construction of Maps for Illustrating the Distribution of Plants, with Reference to the Communication of Mr. Hinds on the Same Subject," *Mag. Nat. Hist.* 9 (1836): 17–21.

43  Watson, *Remarks*, p. viii.

44  Ibid., p. 49. John Barton (1789–1852), for example, in his *Lecture on the Geography of Plants* (London: Harvey and Darton, 1827), concerned himself only with cultivated plants.

45  Ibid., p. 53.

46  Hewett C. Watson, *Topographical Botany*, 2nd ed. (London: Bernard Quaritch, 1883), p. 544. See also D. E. Allen, "Edward Forbes, Manx Botanist," *Journal of the Manx Museum* 6 (1965):254–56; "Hortus Siccus Monensis," *Journal of Botany* 53 (1915):285–86.

47  Edward Forbes, "On the Land and Freshwater Mollusca of Algiers and Bougia," *Ann. Nat. Hist.* 2 (1838–39):250–55; idem, "Notices of a

Botanical Excursion to the Mountains of Ternova in Carniola," *Ann. Nat. Hist.* 3 (1839):236-40.

48  Edward Forbes, "On the Distribution of Terrestrial Pulmonifera in Europe," *Rpt. Brit. Assn.,* 1838, p. 112.

49  *Athenaeum,* 1838, p. 678.

50  William Brand, "On the Proper Mode of Arranging the Society's Herbarium, and Forming a Catalogue for Reference," *Second Annual Report and Proceedings of the Botanical Society of Edinburgh,* 1837-38, pp. 71-75; idem, "Account of a Scheme for Arranging and Classifying the Botanical Society's General Herbarium," *Third Annual Report and Proceedings of the Botanical Society of Edinburgh,* 1839, pp. 108-12.

51  *Athenaeum,* 1838, p. 678.

52  *Rpt. Brit. Assn.,* 1838, p. xxi.

53  W. V. Harcourt, "Objects and Plan of the Association," *Rpt. Brit. Assn.,* 1831-32, pp. 21-41.

54  Wilson and Geikie, *Memoir,* p. 245.

55  W. A. Herdman, "Letter of Professor Edward Forbes on the Marine Zoology of the Irish Sea," *Transactions of the Liverpool Biological Society* 8 (1894):156-58. Forbes penned this rather striking vision of British biology at the age of twenty-three.

56  Harcourt, "Objects and Plan of the Association," pp. 29-30; see also A. D. Orange, "The British Association for the Advancement of Science: The Provincial Background," *Science Studies* 1 (1971):315-29, and the suggestive comments on the importance of the more informal naturalist networks by D. E. Allen in "Natural History and Social History," *Journal of the Society for the Bibliography of Natural History* 7 (1976):509-16.

57  H. C. Watson, *Cybele Britannica,* 4 vols. (London: Longmans, 1847-59).

58  See Harold Stolerman, "Francis Bacon and the Victorians, 1830-1885" (Ph.D. diss., New York University, 1969). The late Susan Cannon referred to this as the period of "Humboldtian science" (*Science in Culture: The Early Victorian Period* [New York: Science History Publications, 1978], chap. 3.).

59  Coincidentally, the Reverend Edward Stanley, one of the founding members of the Manchester Statistical Society and an attendant at the first meeting of the British Association Statistical Section, had been a major source of encouragement to Watson's childhood botanical interests (George Simonds Boulger, "Watson, Hewett Cottrell," *DNB;* and Philip F. Rehbock, "The Origins and Early Years of the Manchester Statistical Society, 1833-1840" [unpublished MS., 1971], pp. 7-8).

60  Harald Westergaard, *Contributions to the History of Statistics* (London: P. S. King, 1932), p. 136. See also Cannon, *Science in Culture,* pp. 240–45.

61  "R.," Review of *Transactions of the Statistical Society of London,* 1837, *London and Westminster Review,* Amer. ed. 29 (1838):37. See also *Oxford English Dictionary.*

62  For example, F.J.F. Meyen included a major section on "The Statistics of Plants" in his *Outlines of the Geography of Plants: With Particular Enquiries Concerning the Native Country, the Culture, and the Uses of the Principal Cultivated Plants on Which the Prosperity of Nations is Based* (London: Ray Society, 1846), trans. of *Grundriss der Pflanzengeographie* (1836). See also William Brand, "Statistics of British Botany," *Third Annual Report and Proceedings of the Botanical Society of Edinburgh,* 1838, pp. 58–66, abstracted in *Rpt. Brit. Assn.,* 1839, pt. 2, p. 89. In this article Brand was concerned with the use of Watson's works on botanical geography as a guide in the arrangement of the herbarium of the Botanical Society of Edinburgh. Also, Gordon, "Notice of the 'New Statistical Account of Scotland,' " *Rpt. Brit. Assn.,* 1834, pt. 2, pp. 692–93; this work was to include statistics on meteorology, hydrography, geology, zoology, and botany. In 1846, Forbes referred to biogeographic data as "the statistics of our science"; see "On the Connexion between the Distribution of the Existing Flora and Fauna of the British Isles . . . ," *Memoirs of the Geological Survey of Great Britain* 1 (1846):398.

63  *Rpt. Brit. Assn.,* 1833, pp. xxviii–xxix, xxxvii, 483–84, 492–95; Frederic J. Mouat, "History of the Statistical Society of London," *Jubilee Volume of the Statistical Society,* 1885, pp. 14–71. See also Frank H. Hankins, *Adolphe Quetelet as Statistician,* Studies in History, Economics, and Public Law, vol. 31, no. 4 (New York: Columbia University Press, 1908); G. M. Jolly and P. Dagnelie, "Adolphe Quetelet, 1796–1874," in R. C. Olby, ed., *Early-Nineteenth-Century European Scientists* (Oxford: Pergamon Press, 1967), pp. 153–79.

64  A. Quetelet, "On the Importance of Keeping Exact Registers in Different Districts," *Rpt. Brit. Assn.,* 1841, pt. 2, p. 96.

65  Jolly and Dagnelie, "Adolphe Quetelet," p. 167.

66  Richard Owen et al., "Report of the Committee . . . Appointed for the Purpose of Reporting on the Registration of Periodical Phaenomena of Animals and Vegetables," *Rpt. Brit. Assn.,* 1845, pt. 1, pp. 321–36.

67  W. Desborough Cooley, "Synopsis of a Proposal Respecting a Physico-Geographical Survey of the British Islands, Particularly in Relation to Agriculture," *Rpt. Brit. Assn.,* 1846, pt. 2, pp. 72–73; Roderick Murchison, Presidential Address, ibid., p. xxxvi.

68  "Registration of the Periodical Phaenomena of Plants and Animals," *Rpt. Brit. Assn.,* 1850, pt. 1, pp. 338–57.

69  R. B. Hinds, "Observations on the Construction of Maps in Geographical Botany," *Mag. Nat. Hist.* 8 (1835):498–501.

70  Edward Belcher, *Narrative of a Voyage Round the World, Performed in Her Majesty's Ship Sulphur, During the Years 1836–1842 . . . ,* 2 vols. (London: H. Colburn, 1843; reprint, Folkestone and London: Dawsons, 1970).

71  R. B. Hinds, "The Physical Agents of Temperature, Humidity, Light, and Soil, Considered as Developing Climate, and in Connexion with Geographic Botany," *Ann. Mag. Nat. Hist.* 9 (1842):169–89, 311–33, 469–75, 521–27.

72  R. B. Hinds, "Memoirs on Geographical Botany," *Ann. Mag. Nat. Hist.* 15 (1845):11–30, 89–104. In his "Report on the Progress of Geographical and Systematic Botany, during the year 1845," August Grisebach criticized Hinds's writings as containing "little more than already known facts and views, not unfrequently mingled with errors, both as regards the facts and deductions" (Arthur Henfrey, ed., *Reports and Papers on Botany,* 2 vols. [London: Ray Society, 1849; New York: Johnson Reprint Corp., 1971], 2:418). And Forbes referred to his work privately as "Hinds' aberation" (Forbes to J. D. Hooker, 6 November 1846, Royal Botanical Gardens, Kew, Hooker Papers, no. 161). Recent authors have been more generous; S. D. McKelvey, for example, described Hinds's *Regions of Vegetation* as including "the first floristic analysis of the vegetation of our west coast made as a result of actual field observation and, as such, a landmark in the botany of the region" (*Botanical Exploration of the Trans-Mississippi West, 1790–1850* [Jamaica Plain, Mass.: Arnold Arboretum, 1955], p. 649).

73  R. B. Hinds, *The Regions of Vegetation; Being an Analysis of the Distribution of Vegetable Forms over the Surface of the Globe in Connexion with Climate and Physical Agents* (London: G. J. Palmer, 1843).

74  Edward Forbes, "Report on the Distribution of Pulmoniferous Mollusca in the British Isles," *Rpt. Brit. Assn.,* 1839, pt. 1, p. 139. These nine naturalists, and the regions for which they provided data, were Leonard Jenyns (Cambridgeshire), William Stanger (southeast England), Joshua Alder (northeast England), William Bean (northeast England), Robert Greville (northeast England), William Thompson (Ireland), and William Jardine, George Johnston, and James Smith (Scotland).

75  Ibid., p. 131.

76  Ibid., pp. 140, 141.

77  Charles Lyell, remarks, *Athenaeum,* 1839, p. 704. On Lyell's percentage method of Cenozoic dating, see *Principles,* vol. 3, chap. V; and M. J. S. Rudwick, "Charles Lyell's Dream of a Statistical Palaeontology," *Palaeontology* 21, pt. 2 (1978):225–44.

78  Lyell, *Principles,* 2:66.

79  Henry T. DelaBeche, *Researches in Theoretical Geology* (New York: F. J. Huntington, 1837), p. 200. (First ed., London, 1834.)

80  Ibid., pp. 335–42.

81  *Rpt. Brit. Assn.,* 1839, p. xxvi.

82  For a more complete account of the evolution of Forbes's motivations for dredging and the results of the British Association Dredging Committee, see my article "The Early Dredgers: 'Naturalizing' in British Seas, 1830–1850," *J. Hist. Biol.* 12 (1979):314–18.

83  Samuel M. Brown and Edward Forbes, *Popular Lectures on the Philosophy of the Sciences* (Edinburgh: n.p., [1840]), p. 7.

84  Edward Forbes, "On the Associations of Mollusca on the British Coasts, Considered with Reference to Pleistocene Geology," *Edinburgh Academic Annual,* 1840, pp. 175–83.

85  The latter hypothesis was suggested to me by Eric Mills, Department of Oceanography, Dalhousie University (personal communication, 7 January 1980).

86  Forbes, "On the Connexion," p. 371.

87  Antonio Risso, *Ichthyologie de Nice; ou, Histoire naturelle des poissons du departement des Alpes maritimes* (Paris: F. Schoell, 1810), pp. xiv–xv; Gören Wahlenberg, *Flora Laponica* (Berlin: Reimer, 1812), as cited in Doty, "Rocky Intertidal Surfaces," p. 538 (see below); J. V. F. Lamoroux; *Histoire des polypiers coralligenes flexibles* (Caen: F. Poisson, 1816), pp. xlvii–lx; Charles D'Orbigny, "Essai sur les plantes marines des cotes du Golfe de Gascogne, et particulièrement sur celles du departement de la Charente-Inferieure," *Mémoires du Muséum d'Histoire Naturelle* 6 (1820):163–203; J. V. F. Lamoroux, "Mémoire sur la géographie des plantes marines," *Annales des Sciences Naturelles* 7 (1826):60–82; H. Milne-Edwards and J. V. Audouin, *Recherches pour servir à l'histoire naturelle du littoral de la France,* 2 vols. (Paris: Crochard, 1832–34); M[ichael] Sars, *Beskrivelser og Iagttagelsor* (Bergen: Thorstein Hallager, 1835). Concurrent with Forbes's work was A. S. Örsted, *De Regionibus Marinis: Elementa Topographiae Historiconaturalis Freti Oresund* (Hauniae: J. C. Scharling, 1844). A valuable bibliography appears in Maxwell S. Doty, "Rocky Intertidal Surfaces," in Joel W. Hedgpeth, ed., *Treatise on Marine Ecology and Paleoecology,* 2 vols., Geological Society of America, Memoir 67 (New York: Geological Society of America, 1957), 1:535–85.

88   Forbes, "On the Associations of Mollusca on the British Coasts," pp.
     182–83.

89   Ibid., p. 178. Italics are Forbes's.

90   Ibid., pp. 179–80.

91   Ibid., p. 177.

92   Ibid., p. 183.

93   In addition to the works discussed, see the following by Forbes: "Zoo-
     geological Considerations on the Freshwater Mollusca," *Ann. Mag.
     Nat. Hist.* 6 (1840–41):241–43; "Notices of Natural History Observa-
     tions Made Since Last Meeting Bearing upon Geology," *Rpt. Brit.
     Assn.,* 1846, pt. 2, pp. 69–70; "Marine Zones of Depth," *Q.J. Geol.
     Soc.* 8 (1852):303; "Note on an Indication of Depth of Primaeval Seas,
     Afforded by the Remains of Colour in Fossil Testacea," *Proc. Roy.
     Soc. Lond.* 7 (1854–55):21–23.

94   Edward Forbes, "Report on the Mollusca and Radiata of the Aegean
     Sea, and on Their Distribution, Considered as Bearing on Geology,
     *Rpt. Brit. Assn.,* 1843, pt. 1, p. 173.

95   Ibid.

96   Karl Möbius's subsequent (1877) definition of the "biocönosis" or
     ecological community stressed the biological side of the species assem-
     blage. In the interim, much attention had been drawn toward inter-and
     intra-species relationships by the *Origin of Species*. See Frank N.
     Egerton, "Studies of Animal Populations from Lamarck to Darwin,"
     *J. Hist. Biol.* 1 (1968):241.

97   Charles Darwin, "Essay of 1842," in Francis Darwin, ed., *The Foun-
     dations of the Origin of Species* (Cambridge: Cambridge University
     Press, 1909), pp. 7–8.

98   Forbes, "Report on the Mollusca and Radiata of the Aegean Sea," pp.
     177–79.

99   Edward Forbes, "On the Light Thrown on Geology by Submarine
     Researches; Being the Substance of a Communication Made to the
     Royal Institution of Great Britain, Friday Evening, the 23rd February
     1844," *Edinb. New Phil. J.* 36 (1844):318–27. An excellent analysis of
     these generalizations is given by Eric L. Mills in his article "Edward
     Forbes, John Gwyn Jeffreys, and British Dredging before the *Chal-
     lenger* Expedition," *Journal of the Society for the Bibliography of Nat-
     ural History* 8 (1978):507–36.

100  Wilson and Geikie, *Memoir,* p. 363.

101  Edward Forbes, "Report on the Investigation of British Marine Zool-
     ogy by Means of the Dredge, Part I: The Infra-littoral Distribution of
     Marine Invertebrata on the Southern, Western, and Northern Coasts
     of Great Britain," *Rpt. Brit. Assn.,* 1850, pt. 1, pp. 192–263.

102  See also Forbes's "On a New Map of the Geological Distribution of Marine Life, and on the Homoiozoic Belts," *Rpt. Brit. Assn.*, 1852, pt. 2, p. 73; idem, "On the Geological Distribution of Marine Animals," *Edinb. New Phil. J.* 54 (1852–53):311–12.

103  Heinrich Karl Wilhelm Berghaus, *Physicalischer Atlas* . . . (Gotha: J. Perthes, 1845; 2nd ed., 1852); see Preston E. James, *All Possible Worlds: A History of Geographical Ideas* (Indianapolis: Bobbs-Merrill, 1972), p. 188. Berghaus and Johnston had collaborated at least as early as 1845; see Berghaus and Johnston, *The Physical Atlas: A Series of Maps Illustrating the Geographical Distribution of Natural Phenomena* [prospectus] (Edinburgh: J. Johnstone, 1845).

104  J. H. Balfour, "Sketch of the Life of the Late Professor Edward Forbes," *Ann. Mag. Nat. Hist.*, 2nd ser. 14 (1855):46.

105  Sven Ekman, *Zoogeography of the Sea* (London: Sidgwick and Jackson, 1953).

106  Edward Forbes, *The Natural History of the European Seas*, edited and continued by Robert Godwin-Austen (London: John Van Voorst, 1859), pp. 222–25.

107  Ibid., p. 225. Forbes had discussed outliers at least as early as 1846, in "On the Connexion," pp. 387–90.

108  Arthur Henfrey, *The Vegetation of Europe, Its Conditons and Causes* (London: John Van Voorst, 1852). This was a companion volume to Forbes's *European Seas* in Van Voorst's innovative series, "Outlines of the Natural History of Europe." The third work in the series, Godwin-Austen's *Geological History of the European Area, Natural and Physical*, never reached print.

109  Henfrey, *Vegetation of Europe*, pp. 42–43. Italics are Henfrey's.

110  Ibid., p. 44.

### Chapter 5: Whence Came the Flora and Fauna?

1  This was the theme of Nils von Hofsten's classic historical monograph "Zur älteren Geschichte des Diskontinuitätsproblems in der Biogeographie," *Zoologische Annalen* 7 (1919):197–349. In the present introduction I have depended heavily on this monograph, which is probably the most extensive contribution to the history of historical biogeography yet to appear. It covers not merely the problem of biogeographic discontinuity from antiquity to the twentieth century, but biogeographic theory in general. Also useful for the early development of the major types of literature on plant geography is A. Engler, "Die Entwicklung der Pflanzengeographie in den letzten hundert Jahren

und weitere Aufgaben derselben," in *Wissenschaftliche Beiträge zum Gedächtnis der hundert-jährigen Wiederkehr des Antritts von Alexander von Humboldts Reise nach Amerika am 5 Juni 1799* (Berlin: W. H. Kuhl, 1899), pp. 1–247.

2   Gareth Nelson, "From Candolle to Croizat: Comments on the History of Biogeography," *J. Hist. Biol.* 11 (1978):269–305.

3   C. Linnaeus, "On the Increase of the Habitable Earth," translation by F. J. Brand of *Oratio de Telluris Habitabili Incremento* (1744), in *Select Dissertations from the Amoenitates Academicae, A Supplement to Mr. Stillingfleet's Tracts Relating to Natural History,* 2 vols. (London: G. Robinson, 1781), 1:71–127.

4   Joachim Frederik Schouw, *Grundzüge einer allgemeinen Pflanzengeographie* (Berlin: Reimer, 1823), from the original Danish *Gruntraek hil en almindelig Plantegeographie* (Copenhagen, 1822); see also Schouw, *The Earth, Plants, and Man,* trans. and ed. Arthur Henfrey (London: Henry G. Bohn, 1859), pp. 17–21; K. A. Rudolphi, *Beyträge zur Anthropologie und allgemeinen Naturgeschichte* (Berlin: Haude und Spener, 1812), pp. 125, 129; A. Desmoulins, "Mémoire sur la distribution géographique des animaux vertébrés, moins les oiseaux," *Journal de Physique* 94 (1822):19–28. See von Hofsten, "Diskontinuitätsproblems" pp. 268–69.

5   William Kirby and William Spence, *An Introduction to Entomology,* 4 vols. (London: Longman, Hurst, Rees, Orme and Brown, 1815–26); William Swainson, *A Treatise on the Geography and Classification of Animals* (London: Longman, Rees, Orme, Brown, Green and Longman, 1835), chap. 1; Louis Agassiz, *Recherches sur les Poissons fossiles,* 5 vols. (Neuchatel: Imprimerie de Petitpierre, 1833–43); idem, "Geographical Distribution of Animals," *Christian Examiner and Religious Miscellany,* 1850, pp. 181–204, republished in *Edin. New Phil. J.* 49 (1850):1–33.

6   Swainson, *Geography and Classification,* pp. 3, 9.

7   Von Hofsten ("Diskontinuitätsproblems," p. 277) uses the term to characterize Humboldt's position.

8   See von Hofsten (ibid., pp. 262, 280–81), who refers to Humboldt and Wahlenberg as "the founders of exact descriptive and physical plant geography" (p. 262).

9   H. F. Link, *Die Urwelt und das Alterthum, erläutert durch die Naturkunde,* 2 vols. (Berlin: Ferdinand Dümmler, 1821–22); Isidore Geoffroy St. Hilaire, "Mammifères," *Dictionnaire classique d'Histoire naturelle* (1826). See von Hofsten, "Diskontinuitätsproblems," pp. 267, 272.

10    Von Hofsten, "Diskontinuitätsproblems," pp. 265–66.

11    Robert Knox wrote that it was Buffon "who discovered and first spoke of 'centres of creation.' " He then chastised Edward Forbes, "who assuredly never claimed it in his own name. But he ought to have disavowed it when ascribed to him by others, whose motives for doing so may very readily be guessed at" (Robert Knox, trans., *A Manual of Zoology*, by Henri Milne-Edwards, ed. C. Carter Blake, 2nd ed. [London: Henry Renshaw, 1863], p. 541). For Zimmermann, see chap. 4, n. 6, above. K. L. Willdenow, *Grundriss der Kräuterkunde* (Berlin: Haude und Spener, 1792), translated as *The Principles of Botany, and of Vegetable Physiology* (Edinburgh: William Blackwood, 1805). See also von Hofsten, "Diskontinuitätsproblems," pp. 251–57, 266.

12    Link, *Die Urwelt und das Alterthum;* A. P. DeCandolle, "Géographie botanique," *Dictionnaire des Sciences Naturelles* (1820); Leopold von Buch,"Allgemeine Übersicht der Flora auf den Canarischen Inseln," *Abhandlungen der Königlichen Akademie der Wissenschaften zu Berlin,* 1816–17, pp. 337–84; von Hofsten, "Diskontinuitätsproblems," pp. 265–66.

13    Charles Lyell, *Principles of Geology,* 3 vols. (London: John Murray, 1830–33; reprint, New York: Johnson Reprint Corp., 1969), 2:124–25.

14    Ibid., vol. 2, chaps. 5–6.

15    Ibid., 2:177.

16    Ibid., p. 172.

17    Ibid., 1:93–95.

18    Ibid., pp. 100–101.

19    Lyell did discuss, at considerable length, the changes in the relative levels of land and sea, especially during the Tertiary period, but only to show how such changes altered climate (ibid., chap. 8).

20    Speculation on the climate of Britain in earlier geologic epochs dates at least to Robert Hooke's *Tractatus de Terrae motis,* published in 1705 (though written in 1688). Hooke believed that England had once enjoyed a warmer climate, based on the discovery of fossil turtles and ammonites. Similar reasoning was employed by Buffon (*Epoques de la Nature*) to explain the existence of mammoths in Siberia. And by the early nineteenth century it was generally accepted that a warmer climate had prevailed worldwide during the Carboniferous period, based on the presence of fossils of tropical floras in temperate regions.

21    Von Hofsten, "Diskontinuitätsproblems," pp. 251–52, 276–77, 281.

22    The ethnologist James Cowles Prichard (1786–1848) preceded Lyell in the discussion of centers of creation in his *Researches into the Physical History of Mankind,* 2nd ed., 2 vols. (London: John and Arthur

Arch, 1826); see M. P. Kinch, "Geographical Distribution and the Origin of Life: The Development of Early-Nineteenth-Century British Explanations," *J. Hist. Biol.* 13 (1980):99–103.

23  Edward Forbes to Andrew Ramsay, Dublin, 5 January 1848, Imperial College Archives, Ramsay Correspondence; published in part in George Wilson and Archibald Geikie, *Memoir of Edward Forbes, F.R.S.* (Cambridge: Macmillan, 1861), p. 429.

24  In the eighth edition of the *Principles* (London: John Murray, 1850), Lyell stated (p. 608) that naturalists had adopted "very generally *the doctrine of specific centres.*" See also [S. G.] Morton, "Doctrine of Specific Organic Centers," *Edinb. New Phil. J.* 51 (1851):197–98. There were still noteworthy opponents, however; see John Fleming, "Remarks on the Origin of Plants and the Physical and Geographical Distribution of Species," *Ann. Mag. Nat. Hist.*, 2nd ser. 4 (1849):202–3; and R. B. Hinds, "Memoirs on Geographic Botany," *Ann. Mag. Nat. Hist.* 15 (1845):11–30, 89–104.

25  Wilson and Geikie, *Memoir*, p. 168.

26  Edward Forbes, "Lectures on the Zoology of the British Seas," *Manx Sun*, 20 March 1840, p. 2.

27  Edward Forbes to Leonard Horner, London, 22 January 1845, British Museum (Natural History) Library, Forbes Tracts, L.60F(3). I heartily thank Dr. Janet Browne for bringing this letter to my attention.

28  Edward Forbes, "Report on the Mollusca and Radiata of the Aegean Sea, and on Their Distribution, Considered as Bearing on Geology," *Rpt. Brit. Assn.*, 1843, pt. 1, p. 173. Although Forbes spoke of the representative species concept as though it were new, Prichard had written in 1826 of "corresponding species of the same genus found in two distinct and entirely separate regions" (*Researches*, 1:79). See R. A. Richardson, "The Development of the Theory of Geographical Race Formation: Buffon to Darwin" (Ph.D. diss., University of Wisconsin, 1968), pp. 90–92.

29  [John Fleming], "Botanical Geography," *North British Review* 20 (1854):520–22.

30  I have discussed this episode in greater detail in "The Early Dredgers: 'Naturalizing' in British Seas, 1830–1850," *J. Hist. Biol.* 12 (1979): 314–18.

31  See Forbes's initial exercise in geological theorizing, "On a Shell-Bank in the Irish Sea, Considered Zoologically and Geologically," *Ann. Nat. Hist.* 4 (1839–40):217–23. Changes in climate and local elevations of strata were both discussed in Forbes's "Report on the Mollusca and Radiata of the Aegean Sea," pp. 172–79.

32  Edward Forbes, "Report on the Collection of Fossils from Southern India, presented by C. J. Kaye, Esq., F.G.S., and the Rev. W. H. Egerton, F.G.S.," *Q.J. Geol. Soc.* 1 (1845):79–81 (read 31 January 1844); idem, "Report on the Fossil Invertebrata from Southern India, Collected by Mr. Kaye and Mr. Cunliffe," *Trans. Geol. Soc.* 7 (1845): 167–69.

33  On this point see Forbes, *A History of British Starfishes, and Other Animals of the Class Echinodermata* (London: John Van Voorst, 1841), p. 122.

34  Wilson and Geikie, *Memoir*, p. 360.

35  Edward Forbes, "On the Distribution of Endemic Plants, More Especially Those of the British Islands, Considered with Regard to Geological Changes," *Rpt. Brit. Assn.*, 1845, pt. 2, pp. 67–68; abbreviated, but with audience discussion, in *Athenaeum*, 1845, p. 678.

36  The term "Pleistocene" had been proposed by Lyell in 1839 to replace his previous "Newer Pliocene"; the "Older Pliocene" then became simply the "Pliocene." In Lyell's system, Pleistocene referred to strata containing a very high percentage of recent species, particularly those strata he had examined in Sicily. Forbes adopted the term almost immediately, extending it to the formations of the glacial epoch in Britain (believed to be synchronous with the deposition of the Sicilian strata). Most geologists continued to use "Newer Pliocene" through the 1840s, but eventually "Pleistocene" became the accepted term for the epoch of glaciation. Lyell later had doubts about the usefulness of the term. In 1865 he advocated (somewhat equivocally) that "Pleistocene" be avoided because of confusion over its meaning which he attributed partially to Forbes. See Lyell, *Elements of Geology* (New York: Appleton, 1868), pp. 107–8. See also William B. N. Berry, *Growth of a Prehistoric Time Scale* (San Francisco: W. H. Freeman, 1968), p. 111.

37  Forbes, "On the Distribution of Endemic Plants," *Athenaeum*, 1845, p. 678.

38  Edward Forbes, "On the Question in Natural History, Have Genera, Like Species, Centres of Distribution?" *Edinb. New Phil. J.* 45 (1848): 175–76.

39  Criticism of this assumption was central in August Grisebach's assessment. See his "Report on Geographical and Systematic Botany for 1845," in Arthur Henfrey, ed., *Reports and Papers on Botany*, 2 vols. (London: Ray Society, 1849; New York: Johnson Reprint Corp., 1971), 2:420–22.

40  For example, in a letter to William Thompson of Belfast, Forbes theorized that aquatic plants common to Europe and North America must have been transported by migratory birds (Wilson and Geikie,

*Memoir,* p. 475). See also Forbes, "On the Distribution of Freshwater Animals and Plants," *Athenaeum,* 1850, p. 290.

41 Forbes, "On the Distribution of Endemic Plants," p. 67.

42 See Martin Fichman, "Wallace: Zoogeography and the Problem of Land Bridges," *J. Hist. Biol.* 10 (1977):45–63.

43 Edward Forbes, "On the Question, Whence and When Came the Plants and Animals Now Inhabiting the British Isles and Seas?" *Athenaeum,* 1846, pp. 247–48; Wilson and Geikie, *Memoir,* p. 395.

44 Edward Forbes, "On the Connexion Between the Distribution of the Existing Flora and Fauna of the British Isles, and the Geological Changes Which Have Affected Their Area, Especially During the Epoch of the Northern Drift," *Mem. Geol. Surv.* 1 (1846):336–432, with 2 plates.

45 Ibid., p. 350.

46 Ibid., p. 351. Darwin's manuscripts indicate that he anticipated Forbes in this theory, though Forbes was the first to publish it (*More Letters of Charles Darwin,* ed. Francis Darwin and A. C. Seward, 2 vols. [New York: D. Appleton and Co., 1903], 1:408). See also Michael T. Ghiselin, *The Triumph of the Darwinian Method* (Berkeley and Los Angeles: University of California Press, 1969), p. 39; Charles Darwin and Alfred Russel Wallace, *Evolution by Natural Selection* (Cambridge: Cambridge University Press, 1958), pp. 178–81.

47 Forbes, "Connexion," p. 349.

48 W. H. Harvey, *A Manual of the British Algae* (London: Van Voorst, 1841), pp. xvi–xvii. A coastal origin for the floating *Sargassum* was accepted for some time, though it was usually thought to have come from the West Indies. This idea is now discounted; see Sven Ekman, *Zoogeography of the Sea* (London: Sidgewick and Jackson, 1953), p. 333.

49 Forbes, "Connexion," pp. 363–65.

50 Ibid., p. 345.

51 Hence the inclusion in the title of the work of the words "the Geological Changes . . . During the Epoch of the Northern Drift."

52 Darwin, *More Letters,* 1:95.

53 This important transformation in Western intellectual history is admirably described in Stephen Toulmin and June Goodfield, *The Discovery of Time* (New York: Harper & Row, 1965). It is also a major theme in Michel Foucault, *The Order of Things: An Archaeology of the Human Sciences* (New York: Random House, 1970).

54 Louis Agassiz, *Études sur les glaciers* (Neuchatel: Jent et Gassmann, 1840). See M. J. S. Rudwick, "The Glacial Theory," *Hist. Sci.* 13 (1975):136–57.

55   Forbes, "Connexion," p. 400. In 1841 Forbes seems to have been a *supporter* of Agassiz's views on glaciation. In a letter (13 February 1841) Forbes told Agassiz: "I mean during the summer to collect data on . . . the decidedly arctic character of the pleistocene fauna . . . in order to present a mass of geological proofs of your theory" (*Louis Agassiz, His Life and Correspondence,* ed. Elizabeth Cary Agassiz, 2 vols. [Boston: Houghton, Mifflin, 1888], 1:338). Forbes went to the Aegean during the summer instead. By 1845 his views on glaciation had changed.

56   Forbes, "Connexion," p. 363.

57   For a discussion of the impact of the discovery of the Irish elk on the diluvialist-uniformitarian controversy and an illustration of Owen's reconstruction of the elk, see M. J. S. Rudwick, *The Meaning of Fossils: Episodes in the History of Palaeontology,* 2nd ed. (New York: Neale Watson Academic Publications, 1976), pp. 172–73. *Megaloceros* continues to excite the imagination of scientists and laymen, generating speculations on the functions of the antlers and their interpretation within evolutionary theory; see Stephen Jay Gould, "The Origin and Function of 'Bizarre' Structures: Antler Size and Skull Size in the 'Irish Elk,' *Megaloceros giganteus*," *Evolution* 28 (1974):191–220; idem, "The Misnamed, Mistreated, and Misunderstood Irish Elk," *Natural History,* March 1973, pp. 10–19.

58   James Parkinson, *Organic Remains of a Former World,* 3 vols. (London: Sherwood, Neely, and Jones, 1804–11). Parkinson refers to *Megaloceros* as "the Fossil Elk of Ireland" (3:313–19, plate xx, fig. ii). Books Forbes used in his youth are mentioned in Hugh Miller, "The late Professor Edward Forbes," *Edinb. New Phil. J.,* n.s. 1 (1855):135, originally an address to the Royal Physical Society, 29 November 1854.

59   Edward Forbes, "On a Pleistocene Tract in the Isle of Man, and the Relations of its Fauna to that of the Neighbouring Sea," *Rpt. Brit. Assn.,* 1840, pt. 2, pp. 104–5.

60   Edward Forbes, "Note on the age of the Manx elk," dated June 1843, Scottish National Library MSS., vol. 3813, nos. 167–68.

61   Ibid.

62   Forbes's manuscript reads in part: "The pleistocene [tract] is not a raised beach but a raised sea bottom, the fossils in its highest positions being such as indicate a depth of 20 fathoms or more. Elk bones are never found in it; only in the freshwater basins which it includes; therefore the Elk *must have existed posterior to the elevation of the* pleistocene (which was *probably continuous with* that of Liverpool & *the*

*Clyde, forming a great plain extending from Scotland to Cheshire,* where the sea now is), & as the pleistocene has been referred to the age of the till, posterior to that deposit." The portions in italics are repeated verbatim in Richard Owen, *A History of British Fossil Mammals and Birds* (London: John Van Voorst, 1846), p. 467; the latter work was based on reports presented to the British Association in 1842–43.

63 Thomas Molyneux, "A Discourse concerning the Large Horns frequently found under Ground in Ireland, Concluding from them that the great American Deer, call'd a Moose, was formerly common in that Island: with remarks on some other things Natural to that Country," *Phil. Trans.* 19 (1697):489–512.

64 Molyneux was convinced that a provident Creator would not permit a species to become extinct. Therefore the absence of the elk in modern Ireland implied that the species must still be preserved elsewhere. None had been seen in Europe, but reports of the moose coming from the New World were taken as proof of the elk's existence there.

65 *Molyneux,* "Discourse," p. 507. Italics in original.

66 Forbes, "Note on the age of the Manx elk," p. 2.

67 Forbes, "On the Distribution of Endemic Plants," p. 67.

68 Edward Forbes to Charles Lyell, 1 March 1847, American Philosophical Society, Lyell Papers, no. 180. The lecture referred to was "On the Question, Whence and When Came the Plants and Animals Inhabiting the British Isles and Seas?" *Athenaeum,* 1846, pp. 247–48.

69 See especially the chart opposite p. xlvi in Owen's *History of British Fossil Mammals and Birds.*

70 This second point was suggested to me by Frank N. Egerton, Personal communication, 19 June 1974.

71 Wilson and Geikie, *Memoir,* p. 384. Italics are Forbes's.

72 Forbes to Lyell, 1 March 1847.

73 Edward Forbes to J. E. Gray, postmarked 28 March 1840, American Philosophical Society, J. E. Gray Papers.

74 Edward Forbes, "On the Phrenological Developments of the Cheese-Mite," *University Journal of Literature and Science,* January 1834, pp. 19–22. Unfortunately, no correspondence between Watson and Forbes survives.

75 Hewett C. Watson to C. C. Babington, 1846, Cambridge University Herbarium, Watson Papers. For copies of this and other Watson manuscripts, not to mention many original ideas regarding Watson's career, I am very much indebted to Professor Frank N. Egerton. For another rendering of the Forbes-Watson rivalry, see Egerton's forthcoming biography of Watson.

76  Hewett C. Watson, *Cybele Britannica*, 4 vols. (London: Longmans, 1847–59), 1:55 and appendix.

77  Watson instanced Robert Chamber's supplementary "Explanations" to the *Vestiges of the Natural History of Creation*. See [Robert Chambers], *Vestiges of the Natural History of Creation*, 4th ed. (New York: Wiley and Putnam, 1846), "Explanations," pp. 117–18.

78  Watson, *Cybele Britannica*, 1:468, 469.

79  Ibid., p. 471.

80  Forbes, "Connexion," p. 342.

81  [Edward Forbes], "Plants and Botanists," *Westminster Review* (American ed.), October 1852, p. 212.

82  Forbes was aware, before the fact, of Watson's intention to publish an attack; see Forbes to William Thompson, 10 October 1846, Manx Museum, MS 2148/17A, p. 8.

83  Joseph Hooker to Charles Darwin, 28 September 1845, Cambridge University Library, Darwin Papers, vol. 100, fols. 71–72.

84  Hooker to Darwin, 10 April 1846, in *Life and Letters of Sir Joseph Dalton Hooker*, ed. Leonard Huxley, 2 vols. (New York: D. Appleton and Co., 1918), 1:444.

85  Darwin to Hooker, February 1846, in Darwin, *More Letters*, 1:56. See also Wilson and Geikie, *Memoir*, p. 366.

86  Forbes to Hooker, 31 October 1846, Archives, Royal Botanic Gardens, Kew, Letters to Sir Joseph Dalton Hooker, vol. 8, nos. 159–60.

87  Forbes to Hooker, 22 April 1847, Letters to Hooker, vol. 8, nos. 163–64.

88  Watson to Darwin, undated, Cambridge University Library, Darwin Papers, vol. 47, fol. 163.

89  [John Fleming], "Botanical Geography," *North British Review* 20 (1854):513–14.

90  Watson, *Cybele Britannica*, 4:125, 442, 518–19. For example, Watson stressed that the writing of a true history of the British flora must be done "under a worthier ambition than that of 'getting up some sort of paper, likely to make talk among the geologists, at the Meeting of the British Association'" (p. 125). The source of Watson's quotation is not known.

91  Ibid., p. 8.

92  Wilson and Geikie, *Memoir*, p. 395.

93  William King, "First Series of Supplementary Notes to a Former Paper, Entitled 'An Account of Some Shells and Other Invertebrate Forms Found on the Coast of Northumberland and of Durham,'"

*Ann. Mag. Nat. Hist.* 19 (1847):334; Ch[arles] Martins "On the Vegetable Colonisation of the British Islands, Shetland, Feroe, and Iceland," *Edinb. New Phil. J.* 46 (1848):44.

94    Roderick Murchison, "Presidential Address," *Rpt. Brit. Assn.,* 1846, p. xxxiii.

95    Ibid., p. xxxiv.

96    Charles Lyell, *Life, Letters, and Journals,* 2 vols. (London: John Murray, 1881), 2:106, quoted from a letter to Forbes, dated 14 October 1846. See also p. 105, and Lyell, *Principles of Geology,* 7th ed. (London: John Murray, 1847), pp. 88, 676.

97    Lyell, *Life, Letters, and Journals,* 2:107.

98    Ibid., p. 106.

99    Forbes to Lyell, 18 October 1846, ibid., 2:111. Italics are Forbes's. At the time of writing the "Connexion" essay (spring 1846) Forbes wrote to Darwin, "From the hurry and pressure which unfortunately attend all my movements and doings I rarely have time to spare, in preparing for publication, to do more than give brief and unsatisfactory abstracts, which I fear are often extremely obscure" (Darwin, *More Letters,* 1:53).

100    Lyell, *Life, Letters, and Journals,* 2:111–12. See also Forbes to Lyell, 1 March 1847, American Philosophical Society, Lyell Papers, no. 180.

101    Leonard Horner, "Anniversary Address of the President," *Q.J. Geol. Soc.* 3 (1847):lv. Charles Daubeny repeated these praises in his address to the British Association nine years later (*Athenaeum,* 1856, p. 998).

102    Joseph Hooker, *The Botany of the Antarctic Voyage of H.M. Discovery Ships "Erebus" and "Terror," in the Years 1839–1843,* vol. 2, *Flora Novae-Zelandiae* (London: Lovell Reeve, 1853–55), pp. xxii–xxiii. See also vol. 3, *Flora Tasmaniae* (1860), pp. xviii–xix. A second botanical defender of Forbes's theories was Arthur Henfrey, in *The Vegetation of Europe: Its Conditions and Causes* (London: John Van Voorst, 1852), p. 383.

103    Darwin, *More Letters,* 1:461.

104    Ibid., pp. 411–12.

105    Ibid., pp. 53–55.

106    Ibid., p. 412.

107    Ibid., p. 93.

108    Forbes to Lyell, 27 June 1850, American Philosophical Society, Lyell Papers, no. 182.

109    See, by Forbes, "Report on the Investigation of British Marine Zoology by means of the Dredge," *Rpt. Brit. Assn.,* 1850, pt. 1, p. 263; Report of Section D of the British Association, *Literary Gazette,* 1851,

pp. 483–84; "On Recent Researches into the Natural History of the British Seas," *Edinb. New Phil. J.* 50 (1850–51):335–39; "On the Extinct Land-Shells of St. Helena," *Q.J. Geol. Soc.* 8 (1852):197–99.

110 Robert M'Andrew, "On the Mollusca of Vigo Bay in the North-west of Spain," *Ann. Mag. Nat. Hist.,* 2nd ser. 3 (1849):507–13; Forbes to A. C. Ramsay, May 1849, Imperial College Archives, Ramsay Correspondence. M'Andrew's discovery was commemorated in a poem probably composed by Forbes for a social gathering of the Geological Survey "Royal Hammerers" ("Account of a New Discovery lately Made by a Red Lion on the Coast of Spain," Institute of Geological Sciences Library, London, "Royal Hammers' Songs: unnamed," GSM 1/145).

111 Alphonse De Candolle, *Géographie Botanique Raisonnée,* 2 vols. (Paris: Victor Masson, 1855), 2:1315. See also De Candolle's "On the Causes Which Limit Vegetable Species Towards the North," *Annual Report of the Smithsonian Institution,* 1858, p. 245, read before the Académie des Sciences in 1847.

112 Oswald Heer, "On the Probable Origin of the Organized Beings Now Living in the Azores, Madeira, and the Canaries," *Ann. Mag. Nat. Hist.,* 2nd ser. 18 (1856):183. See also Heer's "Über die fossilen Pflanzen von St. Jorge in Madeira," *Neue Denkschriften der allgemeinen Schweizerischen Gesellschaft für die gesammten Naturwissenschaften* 15 (1857):15–24.

113 Possibly in Maury's *Physical Geography of the Sea* (New York: Harper and Brothers, 1855).

114 Heer, "Probable Origin," p. 184.

115 Asa Gray, "Diagnostic Characters of New Species of Phaenogamous Plants, Collected in Japan by Charles Wright, Botanist of the U.S. North Pacific Exploring Expedition. . . . With Observations upon the Relations of the Japanese Flora to that of North America and of other Parts of the North Temperate Zone," *Memoirs of the American Academy of Arts and Sciences,* n.s. 6, pt. 2 (1858):377–452, esp. 442. Lyell inclined toward Gray's suggestion while retaining a belief in Forbes's hypothesis of a westward extension of Europe during the Miocene; see his *Elements of Geology,* 6th ed. (New York: D. Appleton and Co., 1868), pp. 268–76. A similar position was taken in Daniel Oliver, "The Atlantis Hypothesis in its Botanical Aspect," *Natural History Review* 2 (1862):149–70; and Andrew Murray, *The Geographical Distribution of Mammals* (London: Day and Son, 1866), chap. 4.

116 Franz Unger, "The Sunken Island of Atlantis," *Journal of Botany* 3 (1865):17–18, translated from *Die Versunkene Insel Atlantis* (Vienna: Braunmüller, 1860). Italics are Unger's.

117 Ibid., p. 22.
118 Ibid., p. 25.
119 Darwin, *Life and Letters,* 1:431–36. See S. P. Woodward, *A Manual of the Mollusca* (London: Virtue Brothers, 1866); Thomas Vernon Wollaston, *Insecta Maderensia; Being an Account of the Insects of the Islands of the Madeiran Group* (London: John Van Voorst, 1854), pp. xiii–xiv; and idem, *On the Variation of Species with Special Reference to the Insecta; Followed by an Inquiry into the Nature of Genera* (London: John Van Voorst, 1856), chap. 5.
120 Darwin to Lyell, 16 June 1856, in Darwin, *Life and Letters,* 1:431.
121 Joseph Hooker to Charles Darwin, 31 July 1866, in Hooker, *Life and Letters,* 2:99–100. Hooker's supposition about Wallace was incorrect by this time, as Wallace had gone over to the migrationist camp; see Martin Fichman, "Wallace: Zoogeography and the Problem of Land Bridges," *J. Hist. Biol.* 10 (1977):45–63.
122 Joseph Hooker, "On Insular Floras: A Lecture," *Journal of Botany, British and Foreign,* 5 (1867):23–31.
123 Joseph Hooker, "On Geographical Distribution," *Rpt. Brit. Assn.,* 1881, p. 733.
124 Hooker, *Life and Letters,* 2:98.
125 For the turn of the century, see, for example, R. F. Scharff, *The History of the European Fauna* (London: Walter Scott, 1899), and Hans Gadow, *The Wanderings of Animals* (Cambridge: Cambridge University Press, 1913). As a demonstration of the absurdity of continued extensionism, the many hypothesized land bridges were assembled together on the same map (with virtually no ocean areas remaining) in Anton Handlirsch, "Beiträge zur exacten Biologie," *Sitzungsberichte der Akademie der Wissenschaften in Wien* (m.-n.Kl.) 122, Abt. 1 (1913): 361–481, cited in Richard Hesse et al., *Ecological Animal Geography,* 2nd ed. (New York: John Wiley and Sons, 1951), pp. 10, 14.
126 Suggestive thoughts to this effect appear in Gareth Nelson, "From Candolle to Croizat: Comments on the History of Biogeography," *J. Hist. Biol.* 11 (1978):269–305.

## Chapter 6: A Darwinian Epilogue

1 Robert Knox, "Zoology: Its Present Phasis and Future Prospects," *Zoologist* 15 (1857):5475.
2 Charles Darwin, *On the Origin of Species,* facsimile of the first edition (New York: Atheneum, 1967), p. 206.
3 E. R. Lankester, "On the Use of the Term Homology in Modern Zoology, and the Distinction between Homogenetic and Homoplastic

Agreements," *Ann. Mag. Nat. Hist.,* 4th ser. 6 (1870):34–43; Stuart A. Kauffman, "Biological Homologies and Analogies," *Dictionary of the History of Ideas* (New York: Charles Scribner's Sons, 1968), 1:236–42.

4   *The Anatomical Memoirs of John Goodsir,* ed. William Turner, 2 vols. (Edinburgh: Adam and Charles Black, 1868), 1:265. For other anti-evolutionary arguments, see ibid., pp. 208–10.

5   *More Letters of Charles Darwin,* ed. Francis Darwin and A. C. Seward, 2 vols. (New York: D. Appleton and Co., 1903), 1:77. Other disparaging comments, on quinarianism as well as polarity, appear in letters on pp. 84, 128, and 305. See also David L. Hull, *Darwin and His Critics: The Reception of Darwin's Theory of Evolution by the Scientific Community* (Cambridge: Harvard University Press, 1973), pp. 74–75.

6   R. C. Stauffer, ed., *Charles Darwin's Natural Selection: Being the Second Part of His Big Species Book Written from 1856 to 1858* (London: Cambridge University Press, 1975), chap. 11.

7   Useful references toward such a history include Donald Worster, *Nature's Economy: The Roots of Ecology* (San Francisco: Sierra Club Books, 1977), chap. 10; Frank N. Egerton, "Ecological Studies and Observations before 1900," in B. J. Taylor and T. J. White, eds., *Issues and Ideas in America* (Norman: University of Oklahoma Press, 1976); and the works by Von Hofsten, Engler, Fichman, and Nelson cited in Chapter 5, above.

8   John Theodore Merz, *A History of European Scientific Thought in the Nineteenth Century,* 2 vols. (New York: Dover, 1965; 1st ed. 1904–12), 2:274.

9   D'Arcy Wentworth Thompson, *On Growth and Form* (Cambridge: Cambridge University Press, 1917). See also Stephen Jay Gould, "D'Arcy Thompson and the Science of Form," *New Literary History* 2 (1971):229–58; and idem, "The Shape of Things to Come," *Systematic Zoology* 22 (1973):401–4.

10   For the media's summary of these undercurrents at their peak in the early 1970s, see "Reaching beyond the Rational," *Time,* 23 April 1973, pp. 83–86.

# Bibliography

## Works by the Philosophical Naturalists and Their Contemporaries

Abernethy, John. *Physiological Lectures, Exhibiting a General View of Mr. Hunter's Physiology, and of His Researches in Comparative Anatomy.* London: Longman, Hurst, Rees, Orme, and Brown, 1817.

Agassiz, Elizabeth Cary, ed. *Louis Agassiz, His Life and Correspondence.* 2 vols. Boston: Houghton, Mifflin, 1888.

Agassiz, Louis. *Recherches sur le poissons fossiles.* 5 vols. Neuchatel: Imprimerie de Petitpierre, 1833–43.

——. *Études sur le glaciers.* Neuchatel: Jent et Gassmann, 1840.

——. "Geographical Distribution of Animals." *Christian Examiner and Religious Miscellany,* 1850, pp. 181–204.

Babbage, Charles. *Reflections on the Decline of Science in England and on Some of its Causes.* London: B. Fellows, 1830.

Baer, K. E. Von. "Fragments Relating to Philosophical Zoology." Trans. T. H. Huxley. In Arthur Henfrey and Thomas Henry Huxley, eds., *Scientific Memoirs . . . ,* pp. 176–238. London: Taylor and Francis, 1853; reprint, New York and London: Johnson Reprint Corp., 1966.

Balfour, John Hutton. *A Manual of Botany, being an Introduction to the Study of the Structure, Physiology, and Classification of Plants.* London: Griffin, 1849.

Barclay, John. *Introductory Lectures to a Course of Anatomy . . . with a Memoir of the Life of the Author, by George Ballingall, M.D.* Edinburgh: Maclachlan and Stewart, 1827.

Barry, Martin. "On the Unity of Structure in the Animal Kingdom." *Edinb. New Phil. J.* 22 (1836–37):116–41.

——. "Further Observations on the Unity of Structure in the Animal Kingdom, and on Congenital Anomalies, including 'Hermaphrodites'; with some Remarks on Embryology, as facilitating Animal Nomenclature, Classification, and the study of Comparative Anatomy." *Edinb. New Phil. J.* 22 (1836–37):345–64.

——. "Researches in Embryology." *Phil. Trans.* 128 (1838):301–41; 129 (1839):307–80.

——. "A Contribution to the Physiology of Cells." *Phil. Trans.* 130 (1840):529–93.

Barton, John. *A Lecture on the Geography of Plants.* London: Harvey and Darton, 1827.

Béclard, Pierre Auguste. *Elements of General Anatomy.* Translated from the last edition of the French, . . . with notes and corrections, by Robert Knox. Edinburgh: Maclachlan and Stewart, 1830.

Belcher, Edward. *Narrative of a Voyage Round the World, Performed in Her Majesty's Ship "Sulphur," During the Years 1836–1842.* . . . 2 vols. London: H. Colburn, 1843; reprint, Folkstone and London: Dawsons, 1970.

Berghaus, Heinrich Karl Wilhelm. *Physicalischer Atlas.* . . . Gotha: J. Perthes, 1845; 2nd ed., 1852.

Berghaus, Heinrich Karl Wilhelm, and Johnston, Alexander Keith. *The Physical Atlas; a Series of Maps Illustrating the Geographical Distribution of Natural Phenomena* [prospectus]. Edinburgh: J. Johnstone, 1845.

Brand, William. "On the Proper Mode of Arranging the Society's Herbarium, and Forming a Catalogue for Reference." *Second Annual Report and Proceedings of the Botanical Society of Edinburgh,* 1837–38, pp. 71–75.

——. "Statistics of British Botany." *Third Annual Report and Proceedings of the Botanical Society of Edinburgh,* 1839, pp. 58–66, abstracted in *Rpt. Brit. Assn.,* 1839, pt. 2, p. 89.

——. "Account of a Scheme for Arranging and Classifying the Botanical Society's General Herbarium." *Third Annual Report and Proceedings of the Botanical Society of Edinburgh,* 1839, pp. 108–12.

[Brown, John.] "Dr. Samuel Brown." *North British Review* 26 (1857):376–406.

Brown, Robert. "On the Proteaceae of Jussieu." *Transactions of the Linnean Society of London* 10 (1810–11):15–226.

——. "General Remarks, Geographical and Systematical, on the Botany of Terra Australis." An appendix to Matthew Flinders. *A Voyage to Terra Australis*, vol. 2. London: G. & W. Nicol, 1814.

Brown, Samuel M. "Experimental Researches on the Production of Silicon from Paracyanogen." *Proc. Roy. Soc. Edinb.* 1 (1841):341–43.

———. *Two Processes for Silicon.* Edinburgh: A. and D. Black, 1843.

———. *Testimonials in Favour of Dr. Samuel Brown, now a candidate for the Chair of Chemistry in the University of Edinburgh.* Edinburgh: Neill and Company, 1843.

———. "Sir Humphrey Davy." *North British Review* 2 (1844):53–86.

———. *Some Account of Itinerating Libraries and Their Founder.* Edinburgh: William Blackwood and Sons, 1856.

———. *Lectures on the Atomic Theory, and Essays Scientific and Literary.* 2 vols. Edinburgh: T. Constable and Co., 1858.

Brown, Samuel M., and Forbes, Edward. *Popular Lectures on the Philosophy of the Sciences.* Edinburgh: n.p., [1840].

Brown, Thomas. *The Elements of Conchology.* London: Lackington, Allen and Co., 1816.

Buch, Leopold von. "Allgemeine Übersicht der Flora auf den Canarischhen Inseln." *Abhandlungen der Königlichen Akademie der Wissenschaften zu Berlin,* 1816–17, pp. 337–84.

———. "On the Cystidea (a New Family of Radiated Animals), Introduced by an Account of the *Caryocrinus ornatus,* Say." *Q.J. Geol. Soc.* 2, pt. 2 (1845–46):20–42.

Carpenter, William B. "On the Structure and Functions of the Organs of Respiration, in the Animal and Vegetable Kingdoms." *West of England Journal of Science and Literature,* no. 4 (1835), pp. 217–28; no. 5 (1836), pp. 279–87.

———. "On the Unity of Function in Organized Beings." *Edinb. New Phil. J.* 23 (1837):92–114.

———. "Physiology an Inductive Science." *British and Foreign Medical Review* 5 (1838):317–42.

———. *Principles of General and Comparative Physiology, Intended as an Introduction to the Study of Human Physiology, and as a Guide to the Philosophical Pursuit of Natural History.* London: J. Churchill, 1839; 2nd ed., 1841; 3rd ed., 1851; 4th ed., 1854.

[———]. "Professor Owen *on the Comparative Anatomy and Physiology of the Vertebrate Animals.*" *British and Foreign Medico-Chirurgical Review* 23 (1847):472–92.

———. *Nature and Man: Essays Scientific and Philosophical With an Introductory Memoir by J. Estlin Carpenter, M.A.* New York: D. Appleton and Co., 1889.

Chambers, Robert. *Vestiges of the Natural History of Creation.* 4th ed. New York: Wiley and Putnam, 1846.

*Commissioners for the Universities of Scotland, 1826 and 1830. Evidence,* vol. 1, *University of Edinburgh.* London: 1837.

Cooley, W. Desborough. "Synopsis of a Proposal Respecting a Physico-Geographical Survey of the British Islands, Particularly in Relation to Agriculture." *Rpt. Brit. Assn.,* 1846, pt. 2, pp. 72–73.

Costa, Emanuel Mendes da. *Elements of Conchology.* London: Benjamin White, 1776.

Couch, R. Q. "On the Morphology of the Different Organs of Zoophytes." *Ann. Mag. Nat. Hist.* 15 (1845):161–66.

Darwin, Charles. *Journal of Researches into the Geology and Natural History of the various countries visited by H.M.S. "Beagle."* . . . London: Henry Colburn, 1839; facsimile reprint, New York: Hafner Publishing Co., 1952.

———. *On the Origin of Species.* Facsimile of the first edition. New York: Atheneum, 1967.

Darwin, Charles, and Wallace, Alfred Russel. *Evolution by Natural Selection.* Cambridge: Cambridge University Press, 1958.

Darwin, Francis, ed. *The Foundations of the Origin of Species.* Cambridge: Cambridge University Press, 1909.

Darwin, Francis, and Seward, A. C., eds. *More Letters of Charles Darwin.* 2 vols. New York: D. Appleton and Co., 1903.

Davy, Humphrey. *Elements of Chemical Philosophy.* London: J. Johnson and Co., 1812.

DeBlainville, Henri Marie. "The Comparative Osteography of the Skeleton and Dentar System, in the Five Classes of Vertebral Animals, Recent and Fossil." Edited (from the French) and additionally illustrated with numerous notes, observations and drawings, by Robert Knox. *Lancet,* September–November 1839, pp. 137–45, 185–92, 217–22, 297–307.

DeCandolle, Alphonse. "Mémoires sur la Géographie Botanique de la Suisse, par M. Oswald Heer." *Bibliotheque Universelle des Sciences, Belle-lettres et Arts, Sciences* 7 (1837):198–201.

———. *Géographie Botanique Raisonnée.* 2 vols. Paris: Victor Masson, 1855.

———. "On the Causes Which Limit Vegetable Species Towards the North." *Annual Report of the Smithsonian Institution,* 1858, pp. 237–45.

DeCandolle, Augustin-Pyramus. "Géographie botanique." In *Dictionnaire des Sciences Naturelles* 18 (1820):359–422.

DeCandolle, Augustin-Pyramus, and Sprengel, K. *Elements of the Philosophy of Plants.* Edinburgh: W. Blackwood, 1821.

DelaBeche, Henry T. *Researches in Theoretical Geology.* New York: F. J. Huntington, 1837.

Desmoulins, A. "Mémoire sur la distribution géographique des animaux vertébrés, moins les oiseaux." *Journal de Physique* 94 (1822):19–28.

Donovan, E. *The Natural History of British Shells.* 5 vols. in 3. London: printed for Donovan and for F. and C. Rivington, 1799–1803.

D'Orbigny, Charles. "Essai sur les plantes marines des cotes du Golfe de Gascogne, et particulièrement sur celles du departement de la Charente-Inferieure." *Mémoires du Muséum d'Histoire Naturelle* 6 (1820):163–203.

Fabricius, J. C. *Philosophia Entomologica.* Hamburg: C. E. Bohnii, 1778.

Fleming, John. *The Philosophy of Zoology.* 2 vols. Edinburgh: Archibald Constable, 1822.

———. *Molluscous Animals.* Edinburgh: Adam and Charles Black, 1837.

———. *History of British Animals.* London: Duncan and Malcolm, 1828; 2nd ed., 1842.

———. *The Institutes of Natural Science.* Edinburgh: privately printed, [1846].

———. "Remarks on the Origin of Plants and the Physical and Geographical Distribution of Species." *Ann. Mag. Nat. Hist.,* 2nd ser. 4 (1849): 202–3.

[———.] "Botanical Geography." *North British Review* 20 (1854):501–22.

———. *The Lithology of Edinburgh.* Edinburgh: William P. Kennedy, 1859.

Forbes, Edward. "On the British Species of the Genus *Patella.*" [Edinburgh] *University Journal,* January 1834, p. 6.

———. "Notice of Sixteen Species of Testacea new to Scotland." *Athenaeum,* 1836, p. 634.

———. "On the Comparative Elevation of Testacea in the Alps." *Magazine of Zoology and Botany* 1 (1837):257–59.

———. "On the Distribution of Terrestrial Pulmonifera in Europe." *Rpt. Brit. Assn.,* 1838, p. 112.

———. "On the Land and Freshwater Mollusca of Algiers and Bougia." *Ann. Nat. Hist.* 2 (1838–39):250–55.

———. "Notices of a Botanical Excursion to the Mountains of Ternova in Carniola." *Ann. Nat. Hist.* 3 (1839):236–40.

———. "Report on the Distribution of Pulmoniferous Mollusca in the British Isles." *Rpt. Brit. Assn.,* 1839, pt. 1, pp. 127–47.

———. "On a Shell-Bank in the Irish Sea, Considered Zoologically and Geologically." *Ann. Nat. Hist.* 4 (1839–40):217–23.

———. "Lectures on the Zoology of the British Seas." *Manx Sun,* 20 March 1840, p. 2.

———. "On a Pleistocene Tract in the Isle of Man, and the Relations of its

Fauna to that of the Neighbouring Sea." *Rpt. Brit. Assn.,* 1840, pt. 2, pp. 104–5.

———. "On the Associations of Mollusca on the British Coasts, considered with Reference to Pleistocene Geology." *Edinburgh Academic Annual,* 1840, pp. 175–83.

———. "Zoo-geological Considerations on the Freshwater Mollusca." *Ann. Mag. Nat. Hist.* 6 (1840–41):241–43.

———. *A History of British Starfishes, and Other Animals of the Class Echinodermata.* London: John Van Voorst, 1841.

———. *An Inaugural Lecture on Botany, Considered as a Science, and as a Branch of Medical Education.* London: John Van Voorst, 1843.

———. "Report on the Mollusca and Radiata of the Aegean Sea, and on Their Distribution, Considered as Bearing on Geology." *Rpt. Brit. Assn.,* 1843, pt. 1, pp. 130–93.

———. "On the Light Thrown on Geology by Submarine Researches; Being the Substance of a Communication Made to the Royal Institution of Great Britain, Friday Evening, the 23rd February 1844." *Edinb. New Phil. J.* 36 (1844):318–27.

[———.] "Carbon and Silicon." *Literary Gazette,* 1844, pp. 39–40.

———. "On the Morphology of the Reproductive System of Sertularian Zoophytes, and its Analogy with that of the Flowering Plants." *Rpt. Brit. Assn.,* 1844, pt. 2, pp. 68–69.

———. "On Some Important Analogies Between the Animal and Vegetable Kingdoms." *Athenaeum,* 1845, p. 199.

———. "On the Distribution of Endemic Plants, More Especially Those of the British Islands, Considered with Regard to Geological Changes." *Rpt. Brit. Assn.,* 1845, pt. 2, pp. 67–68; abbreviated in *Athenaeum,* 1845, p. 678.

———. "Report on the Collection of Fossils from Southern India, presented by C. J. Kaye, Esq., F.G.S., and the Rev. W. H. Egerton, F.G.S." *Q.J. Geol. Soc.* 1 (1845):79–81.

———. "Report on the Fossil Invertebrata from Southern India, Collected by Mr. Kaye and Mr. Cunliffe." *Trans. Geol. Soc.* 7 (1845):97–174.

———. "On the Connexion Between the Distribution of the Existing Flora and Fauna of the British Isles, and the Geological Changes Which Have Affected Their Area, Especially During the Epoch of the Northern Drift." *Mem. Geol. Surv.* 1 (1846):336–432.

———. "Notices of Natural History Observations Made Since Last Meeting Bearing upon Geology." *Rpt. Brit. Assn.,* 1846, pt. 2, pp. 69–70.

———. "On the Question, Whence and When Came the Plants and Animales Now Inhabiting the British Isles and Seas?" *Athenaeum,* 1846, pp. 247–48.

———. "On the *Cystideae* Found in British Rocks, and on Recent Additions to our Knowledge of the Fossil Echinodermata." *Athenaeum,* 1847, p. 744.

———. "On the Question in Natural History, Have Genera, Like Species, Centres of Distribution?" *Edinb. New Phil. J.* 45 (1848):175–76.

———. "On the Cystideae of the Silurian Rocks of the British Islands." *Mem. Geol. Surv.* 2 (1848):483–534.

———. "Report on the Investigation of British Marine Zoology by Means of the Dredge, Part I: The Infra-littoral Distribution of Marine Invertebrata on the Southern, Western, and Northern Coasts of Great Britain." *Rpt. Brit. Assn.,* 1850, pt. 1, pp. 192–263.

———. "On the Distribution of Freshwater Animals and Plants." *Athenaeum,* 1850, p. 290.

———. "On Recent Researches into the Natural History of the British Seas." *Edinb. New Phil. J.* 50 (1850–51):335–39.

———. Report of Section D of the British Association. *Literary Gazette,* 1851, pp. 483–84.

———. "On the Extinct Land-Shells of St. Helena." *Q.J. Geol. Soc.* 8 (1852):197–99.

———. "Marine Zones of Depth." *Q.J. Geol. Soc.* 8 (1852):303.

[———.] "Plants and Botanists." *Westminster Review* (American edition), October 1852, pp. 207–14.

[———.] "The Future of Geology." *Westminster Review,* n.s. 2 (1852):67–94.

———. "On the Supposed Analogy Between the Life of an Individual and the Duration of a Species." *Edinb. New Phil. J.* 53 (1852):130–35.

———. "On a New Map of the Geological Distribution of Marine Life, and on the Homoiozoic Belts." *Rpt. Brit. Assn.,* 1852, pt. 2, p. 73; *Edinb. New Phil. J.* 54 (1852–53):311–12.

[———.] Obituary on Leopold von Buch. *Literary Gazette,* 1853, p. 253.

———. "Anniversary Address of the President." *Q.J. Geol. Soc.* 10 (1854): xxii–lxxxi.

———. "On the Manifestation of Polarity in the Distribution of Organized Beings in Time." *Proc. Roy. Inst.* 1 (1851–54):428–33.

[———.] "Siluria." *Quarterly Review* 95 (1854):363–94.

———. "Note on an Indication of Depth of Primaeval Seas, Afforded by the Remains of Colour in Fossil Testacea." *Proc. Roy. Soc. Lond.* 7 (1854–55):21–23.

————. "Inaugural Lecture." *Monthly Journal of Medical Science* 18 (1854): 560–68.

————. "Map of the Distribution of Marine Life Illustrated Chiefly by Fishes, Molluscs and Radiata. Showing also the Extent and Limits of the Homoiozoic Belts." In Alexander Keith Johnston, *Physical Atlas of Natural Phenomena,* new and enlarged ed., plate xxxi, with notes, pp. 99–102. Edinburgh: W. and A. K. Johnston, 1856.

Forbes, Edward, and Godwin-Austen, Robert. *The Natural History of the European Seas.* London: John Van Voorst, 1859.

Forbes, Edward, and Goodsir, John. "Notice of Zoological Researches in Orkney and Shetland During the Month of June 1839." *Rpt. Brit. Assn.,* 1839, pt. 2, pp. 79–83.

————. "On Some Remarkable Marine Invertebrata New to the British Seas." *Trans. Roy. Soc. Edinb.* 20 (1853):307–16.

Forbes, Edward, and Hanley, Sylvanus. *A History of British Mollusca and their Shells.* 4 vols. London: John Van Voorst, 1848–53.

Fries, Elias Magnus. *Systema Orbis Vegetabilis: Primas Lineas Novae Constructionis.* Lund: Typographia Academica, 1825.

Gadow, Hans. *The Wanderings of Animals.* Cambridge: Cambridge University Press, 1913.

Geoffroy Saint-Hilaire, Etienne. *Philosophie Anatomique.* 2 vols. Paris: Mequignon-Marvis, 1818; privately printed by the author, 1822.

Geoffroy Saint-Hilaire, Isidore. "Mammifères." *Dictionnaire classique d'Histoire naturelle,* vol. 10 (1826).

Goethe, J. W. von. *Versuch, die Metamorphose der Pflanzen zu erklaren.* Gothe, 1790. Trans. Agnes Arber as "Goethe's Botany," *Chronica Botanica* 10 (1946):63–126.

Goodsir, John. "On the Origin and Development of the Pulps and Sacs of the Human Teeth." *Edinburgh Medical and Surgical Journal* 51 (1839):1–38.

Goodsir, John, and Goodsir, Harry D. S. *Anatomical and Pathological Observations.* Edinburgh: Myles Macphail, 1845.

Graham, Robert, and MacKay, James Townsend. "Comparative View of the More Remarkable Plants Which Characterize the Neighbourhood of Dublin, the Neighbourhood of Edinburgh, and the Southwest of Scotland." *Rpt. Brit. Assn.,* 1836, pt. 1, pp. 253–57.

Gray, Asa. "Diagnostic Characters of New Species of Phaenogamous Plants, Collected in Japan by Charles Wright, Botanist of the U. S. North Pacific Exploring Expedition. . . . With Observations upon the Relations of the Japanese Flora to that of North America and of other Parts of the North Temperate Zone." *Memoirs of the American Academy of Arts and Sciences,* n.s. 6, pt. 2 (1858):377–452.

Grierson, James. "General Observations on Geology and Geognosy, and the Nature of These Respective Studies." *Memoirs of the Wernerian Society* 5 (1823–25):401–10.

Haeckel, Ernst. *Generelle Morphologie der Organismen.* 2 vols. in 1. Berlin: Georg Reimer, 1866.

Hamilton, William. *Discussions on Philosophy and Literature, Education and University Reform.* London: Longman, Brown, Green and Longmans, 1852.

Harvey, W. H. *A Manual of the British Algae.* London: Van Voorst, 1841.

Hay, D. R. *The Geometric Beauty of the Human Figure Defined, To Which Is Prefixed a System of Aesthetic Proportion Applicable to Architecture and Other Formative Arts.* Edinburgh and London: William Blackwood and Sons, 1851.

Heer, Oswald. "On the Probable Origin of the Organized Beings Now Living in the Azores, Madeira, and the Canaries." *Ann. Mag. Nat. Hist.,* 2nd ser. 18 (1856):183–85.

————. "Über die fossilen Pflanzen von St. Jorge in Madeira." *Neue Denkschriften der allgemeinen Schweizerischen Gesellschaft für die gesammten Naturwissenschaften* 15 (1857):1–40.

Henfrey, Arthur. *The Vegetation of Europe, Its Conditions and Causes.* London: John Van Voorst, 1852.

————, ed. *Reports and Papers on Botany.* 2 vols. London: Ray Society, 1849; reprint, New York: Johnson Reprint Corp., 1971.

Herdman, W. A. "Letter of Professor Edward Forbes on the Marine Zoology of the Irish Sea." *Transactions of the Liverpool Biological Society* 8 (1894):156–58.

Hinds, R. B. "Observations on the Construction of Maps in Geographical Botany." *Mag. Nat. Hist.* 8 (1835):498–501.

————. "The Physical Agents of Temperature, Humidity, Light, and Soil, Considered as Developing Climate, and in Connexion with Geographic Botany." *Ann. Mag. Nat. Hist.* 9 (1842):169–89, 311–33, 469–75, 521–27.

————. *The Regions of Vegetation; Being an Analysis of the Distribution of Vegetable Forms over the Surface of the Globe in Connexion with Climate and Physical Agents.* London: G. J. Palmer, 1843.

————. "Memoirs on Geographic Botany." *Ann. Mag. Nat. Hist.* 15 (1845):11–30, 89–104.

Hooker, Joseph. *The Botany of the Antarctic Voyage of H.M. Discovery Ships "Erebus" and "Terror," in the Years 1839–1843.* Vol. 2, *Flora Novae-Zelandiae,* London: Lovell Reeve, 1853–55. Vol. 3, *Flora Tasmaniae,* 1860.

———. "On Insular Floras: A Lecture." *Journal of Botany, British and Foreign,* 5 (1867):23–31.

———. "On Geographical Distribution." *Rpt. Brit. Assn.,* 1881, pp. 727–38.

Horner, Leonard. "Anniversary Address of the President." *Q.J. Geol. Soc.* 3 (1847):xxii–xc.

Humboldt, Alexander von. "On Isothermal Lines, and the Distribution of Heat over the Globe." *Edinb. Phil. J.* 3 (1820):1–20, 256–74; 4 (1820–21):23–37, 262–81; 5 (1821):28–39.

———. "New Inquiries into the Laws Which are Observed in the Distribution of Vegetable Forms." *Edinb. Phil. J.* 6 (1822):273–87.

Humboldt, Alexander von, and Bonpland, Aimé. *Essai sur la géographie des plantes.* Paris: Fr. Schoell, 1807.

Hunter, John. *Essays and Observations on Natural History, Anatomy, Physology, Psychology, and Geology.* 2 vols. London: John Van Voorst, 1861.

Huxley, Leonard, ed. *Life and Letters of Thomas Henry Huxley.* 2 vols. London: Macmillan, 1900.

———. *Life and Letters of Sir Joseph Dalton Hooker.* 2 vols. New York: D. Appleton and Co., 1918.

Jenyns, Leonard. "On the Recent Progress and Present State of Zoology." *Rpt. Brit. Assn.,* 1834, pp. 143–251.

Jukes-Brown, A. J. *The Student's Handbook of Historical Geology.* London: George Bell, 1886.

Jussieu, Adrien de. *Géographie botanique.* Paris, [1845]. Reprinted from Charles D'Orbigny's *Dictionnaire universel d'histoire naturelle* (1842–61).

———. *Botanique: Cours élémentaire d'histoire naturelle.* Paris: Victor Masson, 1848.

Kant, Immanuel. *Metaphysical Foundations of Natural Science.* Trans. Ernest Belfort Bax. London: G. Bell and Sons, 1883.

———. *Immanuel Kant's "Critique of Pure Reason."* Trans. Norman Kemp Smith. 2nd impression with corrections. New York: Humanities Press, 1933.

King, William. "First Series of Supplementary Notes to a Former Paper, Entitled 'An Account of Some Shells and Other Invertebrate Forms Found on the Coast of Northumberland and of Durham.'" *Ann. Mag. Nat. Hist.* 19 (1847):334–40.

Kirby, William. "Introductory Address, Explanatory of the Views of the Zoological Club, Delivered at its Foundation, November 29, 1823." *Zoological Journal* 2 (1826):1–8.

Kirby, William, and Spence, William. *An Introduction to Entomology; or,*

*Elements of the Natural History of Insects.* 4 vols. London: Longman, Hurst, Rees, Orme and Brown, 1815–26.

Knox, Robert. "An Account of the *Foramen centrale* of the Retina, Generally Called the *Foramen of Soemmering,* as Seen in the Eyes of Certain Reptiles." *Memoirs of the Wernerian Society* 5 (1823–25):1–7.

———. "On the Wombat of Flinders." *Edinb. New Phil. J.* 1 (1826):104–12.

———. "Observations on the Comparative Anatomy of the Eye." *Trans. Roy. Soc. Edinb.* 10 (1826):43–78.

———. "Observations on the Structure of the Stomach of the Peruvian Lama; to Which are Prefixed Remarks on the Analogical Reasoning of Anatomists, in the Determination *a priori* of Unknown Species and Unknown Structures." *Trans. Roy. Soc. Edinb.* 11 (1831):479–98.

———. "Observations on the Natural History of the Salmon." *Rpt. Brit. Assn.,* 1831–32, pp. 587–89.

———. "Contributions to anatomy and physiology: On some Varieties in Human Structure, with Remarks on the Doctrine of 'Unity of Organization.'" *London Medical Gazette,* n.s. 2 (1843):499–502, 529–32, 554–56, 586–91, 637–40.

———. "Recollections of Researches into the Natural and Economic History of Certain Species of the Clupeadae, Coregoni, and Salmonidae." *Rpt. Brit. Assn.,* 1846, pt. 2, pp. 79–80.

———. "On the Application of the Method, Discovered by the Late Dr. Thibert, of Modeling and Colouring After Nature All Kinds of Fishes." *Rpt. Brit. Assn.,* 1846, pt. 2, p. 80.

———. *The Races of Men: A Fragment.* Philadelphia: Lea & Blanchard, 1850.

———. *Great Artists and Great Anatomists: A Biographical and Philosophical Study.* London: John Van Voorst, 1852; reprint, New York: AMS Press, 1977.

———. *Fish and Fishing in the Lone Glens of Scotland.* London: G. Routledge & Co., 1854.

———. "Xavier Bichat: His Life and Labours. A Biographical and Philosophical Study. *Lancet,* November 1854, pp. 393–96.

———. "Introduction to Inquiries into the Philosophy of Zoology." *Lancet,* June 1855, pp. 625–27.

———. "Some Observations on the *Salmo estuarius,* or Estuary Trout." *Zoologist* 13 (1855):4662–73.

———. "Inquiries into the Philosophy of Zoology." *Zoologist* 13 (1855): 4777–92.

———. "Contributions to the Philosophy of Zoology." *Zoologist* 13 (1855): 4837–42.

———. "On Organic Harmonies: Anatomical Co-relations, and Methods of Zoology and Paleontology." *Lancet,* August 1856, pp. 245–47, 270–71, 297–300.

———. "The Present Position of the Salmon Question, Considered Physiologically." *Zoologist* 14 (1856):4985–92.

———. "Zoology: Its Present Phasis and Future Prospects." *Zoologist* 15 (1857):5473–5502.

———, ed. and trans. *A System of Human Anatomy: Translated from the Fourth Edition of the French of H. Cloquet, M.D., With Notes and a Corrected Nomenclature.* Edinburgh: Maclachlan and Stewart, 1828.

———, ed. *The Anatomy of the Bones of the Human Body; Represented in a Series of Engravings, Copied From the Elegant Tables of Sue & Albinus. By Edward Mitchell, Engraver. With Explanatory References by the late John Barclay, M.D., F.R.S.E.* New ed. Edinburgh: Edward Mitchell, 1829.

Lamoroux, J. V. F. *Histoire des polypiers coralligenes flexibles.* Caen: F. Poisson, 1816.

———. "Mémoire sur la géographie des plantes marines. *Annales des Sciences Naturelles* 7 (1826):60–82.

Lankester, E. R. "On the Use of the Term *Homology* in Modern Zoology, and the Distinction between Homogenetic and Homoplastic Agreements." *Ann. Mag. Nat. Hist.,* 4th ser. 6 (1870):34–43.

Lindley, John. "Some Account of the Spherical and Numerical System of Nature of M. Elias Fries." *Philosophical Magazine* 68 (1826):81–91.

———. *Introduction to Botany.* 4th ed. 2 vols. London: Longman, Brown, Green and Longmans, 1848.

Link, H. F. *Die Urwelt und das Alterthum, erläutert durch die Naturkunde.* 2 vols. Berlin: Ferdinand Dümmler, 1821–22.

Linnaeus, C. *Stationes Plantarum.* Uppsala: L. M. Hojer, 1754.

———. "On the Increase of the Habitable Earth." "On the Police of Nature." In *Select Dissertations from the Amoenitates Academicae: A Supplement to Mr. Stillingfleet's Tracts Relating to Natural History,* 2 vols., trans. F. J. Brand, 1:71–166. London: G. Robinson, 1781.

———. "The Oeconomy of Nature." In *Miscellaneous Tracts relating to Natural History, Husbandry, and Physick,* by B. Stillingfleet, pp. 31–108. London: J. Dodsby, 1791.

———. *L'Équilibre de la Nature.* Translated by Bernard Jasmin with introduction and notes by Camille Limoges. Paris: J. Vrin, 1972.

Lyell, Charles. *Principles of Geology.* 3 vols. London: John Murray, 1830–33; reprint, New York: Johnson Reprint Corp., 1969.

————. *Elements of Geology.* New York: Appleton, 1868.

————. *Life, Letters, and Journals.* 2 vols. London: John Murray, 1881.

M'Andrew, Robert. "On the Mollusca of Vigo Bay in the North-west of Spain." *Ann. Mag. Nat. Hist.,* 2nd ser. 3 (1849):507–13.

M'Cosh, James. "Some Remarks on the Plant, Morphologically Considered." *Botanical Gazette* 3 (1851):118–23.

[————.] "Typical Forms: Goethe, Professor Owen, Mr. Fairbairn." *North British Review* 15 (1851):389–418.

————. "Morphological Analogy Between the Disposition of the Branches of Exogenous Plants and the Venation of Their Leaves." *Literary Gazette,* 1852, p. 716.

————. "Some Further Observations on the Correspondence Between the Leaf-venation and Ramification of the Plant." *Rpt. Brit. Assn.,* 1854, pt. 2, p. 100.

M'Cosh, James, and Dickie, George. *Typical Forms and Special Ends in Creation.* Edinburgh: Thomas Constable and Co., 1856.

MacDonald, W. "On the Homologies of the Vertebrate Skeleton and its Analogies amongst the Invertebrata." *Athenaeum,* 1856, p. 1095.

MacLeay, William S. *Horae Entomologicae; or, Essays on the Annulose Animals.* 1 vol. in 2 pts. London: S. Bagster, 1819–21.

————. "Remarks on the Identity of Certain General Laws Which Have Been Lately Observed to Regulate the Natural Distribution of Insects and Fungi." *Transactions of the Linnean Society of London* 14 (1823–25):46–68.

MacVicar, John Gibson. *Elements of the Economy of Nature; or, The Principles of Physics, Chemistry, and Physiology: Founded on the Recently Discovered Phenomena of Light, Electro-Magnetism, and Atomic Chemistry.* Edinburgh: Adam Black, 1830.

————. "Vegetable Morphology: Its General Principles." *Trans. Bot. Soc. Edinb.* 6 (1860):401–18.

————. "The First Lines of Morphology and Organic Development, Geometrically Considered." *Edinb. New Phil. J.,* n.s. 14 (1861):1–15.

————. *A Sketch of a Philosophy.* 4 vols. London: Williams & Norgate, 1868–74.

Martin, Ch[arles]. "On the Vegetable Colonisation of the British Islands, Shetland, Feroe, and Iceland." *Edinb. New Phil. J.* 46 (1849):40–52.

Maury, Matthew Fontaine. *Physical Geography of the Sea.* New York: Harper and Brothers, 1855.

Meyen, F.J.F. *Outlines of the Geography of Plants: With Particular Enquiries Concerning the Native Country, the Culture, and the Uses of the Principal Cultivated Plants on Which the Prosperity of Nations is Based.* London: Ray Society, 1846.

Milne-Edwards, Henri. *A Manual of Zoology.* Trans. Robert Knox; ed. C. Carter Blake. 2nd ed. London: Henry Renshaw, 1863.

Milne-Edwards, Henri, and Audouin, J. V. *Recherches pour servir à l'histoire naturelle du littoral de la France.* 2 vols. Paris: Crochard, 1832-34.

Mitchell, W. "Analogy between the Serial Arrangements of the Leaves of Plants and Crystalline Forms." *Trans. Bot. Soc. Edinb.* 5 (1857):207-10.

———. "On the Correspondence Between the Serial Internodes of Plants and Serial Crystalline Forms." *Trans. Bot. Soc. Edinb.* 6 (1858):31-35.

Monro *primus,* Alexander. *Essay on Comparative Anatomy.* London: J. Nourse, 1744.

Monro *secundus,* Alexander. *The Structure and Physiology of Fishes Explained, and Compared with Those of Man and Other Animals.* Edinburgh: C. Elliot, 1785.

Morton, S. G. "Doctrine of Specific Organic Centers." *Edinb. New Phil. J.* 51 (1851):197-98.

Moseley, Henry. "On the Geometrical Forms of Turbinated and Discoid Shells." *Phil. Trans.* 128 (1838):351-70.

Murchison, Roderick. "Presidential Address." *Rpt. Brit. Assn.,* 1846.

———. *Siluria: The History of the Oldest Known Rocks containing Organic Remains.* 2nd ed. London: John Murray, 1854.

Murray, Andrew. *The Geographical Distribution of Mammals.* London: Day and Son, 1866.

Newman, Edward. *Sphinx Vespiformis: An Essay.* London: F. Westley and A. H. Davis, 1832.

———. "Further Observations on the Septenary System." *Entomological Magazine* 4 (1837):234-51.

Oken, Lorenz. *Elements of Physiophilosophy.* Translation by Alfred Tulk of *Lehrbuch der Naturphilosophie* (1809). London: Ray Society, 1847.

Oliver, Daniel. "The Atlantis Hypothesis in its Botanical Aspect." *Natural History Review* 2 (1862):149-70.

Orsted, A. S. *De Regionibus Marinis: Elementa Topographiae Historiconaturalis Feti Oresund.* Hauniae: J. C. Scharling, 1844.

Owen, Richard. "A Description of a Specimen of the *Plesiosaurus Macrocephalus,* Conybeare, in the Collection of Viscount Cole, M.P., D.C.L., F.G.S., &c." *Transactions of the Geological Society of London* 5 (1838):515-38.

———. "On the Anatomy of the Dugong." *Proceedings of the Zoological Society of London,* 27 March 1838, p. 43.

———. *Lectures on the Comparative Anatomy and Physiology of the Invertebrate Animals.* London: Longman, Brown, Green, and Longmans, 1843.

———. *Lectures on the Comparative Anatomy and Physiology of the Verte-*

*brate Animals, Delivered at the Royal College of Surgeons of England, in 1844 and 1846.* London: Longman, Brown, Green and Longmans, 1846.

———. *A History of British Fossil Mammals and Birds.* London: John Van Voorst, 1846.

———. "Report on the Archetype and Homologies of the Vertebrate Skeleton." *Rpt. Brit. Assn.,* 1846, pt. 1, pp. 169–340.

———. "On the Homologies of the Bones collectively called 'Temporal' in Human Anatomy." *Athenaeum,* 1846, pp. 968–69.

———. "On the Vertebrate Structure of the Skull." *Athenaeum,* 1846, pp. 1004–5.

———. *On the Archetype and Homologies of the Vertebrate Skeleton.* London: John Van Voorst, 1848.

———. "Presidential Address." *Rpt. Brit. Assn.,* 1858, pp. xlix–cx.

———. "Darwin *on the Origin of Species.*" *Edinburgh Review* 111 (1860): 487–532.

Owen, Richard, et al. "Report of the Committee . . . Appointed for the Purpose of Reporting on the Registration of Periodical Phaenomena of Animals and Vegetables." *Rpt. Brit. Assn.,* 1845, pt. 1, pp. 321–36.

Palmer, James F., ed. *The Works of John Hunter, F.R.S., with Notes.* 4 vols. London: Longman, Rees, Orme, Brown, Green and Longman, 1835–37.

Parkinson, James. *Organic Remains of a Former World.* 3 vols. London: Sherwood, Neely, and Jones, 1804–11.

Powell, Baden. *The Connexion of Natural and Divine Truth; or, The Study of the Inductive Philosophy Considered as Subservient to Theology.* London: John W. Parker, 1838.

Prichard, James Cowles. *Researches into the Physical History of Mankind.* 2nd ed. 2 vols. London: John and Arthur Arch, 1826.

Quetelet, A[dolphe]. "On the Importance of Keeping Exact Registers in Different Districts." *Rpt. Brit. Assn.,* 1841, pt. 2, p. 96.

"R." Review of *Transactions of the Statistical Society of London* (1837). *London and Westminster Review,* American ed., 29 (1838):23–38.

Ramsay, A. C. "On the Former Probable Existence of Palaeozoic Glaciers." *Rpt. Brit. Assn.,* 1854, pt. 2, pp. 93–94.

———. "On the Occurrence of Angular, Subangular, Polished, and Striated Fragments and Boulders in the Permian Breccia of Shropshire, Worcestershire, etc.; and on the Probable Existence of Glaciers and Icebergs in the Permian Epoch." *Q.J. Geol. Soc.* 11 (1855):187–205.

Risso, Antonio. *Ichthyologie de Nice; ou, Histoire naturelle des poissons du departement des Alpes maritimes.* Paris: F. Schoell, 1810.

Roget, Peter Mark. *Animal and Vegetable Physiology Considered with Reference to Natural Theology.* 2 vols. London: William Pickering, 1834.

————. *Outlines of Physiology: with an Appendix on Phrenology.* 1st American ed. Philadelphia: Lea and Blanchard, 1839.

Rudolphi, K. A. *Beyträge zur Anthropologie und allgemeinen Naturgeschichte.* Berlin: Haude and Spener, 1812.

Rylands, Peter. "On the Quinary, or Natural, System of M'Leay, Swainson, Vigors, &c." *Magazine of Natural History* 9 (1836):130–38, 175–82.

Scharff, R. F. *The History of the European Fauna.* London: Walter Scott, 1899.

Schleiden, M. J. *Principles of Scientific Botany; or, Botany as an Inductive Science.* Trans. Edwin Lankester. London: Longman, Brown, Green, and Longmans, 1849; reprint, New York: Kraus Reprint Co., 1969.

Schouw, Joachim Frederik. *Grundzüge einer allgemeinen Pflanzengeographie.* Berlin: Reimer, 1823.

————. *The Earth, Plants, and Man.* Trans. and ed. Arthur Henfrey. London: Henry G. Bohn, 1859.

Stallo, J. B. *General Principles of the Philosophy of Nature.* Boston: Wm. Crosby and H. P. Nichols, 1848.

Stauffer, R. C., ed. *Charles Darwin's Natural Selection: Being the Second Part of His Big Species Book Written from 1856 to 1858.* London: Cambridge University Press, 1975.

Swainson, William. *A Treatise on the Geography and Classification of Animals.* London: Longman, Rees, Orme, Brown, Green and Longman, 1835.

————. "On the Series of Nature, and on the Relations of Animals: Remarks Occasioned by a Review of the Preliminary Discourse on Natural History." *Entomological Magazine* 3 (1835):1–12.

Todhunter, I. *William Whewell, D.D.: An Account of His Writings with Selections from His Literary and Scientific Correspondence.* 2 vols. London: Macmillan and Co., 1876.

Tournefort, Joseph Pitton de. *Relations d'un voyage du Levant.* 2 vols. Paris: L'Imprimerie Royale, 1717.

Treviranus, Gottfried Reinhold. *Biologie; oder, Philosophie der Lebenden Natur für Naturforscher und Aerzte.* 6 vols. in 3. Göttingen: J. F. Röwer, 1802–22.

Turner, Dawson, and Dillwyn, Lewis Weston. *The Botanist's Guide through England and Wales.* 2 vols. London: Phillips and Fardon, 1805.

Turner, William ed. *The Anatomical Memoirs of John Goodsir, with a Biographical Memoir by Henry Lonsdale.* 2 vols. Edinburgh: Adam and Charles Black, 1868.

Turton, W[illiam]. *A Manual of the Land and Fresh-water Shells of the British Islands.* London: Longman, Rees, Orme, Brown and Green, 1831.

Unger, Franz. "The Sunken Island of Atlantis." *Journal of Botany* 3 (1865): 12–26.

Virchow, Rudolph. *Die Cellularpathologie in ihrer Begrundung auf Physiologische und Pathologische Gewebelehre.* Berlin: A. Hirschwald, 1858.

Wallace, Alfred R. "On the Law Which Has Regulated the Introduction of New Species." *Ann. Mag. Nat. Hist.* 2nd ser. 16 (1855):184–96.

———. *Contributions to the Theory of Natural Selection.* London: Macmillan, 1875.

Watson, Hewett C. *Outlines of the Geographical Distribution of British Plants.* Edinburgh: privately printed, 1832. Second edition published as *Remarks on the Geographical Distribution of British Plants; Chiefly in Connection with Latitude, Elevation and Climate.* London: Longman, Rees, Orme, Brown, Green, and Longman, 1835.

———. "Observations Made During the Summer of 1832, on the Temperature and Vegetation of the Scottish Highland Mountains, in Connection With Their Height Above the Sea." *Edinb. New Phil. J.* 14 (1833):317–24.

———. "Observations on the Construction of Maps for Illustrating the Distribution of Plants, with Reference to the Communication of Mr. Hinds on the Same Subject." *Mag. Nat. Hist.* 9 (1836):17–21.

———. *Cybele Britannica.* 4 vols. London: Longmans, 1847–59.

———. *Topographical Botany.* 2nd ed. London: Bernard Quaritch, 1883.

Whewell, William. *History of the Inductive Sciences, from the Earliest to the Present Times.* 3 vols. London: John W. Parker, 1837.

———. *Philosophy of the Inductive Sciences.* 2 vols. London: John W. Parker, 1840.

———. *Indications of the Creator: Extracts, Bearing upon Theology, from the History and the Philosophy of the Inductive Sciences.* 2nd ed. London: Parker, 1846.

———. "On the Idea of Polarity." *Athenaeum,* 1849, pp. 119–20.

Willdenow, K. L. *Grundriss der Kräuterkunde.* Berlin: Haude und Spener, 1792. Translated as *The Principles of Botany, and of Vegetable Physiology.* Edinburgh: William Blackwood, 1805.

Wilson, George. *A Letter from George Wilson, M.D., Lecturer on Chemistry, to the Right Honourable Sir James Forrest, Bart. . . .* Edinburgh: Neill and Company, 1843.

Wilson, George, and Brown, John Crombie. "Account of a Repetition of Several of Dr. Samuel Brown's Processes for the Conversion of Carbon into Silicon." *Trans. Roy. Soc. Edinb.* 15 (1844):547–59; *Proc. Roy. Soc. Edinb.* 1 (1844):468–70.

Wilson, Leonard G., ed. *Sir Charles Lyell's Scientific Journals on the Species Question.* New Haven: Yale University Press, 1970.

Wollaston, Thomas Vernon. *Insecta Maderensia; Being an Account of the Insects of the Islands of the Madeiran Group.* London: John Van Voorst, 1854.

————. *On the Variation of Species with Special Reference to the Insecta; Followed by an Inquiry into the Nature of Genera.* London: John Van Voorst, 1856.

Woodward, S. P. *A Manual of the Mollusca.* London: Virtue Brothers, 1866.

Zimmermann, E.A.W. *Specimen Zoologiae Geographicae Quadrupedum domicilia et migrationes sistens.* Leiden, 1777.

# Index

COMPOSED BY THE COMPOSING ROOM, KIMBERLY, WISCONSIN
MANUFACTURED BY CUSHING-MALLOY, INC.
ANN ARBOR, MICHIGAN
TEXT AND DISPLAY LINES ARE SET IN PLANTIN

Library of Congress Cataloging in Publication Data
Rehbock, Philip F., 1942–
The philosophical naturalists.
(Wisconsin publications in the history of science and
medicine; no. 3)
Bibliography: pp. 253–270.
Includes index.
1. Biology—Great Britain—History. 2. Biology—
Great Britain—Philosophy—History. I. Title.
II. Series.
QH305.2.G7R43 1983     574'.0941     83-47767
ISBN 0-299-09430-8